Greek Theater in Ancient Sicily

Studies of ancient theater have traditionally taken Athens as their creative center. In this book, however, the lens is widened to examine the origins and development of ancient drama, and particularly comedy, within a Sicilian and southern Italian context. Each chapter explores a different category of theatrical evidence, from the literary (fragments of Epicharmus and cult traditions) to the artistic (phlyax vases) and the archaeological (theater buildings). Kate Bosher argues that, unlike in classical Athens, the golden days of theatrical production on Sicily coincided with the rule of tyrants, rather than with democratic interludes. Moreover, this was not accidental, but plays and the theater were an integral part of the tyrants' propaganda system. The volume will appeal widely to classicists and to theater historians.

KATHRYN G. BOSHER was Assistant Professor of Classical Studies at Northwestern University until her death in 2013. She was editor of *Theater Outside Athens: Drama in Greek Sicily and South Italy* (Cambridge, 2012) and co-editor of *The Oxford Handbook of Greek Drama in the Americas* (Oxford, 2015).

EDITH HALL is Professor of Classics at King's College London.

CLEMENTE MARCONI is James R. McCredie Professor of Greek Art and Archaeology at the Institute of Fine Arts, New York University, and Professor of Classical Archaeology at the University of Milan.

Greek Theater in Ancient Sicily

KATHRYN G. BOSHER

Northwestern University, Illinois

Edited By

EDITH HALL

King's College London

CLEMENTE MARCONI

New York University and Università degli Studi di Milano

CAMBRIDGE
UNIVERSITY PRESS

CAMBRIDGE
UNIVERSITY PRESS

University Printing House, Cambridge CB2 8BS, United Kingdom

One Liberty Plaza, 20th Floor, New York, NY 10006, USA

477 Williamstown Road, Port Melbourne, VIC 3207, Australia

314-321, 3rd Floor, Plot 3, Splendor Forum, Jasola District Centre, New Delhi - 110025, India

103 Penang Road, #05-06/07, Visioncrest Commercial, Singapore 238467

Cambridge University Press is part of the University of Cambridge.

It furthers the University's mission by disseminating knowledge in the pursuit of education, learning and research at the highest international levels of excellence.

www.cambridge.org
Information on this title: www.cambridge.org/9781108725651
DOI: 10.1017/9781108663878

© Kathryn G. Bosher 2021

First published 2021
First paperback edition 2022

A catalogue record for this publication is available from the British Library

ISBN 978-1-108-49387-1 Hardback
ISBN 978-1-108-72565-1 Paperback

Contents

Figures

Maps

Tables

Foreword

When Kathryn Bosher died in 2013, her book manuscript remained unpublished. Typically, Kate had been so generous towards others with her time that she had focused on collaborative projects rather than publications authored by her alone. She was the driving force behind the interdisciplinary *Classicizing Chicago* project at Northwestern University. She was the initiator of the magisterial *Oxford Handbook of Greek Drama in the Americas,* of which the other editors were Fiona Macintosh, Justine McConnell, and Patrice Rankine; this was published by Oxford University Press in 2015, two years after her death. Her other major publication was the edited volume *Theater Outside Athens: Drama in Greek Sicily and South Italy,* the results of a pioneering conference she had convened at Northwestern University in 2008, published by Cambridge University Press in 2012. She lived just long enough to read the first of the many favorable reviews of that landmark volume.

She had conducted the research which underlies both this posthumous book and *Theater Outside Athens* at the University of Michigan, under the supervision of Professor Ruth Scodel, as an Assistant Professor of Classical Studies at Northwestern University, and while on a sabbatical in Rome supported by the Loeb Foundation. Kate's passion for the cultural history of the Greek colonies of Sicily and Southern Italy – an area traditionally called "Magna Graecia" by scholars – was immense; she visited almost all of them over the course of her career. It is evidence of the extraordinary breadth of Kate's expertise that not one but two editors, one specializing in material culture and one in literary texts, were required to finalize her manuscript for publication.

In consultation with Kate's husband, LaDale Winling, we decided early in the process to interfere as little as possible with the text of her revised manuscript, which was written in her usual meticulous yet buoyant manner. Michael Sharp at Cambridge University Press, the anonymous reviewers, Professors Eric Csapo at the University of Sydney, and J. R. Green at New South Wales have all provided indispensable advice. Our changes to the main text are small, and for the most part simply promote the flow of the prose or maintain consistency across the chapters. In the footnotes and bibliography, we were slightly more interventionist, in an attempt to make the book accessible to a wider audience. We filled out details of reference works, provided translations, and inserted glosses where the material is particularly unfamiliar or obscure. We also supplemented and updated some technical information and bibliography. But bibliographical comprehensiveness proved impossible, both because the field of regional theater in antiquity is growing so fast, partly as a result of Kate's inspiring contribution, and because new archaeological finds are constantly emerging.

Since the editors of this manuscript completed their work, several pieces of her own were published and new, relevant scholarship has come out. Kate's text was unable to account for them, but they deserve special note. Kate's own work numbers among these publications on theater in Sicily and South Italy, including Bosher (2013b) and Bosher (2014). Reviews of the edited volume *Theater Outside Athens* (2012) in the *Times Literary Supplement* (30 January, 2013) and *Bryn Mawr Classical Review* (https://bmcr.brynmawr.edu/2013/2013.01.08/) also offer assessments of recent scholarship. Other scholarship of note includes Csapo et al. (2014), Carpenter et al. (2014), Ssao et al. (2014), Isler (2017), Kästner and Schmidt (2018), Caminneci et al. (2019), Braund, D., E. Hall, and R. Wyles (eds.) (2019). All of these may be found in the bibliography.

When we were asked if we would help edit this significant monograph, we agreed immediately. The ancient Greeks who lived in Sicily and Southern Italy produced dazzling literature and built imposing theaters: the major part they played in the evolution of European drama deserves to be better understood. But we had a more personal reason. Kate galvanized the lives of everyone she met. She had an unusual gift for bringing together, across continents, people who could complement each other's academic work. We owe a great deal to her. Losing Kate was to lose the most popular, creative, and responsible member of our professional family. Facilitating the publication of her fine monograph has been a pleasure and a privilege.

Edith Hall and Clemente Marconi

Note to the Reader

Work on editing the text and updating the bibliography was completed at the end of 2015. Unfortunately, for various reasons, but in particular the peculiarly difficult process of procuring many of the illustrations required, the final manuscript could not enter production until summer 2019. We trust that the reader will forgive the omission of more recent items of bibliography and details of archaeological discoveries and we are sure that the book's value is not impaired as a result.

1 | Introduction

[...] Say this is patriotic, out of date.
But you are wrong. It never is too late

For nights of stars and feet that move to an
Iambic measure; all who clapped were linked,
The theatre is our treasury and too,
Our study, schoolroom, house where mercy is

Dispensed with justice. Shakespeare has the mood
And draws the music from the dullest heart.
This is our birthright, speeches for the dumb
And unaccomplished. [...]

          – from Elizabeth Jennings, "A Performance of Henry V
                        at Stratford-upon-Avon"

Aeschylus and Aristophanes wrote for a crowd. Like Shakespeare, they did not only cater to the sophisticated and educated, but also drew "music from the dullest heart" and offered speeches for the "dumb and unaccomplished."[1] It is perhaps for this reason that, in the absence of direct written evidence from most citizens of ancient Athens, plays have sometimes been tapped for the views of the audience, and, by extension, for a good segment of the population. The special political circumstances of Athenian theater further encourage the reading of ancient plays as products of a democracy, and as sources for democratic ideas and ideals.[2] Scholars have argued that it was the competition and intellectual vigor encouraged by the democracy that led to the development of theater first in

---

[1] Jennings' poem is printed in Jennings (1986) 209.

[2] For studies of connections between Athenian theater and Athenian democracy, see, for example, Connor (1990); Winkler and Zeitlin (1992); Easterling (1997); Pelling (1997). Here and throughout I use the term democratic in its loosest sense, implying not the minutiae of Athenian institutional procedure but the more general concept of the active participation of the *demos* in government. More important for this argument is the rhetoric of democratic freedom and independence than the detail of governmental organization. It should be noted, however, that cogent arguments against the intrinsically democratic origins and nature of tragedy as a genre have been formulated by Rhodes (2003) and Carter (2004).

Athens.[3] On this model, the plays gave expression to particularly democratic concerns and the audience represented the newly empowered citizen
body.[4] This work has yielded a fairly comprehensive theory of how plays
were part of the democratic machinery of fifth-century Athens. Although
this approach begins by rooting itself in Athens historically, it has led in
many instances to the conclusion that Greek theater *as a medium and
tragedy and comedy as genres* were intrinsically democratic phenomena.[5]

The association between early Greek theater and democracy is compelling, but evidence from outside Athens, in particular from Sicily, compli-
cates the picture. Some of the most important evidence for ancient Greek
theater comes from Sicilian cities controlled by tyrants: the very early comic
fragments of Epicharmus from the fifth century, the comic so-called
"phlyax" vases from the fourth century, and many significant theater
buildings. These three crucial categories of evidence are dated to the
reign of the Syracusan tyrants Gelon and Hieron in the early fifth century,
the tyrant Dionysius I at the beginning of the fourth century, and Hieron II
in the third century. From the brief democratic periods in Sicily, only few
and controversial theatrical artifacts survive.[6] Most notably, during the
latter half of the fifth century, when Athenian theater was at its height,

---

[3] E.g. Henderson (2001) 267: "For poets and spectators alike, drama was not an escape or a time-
out from democratic life, but a form of participation in it."; Saïd (2001); Cartledge (1997). In
a controversial interpretation, Connor (1990) pushes the origins of the City Dionysia to a later
date (ca 501) to coincide with the beginnings of Athenian democracy and argues that tragedy in
its more polished form was introduced to the city at this time. Although he does not suggest that
no theatrical performances were carried out before the beginning of the fifth century, he argues
that any earlier dramas would have been local rural events. This dating of the first official tragic
performances led him to an argument that tragedy itself, like the City Dionysia, which supported
it, portrayed democratic ideals. He goes so far as to suggest that the plays celebrated the freedom
of the people in the newly democratic state in contrast to the tyranny of a few years before. His
argument finds some support in West's recent exposure of the uncertainty of the traditional
dates for the early dramatists, dates which had hitherto been felt to be fairly reliable fixed points:
West (1989). Versnell (1995); Osborne (1993); Martin (1995); and Sourvinou-Inwood (1994) all
disagree with Connor's argument. For different theories about the origins of Greek Theater see,
for example, Nielsen (2000), who traces cult theaters back to the near East; Kinzl (1980), who also
points to Near Eastern beginnings in the dithyramb and the dance; Else (1965) argues for the
evolution of "tragodes" from the "rhapsodes," both professionally and etymologically, and sees
close associations between the Homeric tales and the plots of tragedy.

[4] E.g. Goldhill (1997) 54, "to be in an audience is above all *to play the role of democratic
citizen.*" (sic).

[5] This has often been accepted in the scholarly community beyond Classics. See, for example, Nick
Ridout's summary of Performance Studies theorists' location of the idealized democratic
spectator in classical Athens (Ridout (2008)).

[6] On two fifth-century figurines from Lipari and Camarina, see Bernabò Brea (2001) 23–5, who
suggests they may reflect the comedies of Epicharmus. On vases portraying mythical scenes,
which may be related to tragedy, see, more recently, Taplin (2007).

there is little evidence of large-scale popular theatrical productions in Sicily.[7] Even the evidence for the role of Timoleon, the Corinthian general who became leader of Syracuse in the late 340s, in reviving theater and laying the foundation for monumental theater building in the second half of the fourth century, appears on close examination to be thin, as I argue in Chapter 5. It seems that, in the West, the growth of large-scale, public theater was somehow linked to the tyrants.

Despite this striking association between theater and tyranny, few, if any, studies of western Greek theater examine how drama evolved in Syracuse, or whether it played an important political role there. Instead, western Greek theater is often understood to be derivative of Athenian theater, uprooted from Athens and artificially imported to Syracuse as a foreign luxury good.[8] Most striking, theater is sometimes described as apolitical in a Sicilian context.[9]

It follows that the very important categories of theatrical evidence from the West are also studied, almost exclusively, in relation to Athens. Sicily's opulent theaters, known playwrights, and collections of dramatic figurines and vases have been used to help explain Athens' performance traditions or to paint a picture of Athenian theater imported to the colonies. Despite the widespread assumption that the comic playwright Epicharmus spent most of his working life in Syracuse, the contexts in which we try to understand his plays are often the Panhellenic and far-flung literary and intellectual circle of contemporary Athenian plays and later Hellenistic and Roman theater.[10] Likewise, the "phlyax" vases are now used to help interpret Athenian comedy, as I discuss in Chapter 5, and western theaters are explained as architecturally and symbolically derivative of the theater of Dionysus in Athens (Chapter 6).

---

[7] Tales reported in later sources about the release of Athenians (who had been imprisoned in the quarries of Syracuse after the battle of Syracuse in 413 BCE), if they could sing Euripides' songs, may suggest that the Syracusans were interested in Athenian tragedy (Satyrus, *Life of Euripides* (*POxy.* 1176, fr. 39, col. 19); Plutarch *Nicias* 29). The Syracusans' eagerness to hear songs remembered by prisoners, however, may also suggest that there were not many public performances of Euripides in Syracuse in the latter half of the fifth century BCE.

[8] E.g. Cartledge (1997) 5 on theater buildings. See, however, the new arguments of Csapo (2010), in which he proposes that, by the fourth century, Greek drama was thought of as a Panhellenic art form. In this new schema, Greek plays would not have seemed foreign or identifiably Attic, but more generally Greek. For discussion of this theory, see Chapter 5. In Bosher (2013a) I propose some qualifications of this theory: namely that, even if there was a concept of Greek drama, there were *at the same time* local traditions of theater and performance that were commemorated and celebrated even well into the Roman period.

[9] E.g. Pickard-Cambridge (1962) 239.

[10] E.g. Kherkhof (2001); Pickard-Cambridge (1962). Willi's study (2008), however, considers Epicharmus in the context of other Sicilian writers, see further Chapter 2.

However, given the very significant amount of evidence for theater in the West, and its striking appearance at the same time as the western tyrannies, it seems worthwhile to try to trace the history of Sicilian[11] theater in its own political context. This, then is the main argument of this book: in fifth- and fourth-century Sicily, unlike classical Athens, the golden days of theatrical production coincide with the rule of tyrants, rather than with democratic interludes. I suggest that this was not accidental, but that plays and the theater were an integral part of the tyrants' propaganda system. I aim to present a story of the development of literary western theater, without relying on theories relating to and assuming the existence of a sub-literary farce, which probably did exist as well, but for which we have no certain or clear evidence. I offer a framework within which to understand the continuing tradition of theater in the West, which, I suggest, spanned several centuries from Epicharmus at the beginning of the fifth century to the monumental theaters of the third century.

Scholarly reluctance to interpret Sicilian theater in its own political context is partly due to disparate and insufficient evidence, a condition that is slowly being improved by archaeological finds and new interdisciplinary approaches to older material. Another barrier, however, is theoretical: our understanding of ancient Greek theater has become so intimately tied to the democracy of Athens that it is difficult to interpret theater which is linked to a tyranny.[12] The frequent cultural exchanges between Athens and Syracuse confuse the questions till more. So far, one scholarly solution has been to explain the evidence for Syracusan drama as isolated examples of parasitical rivalry and emulation of the urbane brilliance of Athens. This rivalry, and the wealth and resources that the tyrants had at their disposal to pursue such rivalry, are, moreover, no doubt part of the explanation.

The prevailing scholarly interpretation of classical Greek theater as Athenian and democratic does more, however, than break up the history of Sicilian theater into isolated moments of Athenian literary and cultural colonialism. It leaves us without the means to understand theater in a different political circumstance, like the violent and harsh tyrannies of

---

[11]   In this volume, I use the term Sikeliote for the Greeks on Sicily and Italiote for the Greeks in South Italy; I use the term "natives" to refer to the indigenous people of Sicily and "Italics" to refer to the indigenous people of South Italy. When discussing the tradition of Sicilian Greek theater as a whole, however, I keep the term Sicilian because I do not mean to draw a sharp distinction between the influences and interests of Greeks and indigenous people on early Sicilian dramatic traditions. Nevertheless, it should be clear that the extant fragments and nearly all of the evidence from Sicily are for Greek-language dramas.

[12]   The work of Ann Duncan is likely to change this: see Duncan (2011), (2012), and her forthcoming monograph *Command Performance: Tyranny and Theater in Classical Antiquity*.

Sicily. In foregrounding the communal, interactive function of theater, this interpretation thrusts into the background theater's illusionary and pre-scriptive capacity to manipulate its audience, in addition to, and sometimes rather than, responding to popular opinion and values. The boundaries between manipulation of the audience and reflection of popularly held beliefs are difficult to trace even in today's plays and movies where so much more evidence is at our disposal, but the dual function of theater seems inherent in the genre.

A few extreme modern parallels remind us of the enormous potential of theater as a political tool:

> The National Socialists will reunite people and the stage. We will create a theatre of fifty thousand and hundred thousand; we will draw even the last *Volk* comrade into the magic of dramatic art and enthuse them again and again for the great substance of our national lives.[13]

Thus, Goebbels spelled out a national policy of theater production to German theater directors on May 8, 1933. Mussolini, likewise, used plays to encourage a communal acceptance of Fascist nationalism.[14] Mao[15] and Bolshevik revolutionaries[16] adopted theater as an instrument to further their political goals.[17] Modern dictators take theater seriously in their political planning.

This appeal to modern examples may be a rash starting point for a study of theater under the tyrants of ancient Sicily. Not only have propaganda methods, especially in their practical aspects, evolved in the last twenty-five centuries, but autocratic rulers may well use theater in different ways. Nevertheless, these examples do remind us, even if only in a very general way, that theater has flourished in the most undemocratic of societies.

The power of theater was well known to rulers and to theorists in the ancient world. Plato famously banned independent theater in his ideal republic, replacing it with state-sanctioned public performances.[18]

---

[13] Cited in Fischer-Lichte (2005) 128. Cf. Zortman (1984); Hofstetter (2004); and Stobl (2007).

[14] Mussolini (1933) "La parola del capo del governo," *Bollettino della Societa Italiana degli Autori ed Editori*, 7–9 (cited in Berezin 1994).

[15] E.g. Chen (2002) 58, "[. . .] both Mao and Hitler were interested in the particulars of theater production, and both believe with a passion that great consequences ensued from the way a country managed its theater."

[16] Fischer-Lichte (2005) 97–121, "The Soviet mass spectacles, 1917–1920."

[17] The didactic and political purposes to which theater has been put seem endless. On Napoleon's theatrical reforms, see Lecomte (1912); colonial theater in what was then called Rhodesia (now Zimbabwe), Kaarsholm (1990); theater as a tool for moral pedagogy in Canada, Basourakos (1998).

[18] E.g. Plato, *Laws* 660a, 817a–d. See now the study of theater in Plato's *Laws* by Prauscello (2014).

Aristophanes characterized playwrights as the teachers of the city.[19] Ancient sources record tyrants encouraging the early development of theater.[20] More general studies on tyranny in the ancient world have recognized that theater often developed under the auspices of a tyrant.[21] Theater and tyranny are frequently found together in both the ancient and modern world.

The recognition of theater's susceptibility to political masters encourages the reconsideration of the social forces that allowed, or encouraged, the development of theater in Sicily. Since theater so often engages a group audience and presents its story to a crowd, rather than to a single viewer, it requires a collaborative effort to be successful, but this does not mean that it necessarily expresses a collective or popular point of view.

1.1 Sicily's Network

The very different conditions that obtained in Sicily are not simply an interesting example of the widespread phenomenon of Panhellenic interest in Attic drama; Sicily's political and cultural situation also determined the characteristics, selection, and variety of plays on offer. The island of Sicily is, thus, not an arbitrary geographical boundary for this history. Rather, the boundaries of ancient Sicily identify an ancient context in which we can see a particular strand of the development of Greek theater, and a tradition created under particular conditions to serve a variety of specific masters and audiences.

Irad Malkin has recently argued that old models of center and periphery are not as useful for the study of Greek colonization as they once were.[22] His evocative image of Greeks around the Mediterranean looking in and towards each other, in contrast with the Roman Empire in which Rome was the center spreading its influence out to the rest of the Mediterranean, is tellingly drawn from Plato himself.[23] In antiquity, the Athenians were well aware of the complex networks of literary and artistic development that, together with trade of more practical materials, crisscrossed the

---

[19] E.g. Aristophanes, *Frogs*, 1008–9.

[20] E.g. Herodotus (5.67) on Kleisthenes, tyrant of Sikyon ca 570 BCE, who is said to have instituted tragic choruses in honor of Dionysus; (Pseudo) Plato, *Hipparchos* 228 b–c. Cf. Csapo (1995) 103–4.

[21] Ghiron-Bistagne (1976) 173–4 notes that it is almost invariably under tyrants that theater develops, for they use it as a tool to align themselves with the people against the aristocracy from whose ranks they are attempting to rise.

[22] Malkin (2011); see also Hall (2012) 19–34.   [23] Malkin (2011) 15; Plato *Phaedo* 109b.

Mediterranean enriching each city's culture with infusion of ideas from other Greek cities and, indeed, from outside the Greek world. In this vein, Eric Csapo's new argument that, from at least the fourth century, Greek theater was thought of as a common cultural possession by Greeks throughout the Mediterranean is persuasive and appealing. Whereas modern scholars once imagined Greek theater to have evolved rather like a tree with its roots in Athens only later spreading out to the far reaches of the Mediterranean, Csapo's reassessment allows us to see how other cities contributed to its development and, eventually, could claim a stake in it. In this way, network theory and patterns of de-centralized development in antiquity must apply, in some ways, to the development of ancient Greek theater.

Although the work of Csapo, Malkin, and others opens many new horizons, there are limits to the usefulness of the network-based, collaborative model of cultural development in thinking about ancient theater, and particularly the theater of Greek Sicily. First, developed in the wake of the computer age and drawing very much on the structure of the internet and the much more connected world that the internet has brought about, this model can, deceptively, I think draw us into investigating ancient drama as if it were the drama, or even movies and television, of our own day (a). Secondly, it seems to me that the model does not take enough account of ancient interest in regional traditions, particularly Sicilian, and, later, Roman interest in commemorating and celebrating Sicilian traditions of theater (b).[24]

(a) Internet and networks

As New Historicism has, of course, made clear, our own historical situation inevitably influences our understanding of the past. Network theory's dependence on the internet and modern ease of travel and exchange and the blindness of our own age is perhaps simply like the influence of any other modern situation upon our theories of the past.[25] An *ad hominem* scuffle that began in the larger academic world of the history of Greek colonization has left its mark on recent scholarship on theater outside Athens. The charge was first laid at the feet of the late nineteenth- and early twentieth-century British that they read ancient Greek colonization through the lens of their own

[24] See also Bosher (2013a).

[25] New Historicism, a flexible form of cultural materialism, is usually said to have been founded as a theory of cultural analysis by Greenblatt (1980). Malkin (2011) 9–10.

empire.[26] Italians have likewise been accused of a distorting nationalism that rendered them biased in their judgment of relations between
old Greece and Italy and Sicily.[27] Natives of New Zealand and Australia
were suspected of reading Sicilian and South Italian theatrical vases
through the rose-tinted glasses of their own postcolonial experience;[28]
a charge disputed a few years ago by another New Zealander.[29] "Isms,"
particularly postcolonialism and postmodernism, may also have
sparked unfounded enthusiasm and led scholars astray.[30] As
a Canadian, whose "embarrassingly gradual path to independence," is
a standing joke among our neighbors to the south, I might be wearing
my own particular blinkers.[31] A postcolonial viewpoint, for example,
may inform my own reading of the evidence of "postcolonial" South
Italy and Sicily, and my interest in discerning regional traditions may
be suspect.

In contradistinction to these national and local biases, however, I suggest
that a particularly insidious modern influence that skews our understanding of the theater of earlier periods is constituted by television, movies, and
now increasingly the internet. It is insidious because its influence is so
ubiquitous, crossing rather than accentuating cultural and national boundaries. The internationally available and dominant entertainment industry
of Hollywood reaches the rest of the world in a way unimaginable before
film.[32] Our modern sense of the reach of popular theater and its daily
intrusion into our lives through television and the internet may affect how
we understand the spread of popular theater in other periods, including
ancient Greece. Does the use of Hollywood, or America, as a reference
point for the magnitude of some aspect of the ancient theater industry
inevitably conjure an exaggerated picture of an international and relatively
undifferentiated reception of theater in antiquity?[33] Hollywood, and
American movie and television culture more generally, infiltrate the lives

---

[26] For a recent set of discussions, see Hurst and Owen (2005). Owen (2005) 5, "it has become
something of a truism to state that past studies of Greek 'colonization' have been influenced by,
or even based upon, the colonial experience of Britain and other Western European nations
[…]," with citations.

[27] Taplin (1993) 53.   [28] Taplin (1993) 53.   [29] Robinson (2004) 207, n. 89.

[30] Csapo (2010) 38.

[31] *This American Life*, "Who's Canadian?" originally aired 30 May, 1997, by Sarah Vowel.

[32] Hollywood and other national film collections were already well established and widely
accessible by the time Webster proposed the dominant influence of Attic drama in the West in
1948; during the lifetime of the prolific German archaeologist who published many of the South
Italian theatrical vases, Heinrich Heydemann (1842–1889), by comparison, the moving picture
industry was yet to come.

[33] E.g. Csapo (2010) 87; Bosher (2006) 194; Csapo (2004) 57.

of many in other countries, particularly English speakers, in an ordinary, daily way. Huge posters advertising the latest Hollywood flick can be seen on the street in London, Paris, Rome, and no doubt in most small towns; these signs, and the movies they advertise, are not remarkable or extraordinary.[34] The showing of American movies is not an important social event; rather, movies are widely available and, in most places, inexpensive entertainment.

It may, therefore, be pertinent to reflect how difficult and costly it was to travel to see theater or for theater troupes to travel to perform on tour in the ancient Greek world. Stories of early poets and performers traveling to the West are redolent of adventure and danger. The great wealth that might be gained from such trips to the wealthy city of Syracuse is juxtaposed with the uncertainties and dangers of travel in, for example, the story of Arion and the dolphins.[35] From the later period of the Peloponnesian War, Plutarch's tale of Athenian prisoners freed if they recited Euripides speaks not only to the popularity of the great tragedian, but also, perhaps, to the rarity of performance of Attic drama even in Syracuse.[36] Likewise, Hughes supposes that it might have been too difficult for traveling troupes to reach Paestum and that the painters of comic vases there painted remembered performances from Sicily or even imagined scenes.[37] It is interesting to consider that tales of tragedians traveling abroad often end in their deaths, not as a result of the journey itself, of course, but nevertheless suggesting that such travel was so difficult and arduous that it quite often ended in a permanent move, rather than being a return journey (Euripides in Macedon, Aeschylus, and perhaps even Phrynichus in Sicily).[38] Although the

---

[34] Compare Trendall (1990) 228 on a tragic vase that would have made a "splendid poster" announcing the play. Though vase-paintings, of course, could be created in duplicate or even by the dozen, they could not, like modern posters, be run off on a printing press by the thousands or hundreds of thousands. They did not get passed around by email to millions of viewers. This is obvious, and Trendall is not claiming that they were, but our instinctive interpretation of an ancient image in light of a modern, mass-produced image may lead us to subconsciously overestimate the dissemination of ancient images and of plays.

[35] Hdt. 1.23–4.

[36] Although this may be due to the hostilities between Athens and Syracuse, it also suggests the relative paucity of productions in the West at this time which may be due to the difficulty of bringing performers from an enemy city or from such great distance. (Plut. *Vit. Nic.* 29; Satyr. *Vit. Eur. POxy.* 9.1176 ed. Hunt, fr. 39 col. XIX 11 = Kannicht 189 a–b). See p. 16, n. 7.

[37] Hughes (2003).

[38] Euripides (e.g. *Epigr. Sepulc. AP*, 7, 45=Kannicht 121, Satyr. *Vit. Eur. POxy.* 9.1176 ed. Hunt fr. 39 col. XX 22–XXI=Kannicht 122, Diod. Sic. 13.103.5=Kannicht 123, and others collected in Kannicht); Phrynichus (e.g. Anon. *De com.* 9 p. 7 Kost. = *PCG* 7, T2). The Phrynichus in question may be the comic one, Harvey (2000) 114–15. The details recorded in the Lives of the Poets are suspect (Lefkowitz 1981), but, as a group, they give some record of received views.

traveling players of the Actors of Dionysus guilds are not likely to have sprung up *ex nihilo*, our records for their formal association date to after Alexander the Great.[39] These small indices, scattered though they are, may suggest that the difficulties of travel would promote the development of regional touring groups, or even of local city players.[40] At the very least, I think we must be wary of imputing Hollywood-like influence to Athenian drama: Attic drama must have come to the West, as to other regions, but when it did performances must have been exciting and notable social and dramatic events.

(b)   Regions and origins

Throughout this book, I tackle the second problem of a regional tradition of Sicilian theater and attempt to make the case for it. I argue that it is a tradition defined partly by the content or origin of its plays, but also by their role and appearance in Sicilian society, their reception and reflection in Sicilian art, and their place in the political history of the island.

This effort to distinguish how Sikeliotes and native Sicilians created, thought about, and were influenced by theater is confused by a peculiarly philological instinct to define genres of drama by the evidence of the extant literary texts of plays and to trace traditions back to their origins, and preferably to distinct and autonomous origins in text, cult, society, etc. It is not possible, however, as far as I can tell, to create an accurate stemma of Sicilian theater, even allowing for many complexities. Although a good case can be made for Epicharmus as an originator of comedy, as many ancient authors, including Aristotle, do,[41] and although the argument has been made that Sicilian comedy evolved out of cult rituals in honor of Demeter,[42] this kind of hunt for a historical origin of Sicilian comedy is not my purpose here. Rather, my aim is to collect and examine the disparate evidence for the social and political relevance of theater, both home-grown and Attic, in Sicily. Ancient arguments and celebrations of Epicharmus' role as the inventor of comedy are important as indications of the Sikeliotes' view of their theater and of their pride in it, rather than of some kind of historical origin of comedy, or even Sicilian comedy, in the fragments of Epicharmus.

---

[39] Hugoniot, Hurlet and Milanezi (2004) 11; see Csapo (2004) for discussion of the development of the acting profession; Le Guen (2001) 317, dates the first inscription commemorating the actors of Dionysus in Sicily to the second or the very beginning of the first century BCE.

[40] On traveling theater troupes from Athens, see Lightfoot (2002) and now Taplin (2012) 226–50.

[41] Aristotle *Poetics* 1449b 5–7.   [42] See Chapter 3.

Some problems of definition related to questions of origins and the historical development of Sicilian theater nevertheless obtain here. The first is the problem of distinguishing between cult performance and ritual and formal drama itself. The line between these kinds of performance is difficult to identify in part because of scholarly efforts to find the link between Dionysiac ritual and religion and theater.[43] The association between Dionysus and theater, however, was made also in antiquity, and ancient interest in identifying and commemorating the religious affiliations of theater is a central problem in this book. In Chapter 3, I take up the problem of cult and theater not with a view to tracing some kind of factual historical connection or evolution, but rather in an effort to distinguish the ancient Sikeliote interpretation of relationships between theater and cult from the relationship we often ascribe to Attic drama performed at the festival of Dionysus.

A second problem, likewise introduced by philological frameworks of interpretation, is the expectation that we must cleanly distinguish between various sub-genres of drama or theater. In Athens, tragedy and comedy were distinguished as the two main genres of dramatic performance. Certainly, other performance genres were available to Athenians, including various kinds of choral performance, mime, satyr play (which although formally part of the tragic tetralogy had a recognizably different tone from individual tragedies), recitation, and so on, but the two central categories of Attic drama are nevertheless tragedy and comedy. It is not at all clear that these two genres were as definitive or as dominant in ancient Sicily. Although there were Sikeliotes and Italiotes who traveled to Athens in the fourth century and later and competed in Attic theater festivals for both comedy (e.g. Philemon, Alexis of Thurii) and tragedy (e.g. Dionysius I, Achaeus, Sosiphanes), we do not have good evidence that they or others, like Epicharmus, Aeschylus, or Rhinthon, for example, partook in similar kinds of genre-defined festivals or even presented the same kind of comedy in Sicily or South Italy.[44] As I discuss more fully in Chapters 2 and 4, it is not clear that any of the comic dramas known to have been written by Sikeliotes for Sicilian performance conformed to the norms we might expect of Attic comedy, including the early dramas of Epicharmus. Although mime, as a comic genre, takes a back seat in Athens, in Sicily it comes to the fore with several prominent writers

---

[43] See Scullion (2002) for a summary and discussion of this scholarly effort. I summarize Scullion's argument in Chapter 3.

[44] See also Bosher (2013a) and for the variety of performance in Sicily, see Bosher (2013b).

associated with it (Sophron, Xenarchus, Theocritus). Several of the comic "phlyax" vases may depict Attic comedy (Chapter 5), but none of them definitively represents a chorus, which is not only a key feature of Attic comedy, but also of Attic vases that represent theater. Perhaps even Attic comedy abandoned some of its generic markers in the informal, hybrid, and wealthy theater scenes of ancient Sicily. Attic drama must have provided a reference point of some sort to Sikeliote playwrights and Sikeliote and native Sicilian audiences, but it is far from clear that the Attic model of two dominant genres and competitive festivals was adopted wholesale in Sicily.[45] Indeed, the defining elements of Attic comedy and tragedy, although studied and admired through the generations, have rarely been adopted by subsequent playwrights. Even setting aside formal generic aspects of Attic drama, it may be that tragedy as it manifested itself in Athens has never been recreated, as Daniel Mendelsohn sadly reflected in a talk on our own dramatic responses to the events of 9/11.[46]

1.2 Scope

Without the formal rubric of Attic genres to delimit this study of Sicilian theater, the book is in danger of becoming both diffuse and overblown. In an effort to avoid this, the scope of the book is limited and organized by the major categories of evidence for theater that are found in the Greek West: the fragments of Epicharmus and evidence for early performance traditions (Chapter 2); the problem of the cults of Demeter and Dionysus (Chapter 3); Aeschylus' sojourn in Sicily and the interpretation of early Sicilian comedy by way of imported Athenian tragedy (Chapter 4); South Italian and Sicilian dramatic vases (Chapter 5); and Sicilian theaters (Chapter 6). These categories of evidence are so important to the study of Greek theater in general that, as noted at the outset of this introduction, they are regularly adduced to enrich the history of the Athenian theater. The project of this study, therefore, is to examine these central categories of ancient theatrical evidence in their Sicilian, and sometimes South Italian, context.

This effort is fraught with difficulties, not least the lacunose and fragmentary evidence and the relative paucity of extant literary material from

[45] On competition and choruses in Sicily, see now Wilson (2007).
[46] Mendelsohn seminar at Northwestern University, part of the seminar series, *Aeschylus' Persians: Contemporary Resonances and Fifth-century Meanings*, 21 February, 2007.

plays performed in Sicily. The tale I narrate and the conclusions I draw are provisional and no doubt full of errors of interpretation. Nevertheless, despite the still raw and preliminary character of the book, I offer it here as an attempt to recuperate some of the qualities of a theater scene that inspired so many Sicilian artists to record it on vases and Sicilian tyrants to shelter and celebrate it in monumental theaters.

2 | Out of the Shadows

Epicharmus and Early Performance in Syracuse

The comic playwright Epicharmus produced original dramas acclaimed and influential for many centuries thereafter. His dramas can be better understood in the framework of contemporary Sicilian poetry and performance genres and also with the help of the exiguous records about the context of performance in early Syracuse.

2.1 Epicharmus

That Epicharmus was an important figure in his own time and for many generations thereafter is attested by references in Plato,[1] Ennius,[2] Horace,[3] Columella,[4] and Statius[5] among others. Early histories of ancient theater, such as Norwood's *Greek Comedy* (1931) and Pickard-Cambridge/Webster's *Dithyramb, Tragedy and Comedy* (rev. 1962), and a rash of late nineteenth-century German works on comedy[6] offer thorough syntheses of the known fragments, tracing themes and setting out arguments for his influence on other writers. Most recent scholarship falls into three general categories: philological reconstruction of the texts,[7] piecing together the themes of various plays from literary evidence,[8] and determining his influence on contemporary and later Athenian writers.[9] Thus, perhaps because the fragments, culled from later lexicographers, historians, and a few papyri, are so difficult to interpret, they have remained almost exclusively within the purview of philologists and literary analysts. In the mid-twentieth century, work by Italian scholars, in particular Marcello Gigante, situated Epicharmus and the much later comic playwright Rhinthon in the art

---

[1] *Theaetetus* 152e.

[2] Ennius wrote a poem called the "Epicharmus." For the fragments of which, quoted or referenced in authors including Cicero, Varro, and Priscianus, see Warmington (1935) 410–15.

[3] Horace, *Epistles*, II 1.55–9. [4] Columella, *Res Rustica*, I 1.7. [5] Statius, *Silvae*, V 3.148–51.

[6] E.g. Zielinski (1885); Lorenz (1864). [7] Kassel and Austin (2001) 8–173; Thesleff (1978).

[8] Webster (1962); Barigazzi (1955).

[9] Kerkhof (2001) with a very detailed summary of the history of scholarship on Epicharmus' influence on Attic Comedy, 1–12; Svarlien (1990–1991); Cassio (1985); François (1978); Bonanno (1972); Demand (1971); Gigante (1953).

historical and literary context of South Italy and Sicily. This work was visionary for what might in retrospect be seen as a postcolonial appreciation of the importance of reading the fragments of western Greek comedy on its own terms and in its own historical and social context.[10] In recent years, interdisciplinary attempts to disentangle the complicated history of Sicilian theater concentrate on the influence of Athens on Sicilian and South Italian theater. These new and important interventions show how closely linked the Mediterranean theater world was, and, inevitably perhaps, tend to relegate Epicharmus to a shadowy background. In Oliver Taplin's revolutionary *Comic Angels* (1993), in which he brought back to wide scholarly attention the ever-increasing trove of South Italian and Sicilian comic vases, Epicharmus is not a significant part of the argument.[11] Likewise, Eric Csapo's broad discussion of the development of theater in the Greek and Roman worlds credits Epicharmus with early influence and prestige in the development of a Mediterranean Greek drama, as it were, but argues that any specifically Sicilian form of comedy died with him.[12] The revolutionary arguments made by Taplin and Csapo for the early spread of Attic drama have opened the question of South Italy and Sicily to the wider scholarly community; the present book leans heavily on their work in order to respond to it and to trace what might have been the salient characteristics of a Sicilian theater as it appeared to the generations of Greeks who lived in the brilliant and wealthy city of Syracuse.

An exception in recent work that concentrates on the reception of Attic drama in Sicily is the approach taken by Andreas Willi, who seeks to position Epicharmus in the literary and linguistic world of his Sicilian compatriots, Stesichorus, Empedocles, and Gorgias.[13] In examining Sicilian writers together, he is able to draw general conclusions about the evolution of Sicilan Greek, as well as describe shared thematic and cultural features of these new world texts. He is able to show not only that their language assimilated aspects of the non-Greek native languages of Sicily,[14] but also that these western writers reacted against the literature and culture of their mother cities. He posits a (post-)colonial literature among these early Sicilian writers.[15] What his fascinating book does not take up,

---

[10] E.g. Gigante (1966) and (1971).

[11] The three mentions of Epicharmus fall on the following pages: Taplin (1993) 51 n. 6, 56, 58 n. 8.

[12] Csapo (2010) 39: "Why does a distinctly Sicilian comedy after its early 5th-century efflorescence with Epicharmus and Phormis appear to vanish without a trace?" Cf. Bosher (2013a).

[13] Willi (2008) and (2012) 56–75.   [14] See Willi (2008) chapters 2 and 3.

[15] For his argument for this description, see Willi (2012) 72–3.

however, and what this present work attempts to address, are the socio-political circumstances of Epicharmus' age, and the development of Sicilian theater through the fourth century, when an extraordinary interest in theater is suggested by the comic vases that have appeared so profusely in Sicily and South Italy. Willi makes substantial strides towards bringing to light the literary culture of Sicily before the end of the fifth century. In this book, I attempt to place Epicharmus in the dramatic culture of Sicily from the end of the sixth to the fourth centuries.

The philological and literary approach focused on Sicilian writers that Willi takes allows him to examine Epicharmus' work in great detail, whereas histories of Greek drama tend to marginalize Epicharmus in the history of early drama and in the history of Sicilian theater in particular. This may be because the evidence for his life and work is so scattered and fragmentary. Not only are we uncertain of Epicharmus' city of origin,[16] but we do not know when he began composing comedies (or other writings) in Syracuse. The anonymous writer of the *De comoedia*, a learned treatise on comedy attached to a fourteenth-century manuscript of Aristophanes, but which contains information deriving from Alexandrian scholarship, gives Epicharmus' floruit[17] as 488/4. Likewise, Aristotle gives evidence that he was writing at least as early as 487[18] and the *Suda* 486/5.[19] A reference in one of his plays to Anaxilas of Rhegium is evidence that he was working in the early 470s, perhaps 477.[20] The *Marmor Parium* records that he was working in 472/1.[21] Though no single reference is conclusive on its own, the sheer number of them makes it fairly certain that Epicharmus was working in the two decades between 490 and 470.

Although the central period of Epicharmus' working life can thus be fairly securely dated to the reigns of Gelon and Hieron,[22] the beginning and end are difficult to determine. The famously vague remark of Aristotle that Epicharmus was "long before" Chionides and Magnes is particularly puzzling:

ἀντιποιοῦνται τῆς τε τραγωιδίας καὶ τῆς κωμωιδίας οἱ Δωριεῖς (τῆς μὲν γὰρ κωμωιδίας οἱ Μεγαρεῖς οἵ τε ἐνταῦθα ὡς ἐπὶ τῆς παρ' αὑτοῖς δημοκρατίας γενομένης καὶ οἱ ἐκ Σικελίας, ἐκεῖθεν γὰρ ἦν Ἐπίχαρμος ὁ ποιητὴς πολλῶι

---

[16] The *Suda* (s.v. Epicharmus) offers four possible cities of origin: Krastos, Cos, Samos, and Megara Hyblaea (*PCG* Test. 1); Aristotle's comment that the Megarians claim to be the inventors of comedy (Arist., *Poet.* 1448a 30ff.) supports Megara Hyblaea (*PCG* Test. 4). Theocritus' epigram (*Epigr.* 18.6 (*PCG* Test. 18)) suggests Syracuse.

[17] *PCG* Test. 6 (Anon. *De com.* 4).   [18] *PCG* Test. 4 (Arist. *Poet.* 1448a 30).

[19] *PCG* Test. 1 (*Suda* e 2766).   [20] *PCG* 96.   [21] *PCG* Test. 7 (*Marm. Par.* 239 A 55 Jacoby).

[22] Webster (1961) 453 would put firm dates only in the reign of Hieron.

πρότερος ὢν Χιωνίδου καὶ Μάγνητος· καὶ τῆς τραγωιδίας ἔνιοι τῶν ἐν
Πελοποννήσωι)·

Aristotle, Poetics 1448a 28–34 (PCG Test. 4)[23]

Chionides seems to have performed at the Dionysia at Athens in 487. First,
as Wilamowitz notes, we do not know how long πολλῶι πρότερος means;
secondly, as Butcher and several scholars after him suggest, an οὐ may have
dropped out of the phrase so that it meant "not much earlier."[24] Thus, at
best, this remark does not give us enough proof to place Epicharmus any
earlier than the first decade of the fifth century.[25]

Another piece of evidence brought to bear by Pickard-Cambridge may give
some weight to an earlier date.[26] Epicharmus is often reputed to have followed
Pythagoras.[27] Since the Pythagoreans were persecuted from 510 and
Pythagoras himself withdrew to distant Metapontum, it is likely, as Pickard-
Cambridge suggests, that Epicharmus became involved with the Pythagoreans
before 510 and their persecution in Sicily. If so, we might have reason to date
the beginning of his adult life to before 510. However, since we cannot be
certain of the circumstances of Epicharmus' involvement with the
Pythagoreans, or even whether he was involved with the Pythagoreans at
all,[28] we also cannot be sure that his theatrical career began so early.

The end of his working life is equally difficult to determine, though
a note about his longevity by both Diogenes Laertes and Pseudo-Lucian
and the large number of plays he seems to have written suggest that he had
a long career.[29] The scholiast to Aeschylus' *Eumenides* notes that

---

[23] "The Dorians lay claim to both tragedy and comedy (both the Megarians, from the time when
democracy was developing among them, and those in Sicily, for the poet Epicharmus was there
long before Chionides and Magnes, lay claim to comedy and some of those in the Peloponnese
lay claim to tragedy) making the name out to be significant. For they say that they call the
surrounding villages, κώμας, whereas the Athenians call them 'demes', and thus that the word
comedy comes, not from the verb κωμάζειν, but from wandering about in the κώμας having been
dishonored by the city, and for the verb 'to do' they use δρᾶν whereas the Athenians use
πράττειν."

[24] Butcher (1895), but withdrawn in later editions (Butcher (1907, reprinted 1932) vii n. 1). Cf.
Else (1967) 112–23.

[25] For debate on this subject, see Webster (1961) 453, ". . .either the text is corrupt or the phrase is
an unintelligent interpolation or the Megarians lied."

[26] Pickard-Cambridge (1962) 232–5.

[27] *PCG* Test. 11 (Plut. *Num.* 8.17); *PCG* Test. 9 (Diog. Laert. VIII.78); *PCG* Test. 11 (Anon. *in Plat.
Theat.* 71.12); *PCG* 12 (Iambl. *VP* 266).

[28] Cf. West (1971) 302: "Everyone in Magna Graecia before the reign of Hiero moves in a cloud of
legend. A fair-sized portion of the cloud is Pythagorean territory, and almost anyone is liable to
find himself entendrilled from that quarter, whether he belongs there or not."

[29] Diogenes Laertes VIII, 78 (*PCG* Test. 9) and Pseudo-Lucian, *Makrobioi* (Long Lives) 25 (*PCG*
Test. 9) give him a long life: 90 and 97 years respectively.

Epicharmus made fun of Aeschylus' frequent use of τιμαλφούμενον, the word meaning "honored."[30] Unfortunately, this cannot, as Kerkhof points out, prove that Epicharmus was writing after 458 (the date of the production of the *Oresteia*), since the scholiast does not specify that Epicharmus was mocking the word in the *Eumenides* in particular. Indeed, as Kerkhof has noted, Aeschylus only uses the word twice in the *Eumenides*, at 15 and 626, and once in the Agamemnon at 922.[31] Epicharmus may have been noting a trend in Aeschylus' earlier work.

Pickard-Cambridge and Webster date two plays to the 460s. First, the *Odysseus Nauagos* because a "reference to sycophants excludes a date before the establishment of the democracy in 466 B.C."[32] Secondly, they date the *Pyrrha or Prometheus* to at least 469 because the Prometheus portrayed therein seems to be based on the Prometheus figure first invented by Aeschylus.[33]

Thus it seems safest to estimate Epicharmus' working life between 490 and 466, with the knowledge that it may, in fact, have extended a couple of decades on either side of this mark.

2.2   Literary Traditions in Sicily

At first glance, Epicharmus seems to have emerged suddenly from a society devoid of theater to write comic plays of great literary renown; he seems a solitary genius on the fringes of the Greek world. This image is, in part, created by ancient scholars, who frequently called him the inventor of comedy.[34] Epicharmus' reputation grew until all sorts of extraordinary things were attributed to him, such as the invention of letters of the

---

[30]   *PCG* 221 (Schol. (M) Aesch. *Eum.* 626).

[31]   Kerkhof (2001) 59. Cf. Rodriguez-Noriega Guillen (2012) 85 and n. 40.

[32]   Pickard-Cambridge and Webster (1962) 233 and 258. This fragment of papyrus is now listed in the fragments of the *Odysseus Automolos* (Odysseus the Deserter) by Kassel and Austin (*PCG* 98, fr. 7). It is very damaged along both margins, but the word for fig, *sukon*, appears twice, though not the word "sycophant" itself.

[33]   Cf. Pickard-Cambridge and Webster (1962) 265–8 for a discussion of the character of Prometheus in Aeschylus' now lost satyr play, the *Pyrkaeus*, which was produced with the *Persians* in Athens. When the *Persians* was reproduced for Hieron in, perhaps, 470, the *Pyrkaeus* may have been reproduced with it. This would give the *Pyrrha or Prometheus* a date of no earlier than 469, and, Pickard-Cambridge suggests, probably a much later one.

[34]   Arist. *Poet.* 1449b 5 (*PCG* Test. 5), 1448a 30 (*PCG* Test. 4); Them. *Or.* 27,337 b (*PCG* Test. 5); *Suda* E 2766 (*PCG* Test. 1); Theoc. *Epigr.* 18, 1–2 (AP 9 600, 1–2) (*PCG* Test. 18); Pseudo-Lucian, *Makrobioi* 25 (R-N Test 23); Diom. I 489, 8 Keil (R-N Test. 24); Anon. *De com.* (*Proleg. De com.* III) 9 p. 7 Koster (*PCG* Test. 6).

alphabet,[35] and divine parentage.[36] This glorification set him apart from a literary tradition, and lifted him into the near-mythical range of Homer, for example, or Thespis.[37] Thus, he seems less rooted in his own time and place, but rather a genius set apart from the rest.

This appearance of isolation is increased still further by our lack of information about the literary and cultural world that existed before him, especially in Sicily.[38] There are, nevertheless, several contexts in which Epicharmus might be placed, and these do suggest that he was less isolated and anomalous than he at first appears. The most immediate context of fifth-century Syracuse in which he lived and worked is the subject of this book, but in this chapter I briefly survey some earlier literary traditions on which Epicharmus may have drawn.

2.3 Doric Comedy

One tradition in which Epicharmus has been placed since antiquity is that of speakers of Doric Greek. Aristotle records the Dorians' claim to have been the first to develop the forms of tragedy and comedy, using Epicharmus as proof.[39] Some support for this can be found in other ancient sources that refer to early Doric farces. Athenaeus and the *Suda* record that Sosibius, a Spartan antiquarian of the third or second century BCE, described early Laconian ribald skits performed by δικηλισταί, *dikelistai*, whom Athenaeus equates with other early performers of farce, like the Italian "phlyakes."[40] Hesychius and Plutarch also mention *dikelistai* who entertained the Spartans, explaining that this is the Doric name for mime

---

[35] Pliny *HN* VII 192 (*PCG* Test. 28); *Suda* E 2766 (*PCG* Test. 1).

[36] Ptol. Chenn. apud Phot. *Bibl.* 190, 147 a 7. (*PCG* Test. 24). Ptolemy, however, as Richard Janko pointed out to me, is a known lunatic.

[37] Plato, *Theaetetus* 152e (*PCG* Test. 3).

[38] Some argue that this lack of information simply corresponds to a lack of culture. E.g. in a rather harsh review of M.-P. Loicq-Berger's book, *Syracuse: Histoire culturelle d'une cité grecque* (1967), J. M. Cook writes: "[...] apart from a historical school of some sort, a taste for farce, and very high standards in the selection of die-engravers, Syracuse had no lasting literary or artistic tradition." He continues: "The lesson seems to be that there are few Greek cities whose cultural history adds up to a book and Syracuse is not one of them" (Cook (1968) 241).

[39] See Chapter 2, n. 23.

[40] *PCG* Test. 2 (Athen. XIV p. 621 D); *PCG* Test. 3 (*Suda* C 859). Taplin (1993) 49 points out that Sosibius' testimony is suspect because he was driven by patriotism to see Spartan "mumming" at the origin of the drama of South Italy and Sicily. On the phlyakes, see further Chapter 5. The term "phlyax" or "phlyakes" is now controversial. This is widely recognized and I will henceforth simply use the term without scare quotation marks.

artists.[41] Megarian comedy as a genre is noted by Aristotle (see p. 36), a scholiast to Aristophanes, and in a collection of proverbs, where it is criticized for its crudeness, especially by the Athenians.[42] The origin of the comic figure of a Doric doctor is sought in the character of "Maison."[43] Whether literary Greek comedy as we know it drew on this early Doric farce in its early development, or whether later antiquarians erroneously drew the connection later, is unclear.[44] Modern scholars are often reluctant to confirm this line of dramatic development,[45] though some do trace comedy back to the revels of the Corinthians and Megarians depicted on pots.[46] To what extent Epicharmus drew on early Doric mumming and rough comedy in Syracuse itself is also unclear.[47] The anonymous author of the *De comoedia* (see p. 36) records of Epicharmus that οὗτος πρῶτος τὴν κωμῳδίαν διερριμμένην ἀνεκτήσατο πολλὰ προσφιλοτεχνήσας.[48] Certainly, it is not difficult to imagine that local comic genres that have not survived in the literary record provided material for Epicharmus, but the sources are too scanty to determine whether he represented a more sophisticated version of these early Doric farces in a direct line of development.[49]

Did Epicharmus think of himself as a particularly Doric or even Syracusan playwright? The fragmentary nature of his work means that we will never be certain and even the few fragments that we have tell a mixed story. Later ancient grammarians drew on his plays for examples of Doric

---

[41] *PCG* Test. 4 (Hesych. δ 1821); *PCG* Test. 5 (Plut. *Vit. Ages.* 21.8).

[42] Other references to lowbrow early comic forms from Megara: *PCG* Test. 7 (Arist., *Eth. Nic.* IV 6, p. 1123 a 21); *PCG* Test 8 (scholiast to Aristophanes' *Clouds* 57 b); *PCG* Test. 9 (*Proverbia Bodleianis* 285).

[43] *PCG*. Test. 11–16 (Athen. XIV p. 659 A; Fest. P. 118, 23 L.; Hesych. μ 96; Poll. IV 148; Philod. *Rhet.* IV, vol. I, p. 189 Sudhaus; Diogen. Π)

[44] Recent discussions of Doric comic traditions include Kerkhof (2001) and Csapo and Miller (2007); contra see Breitholtz (1960). As Csapo and Slater (1995) 94 note: "Much of this information [biographical data about 'inventors' . . . who are sometimes said to be Sicilian and Corinthian] is suspect, and the result of learned speculation in antiquity."

[45] Breitholtz (1960). Cf. Cartledge (1997) 4–5, who cuts to the quick of the argument by beginning with the statement that theater "was Athens' peculiar original invention" and that it was Athenian theater which "struck a notably resonant chord in Sicily and South Italy," though he gives a nod to the possibility of early performances (still post-500 BCE) in Icarion, p. 23. Cornford (1961, reprinted 1993, originally 1914) 167–8 argues against the Dorian claim, and points out that Aristotle himself does not seem to support it.

[46] Cf. Cassio (2002) 52; Webster (1970) 8f.; Csapo and Slater (1995) 89–95; Steiner (2009) 244–5.

[47] Kerkhof (2001) 1–38 traces the Doric comic tradition from Megara through Maison and Tettix to Susarion.

[48] "He was the first to put together comedy, which was diffuse, and added much ingenuity" (*PCG* Test. 6, Anon. *De. com.* (*Proleg. De com.* III)).

[49] Cassio (2002) 52 sees a direct line of connection: "Doric comic traditions were imported into Sicily, where a number of decisive developments took place, also prompted by contacts with indigenous cultures and other Greek-speaking colonies in the West."

dialect, and sometimes as evidence for Syracusan or Sicilian dialect. Buck notes that the Sicilian colonies only rarely kept a dialect very close to that of their mother cities because the shifting populations uprooted by the Sicilian tyrants effectively mixed the dialects, creating new hybrid forms of them.[50] Epicharmus seems to have kept to the mixed dialect of Syracuse, the city with which he was primarily associated, rather than adopting a literary Doric like that of his contemporary Pindar, for example.[51] Compared with the Doric of the later Syracusan, Theocritus, Buck observes, Epicharmus and Sophron seem to use rougher and simpler forms. In Epicharmus' fragments, moreover, there are some unusual forms, some from epic, some apparently Rhodian, and some of which may be Sikel or Italic.[52] Nearby Gela was a Rhodian settlement and may have influenced the language.[53] Some words, which seem similar to Latin and unlike Greek, are attributed to Sikel or Italic influence from local tribes that had immigrated to Sicily before the arrival of the Corinthian settlers in the mid-eighth century.[54] Epicharmus did quote Homeric hexameters, and Cassio suggests that, unlike Aristophanes, Epicharmus might often have Doricized Homer's Greek.[55] Since there are so few remaining contemporary inscriptions in Syracusan Doric, however, and no surviving prose or poetry from the late sixth and early fifth centuries, it is difficult to tell whether Epicharmus consciously adopted certain dialectical variants to mark his comedies in some way.[56] Most recently, however, Willi has looked at Epicharmus' work, together with that of his fellow Sikeliotes and Italiotes, Stesichorus, Theagenes of Rhegium, and Xenophanes, and has argued persuasively that "it becomes difficult to deny in the work of all these men the presence of a conscious 'active agency' which is responding to a wish found specifically among colonists of all times and ages: to lay claim to the heritage of the mother-country, but at the same time to free themselves from the weight of that heritage and to oppose it with something new and something of their own."[57]

---

[50] Buck (1955) 14.   [51] Willi (2008) 119–61; Buck (1955) 16.

[52] Hordern (2004) 17; Cassio (2002) 54–5.

[53] Ahrens (1843) 407 proposed Rhodian influence as an explanation for the -μειν (-mein) infinitive endings found in Epicharmus, and this has been generally accepted, but Cassio suggests a more organic development within the Doric dialect itself (Cassio (2002) 54–5).

[54] On the development and characteristics of Sicilian Greek, see Willi (2008) 16–90; Cassio (2002) 67–70.

[55] Cassio (2002) 73: "Epicharmus' Doricized quotation might indicate an attitude of Doric comedy towards the epic tradition different from that of Aristophanes and his colleagues, but one might also suspect that Homeric recitations were more exposed to 'translation' into the local dialect at Syracuse than they were at Athens."

[56] Cassio (2002) 55–6.   [57] Willi (2012) 72–3.

Links between mother cities and their colonies, moreover, do not always seem to have led to the flourishing of theater in Magna Graecia. In mainland Greece, Megara was particularly important for early comedy.[58] However, Megara's colony of Megara Hyblaea never built a theater, as far as we know.[59] Likewise, there is no archaeological evidence for a stone theater at Thurii, founded under the leadership of Athens in the mid-fifth century, although the possibility cannot be discounted that dramatic festivals were introduced there, and the comic poet Diphilus' home town was Thurii.[60] The early writer Aristoxenus of Selinus has left little behind, and it is difficult to be certain that he was primarily a playwright at all. The flourishing of theater in the Corinthian colony of Syracuse was not a foregone conclusion and it may have been as much due to favorable local conditions as to influence and traditions from the mother city.

2.4 Early Literary Influences

Local conditions in Syracuse seem to have been favorable to the arts. Many shadowy poets of the archaic period appear in the historical record of the city. Although the ancient traditions of their visits, and in some cases their very identities, are often suspect, the sheer number of poets and literary figures linked with early Syracuse and Sicily suggests a vibrant literary world. Moreover, many of these are associated with early stages of performance and competition.

The foundation myth of the city of Syracuse is already associated with an elusive but important literary figure: Eumelos. In one myth, one Archias of the ruling class of Corinth, the Bacchiads, was expelled from Corinth or took his leave to relieve the city of a plague brought on by a crime he committed. Taking a group of fellow Corinthians with him, he sailed to Sicily.[61] There, the Corinthians subjugated the native Sikels and founded a colony. Clement of Alexandria draws a link between Archias and Eumelos:

---

[58] Cf. notes 54 and 57.

[59] Regarding Megara Hyblaea, one may notice the provenance from this city of a terracotta theatrical mask dated to the end of the sixth–early fifth century BCE: Bacci and Spigo (2002) 41.

[60] See further Revermann (2010). On Thurii and its relationship to Athens, see Frisone (2008).

[61] Plutarch, *Am. Nat.* 2. Cf. also Diod. Sic. 8.11; Pausanias V, 7, 3; Strabo VI, 2, 4; Pindar *Olympian* 6, 4 ff.

Εὔμηλος δὲ ὁ Κορίνθιος πρεσβύτερος ὢν ἐπιβεβληκέναι ᾿Αρχίαι τῶι Συρακούσας κτίσαντι.[62]

The difficulty in interpreting this passage lies in the word ἐπιβεβληκέναι, *epibeblekenai*, which has been variously translated as "was a contemporary of" and "was a companion of." If the latter translation is correct, and implies that Eumelos accompanied Archias on his voyage to Sicily, then a tradition of epic poetry may have begun in Syracuse from its foundation. Though Eumelos, like so many early writers, does not appear very clearly in the ancient record, there is some helpful biographical information.[63] Indeed, some modern scholars accept him as a single author of several works, though others suspect that later ancient commentators simply attributed all early Corinthian epics to his name out of convenience.[64] Whether or not Eumelos composed all the epics recorded under his name, and whether or not he traveled to Syracuse with Archias, the fragments of epics recorded under his name are nevertheless evidence of early epic among the ruling class of Corinth. Since this early poetic tradition may well have migrated to Syracuse along with early Corinthian settlers, it might have had some influence on Epicharmus' works.[65]

Three epics and a processional hymn are fairly often attributed to Eumelos: a *Titanomachy, Korinthiaka, Europia,* and a *Prosodion.*[66] Very few fragments remain from these epics, but from what little can be determined of their subject matter, they seem to take up a striking number of themes that also appear in the fragments and plays of Epicharmus.

The *Titanomachy* seems to have taken up myths about the older generations of the gods, including Earth and Sea, Prometheus,[67] Cyclops, and Cheiron. Among the extant titles of Epicharmus' plays

---

[62] Clemens Alexandrinus *Strom.* I, 131, 8: "Eumelos, the Corinthian, who was older, was a companian to/lived at the same time as Archias who founded Syracuse."

[63] West (2002) 109: "Among the reputed authors of early epic poems, few of whom can be pinned down as creatures of flesh and blood, Eumelos of Corinth stands out as one of the solider figures. We are offered more definite biographical information about him than about most of that crepuscular fraternity."

[64] West (2002) 109–10; Janko (1982) 231–3.

[65] Bowra (1963) 2–3 thinks it likely that Eumelos was associated with Archias and may have been involved with the founding of Syracuse. Cf. Loicq-Berger (1967) 53, who argues that Eumelos seems to have been in the Hesiodic tradition and therefore did not introduce Homeric poetry, *per se*, to Syracuse.

[66] A *Homecoming of the Greeks* (Schol. Pind. *Ol.* 13.31 a) and a *Bougonia* (Eusebius (Hieron.) *Chron. Ol.* 5.1) are also attributed to him. Cf. West (2002) 109.

[67] Cf. West (1994) 146–7, who argues that there is no clear evidence that Prometheus played a role in the *Titanomachy*. Cf. also Kerkhof (2001) 136–40, who draws connections between the *Prometheus Bound* attributed to Aeschylus and Epicharmus' *Pyrrha and Prometheus*.

there are also *Earth and Sea,* a *Prometheus,* a *Cyclops,* and (among the Pseudepicharmeia) a *Cheiron.*[68] Stephanie West suggests that the *Titanomachy* introduced the story of the flood. This story of the flood, however, can be identified securely first in extant works of Pindar and Epicharmus, which may suggest an even more direct connection between Eumelos and the early writers of Syracuse.[69] Eumelos' *Korinthiaka* included a significant section on the figure of Medea, and Epicharmus also wrote a play of that name. The *Europia* seems, in large part, to have been about Dionysus. As I discuss in Chapter 3, Dionysus and Bacchus figure prominently in Epicharmus' plays, although there is a striking absence of evidence of cults devoted to him in early Syracuse. Dionysus (or Bacchus) was, as his name suggests, an important god for the Bacchiads, the ruling family of Corinth at the time when Syracuse was founded. Perhaps Epicharmus looked back to the epic tradition of Corinth, such as the *Europia,* for the inspiration to write about Bacchus, rather than or in addition to the Athenian preoccupation with Dionysus and theater.

Archilochus and iambic poetry, Sappho and monody are associated with the island early, but tenuously. Archilochus' fragment about the foundation of Syracuse has led to the suggestion that he visited the island. In one fragment, Archilochus describes Ethiops of Corinth, who, on the first Corinthian expedition to Sicily, exchanged his plot of land in Sicily for a honey cake.[70] The *Marmor Parium* records that Sappho "set sail for Sicily when Critias was archon at Athens and the *gamoroi* governed Syracuse."[71] Cicero also records that a statue of Sappho stood in the prytaneum of the city.[72] Both Archilochus and Sappho speak of travels or exile in their own writing, though they do not explicitly mention Syracuse. As Loicq-Berger notes on the subject of Archilochus, their circles and their centuries "étaient assurement ouverts à toute connaissance de l'étranger."[73] Thus, their knowledge of Syracuse or Sicily need not mean that they ever traveled to the city. On the other hand, frequent traveling among the upper classes, as well as the traffic of merchant ships, which operated busily in the Mediterranean, suggest that the poetry of Archilochus and Sappho, if not the persons, may also have been known to the Syracusans.

---

[68] Wilamowitz thought a reference to a Titan in another unattributed Doric fragment was from Epicharmus (*PCG.* Anon. Dor. 9).

[69] West (2002) 130.   [70] Archilochus, fragment 216 L-B; Athenaeus IV 176 D.

[71] *Marmor Parium, FGrH,* II B, 239, F 36 A.   [72] Cicero, *In Verrem* 2.4.126–7.

[73] Loicq-Berger (1967) 54.

Arion, credited with instituting choral performances in Corinth, and introducing tragedy to Athens,[74] is reported by Herodotus to have grown wealthy in Syracuse.[75] Fantastical (or perhaps symbolic) as Herodotus' story of Arion's rescue by dolphins after being thrown overboard by pirates is, it does suggest that there were early performances of dithyramb in Syracuse, and that there was money to be made there. Polacco and Anti suggest that it was through Arion's dionysiac dithyrambs that the cult of Dionysus was introduced to Sicily.[76] The popularity of the dithyramb in Syracuse is suggested by a number of dithyrambists who worked several centuries later at the court of Dionysius I.[77]

Stesichorus, too, is said to have lived in Himera on the northern coast of Sicily.[78] He took up a wide range of subjects in his poems, some of which also appear among the plays of Epicharmus. For example, both wrote on the subject of the Trojan War. Stesichorus wrote a *Sack of Troy* and *Homecomings*; likewise, Epicharmus seems to have written three plays about Odysseus and one called the Trojans. Both also wrote on the adventures of Heracles (Stesichorus appears to have written three poems about Heracles suggestive of Epicharmus' three Heracles plays). As Malkin has shown, Heracles was a particularly important figure in Sicilian lore about the Greek colonization of the island. He is figured as late as Diodorus Siculus as the earliest colonizer, and yet, as Malkin points out, he proved to be a point of contact with the Phoenician/Punic world on the west side of Sicily.[79] Their god Melqart had much in common with Heracles and the two groups could find a shared interest in the worship of Melqart/Heracles. Although these subjects are too general and too popular to prove a direct connection between the two poets, they do confirm that both were working with a similar set of myths. Stesichorus' poems may, moreover, have been meant for choral performance and would then have been best suited to larger outdoor performances, as Burkert suggests.[80]

---

[74] *Suda* s.v. *Arion*; John the Deacon, *Commentary on Hermogenes* (= Solon 30a); Scholion to Aristophanes, *Birds* 1403.

[75] Herodotus I, 23.

[76] Polacco and Anti (1981/1990) 32: "Arione è ritenuto dagli antichi il creatore del ditirambo dionisiaco e probabilmente per questa via penetrò in Occidente il culto di Dioniso, legato a sua volta all'esplosione dell'orfismo che ha soprattutto a Siracusa uno dei suoi centri maggiori."

[77] Polacco and Anti (1981/1990) 32. Telestes (*Mar. Par., FrGrH,* II B 239, F 65 A; Ath. XIV, 616F, 625 F; Diod. Sic. 14.466) and Philoxenus (Paus. I, 2, 3; Diod. Sic. 15.6; Hsch., s.v. δουλονα).

[78] Plato, *Phaedrus* 244a. West (1971) has collected the biographical testimonia.

[79] Malkin (1994) 219–35.

[80] Burkert (1987) 52–3. Cassio (2002) 56 notes that choral Doric may have influenced Epicharmus, but that it is difficult to identify precisely how.

Rhapsodic competition, too, is reported at Syracuse by a scholiast to Pindar who notes that one Kynaithos of Chios recited Homer at Syracuse in 504/1 BCE.[81] This note is now further supported by an inscription, which records the presence of a Kynaithos in Gela, not far down the coast from Syracuse. Burkert notes that the name Kynaithos is extremely rare and concludes that "the identification remains a distinct possibility."[82] Janko agrees with Burkert that the reference refers to the beginning of rhapsodic competition in Syracuse, and he draws attention to the parallel of Pisistratid encouragement of rhapsodic contests at the Panathenaia.[83]

These figures, then, Eumelos, Arion, Stesichorus, Kynaithos, and perhaps Archilochus and Sappho associate epic, dithyramb, choral and monodic lyric, and rhapsodic competition with Syracuse. Though no single attribution may be completely trusted, in conjunction they suggest that there was a thriving culture of poetry and performance of literary works in Sicily, and especially in Syracuse, before Epicharmus began composing his plays.

2.5   Epicharmus, Early Performance, and Comic Competitions

Thus, from an early period, Syracuse is likely to have been the site of large-scale productions of various kinds of poetry and drama performed before many spectators. As discussed in Chapter 3, moreover, there were many festivals at which plays might have been performed. How were performances organized? Were they simply presented piecemeal, as the playwrights wrote a new piece, or at the whim of the tyrants? Or were they part of a more formal system, as at Athens?

A fragment quoted as a proverb by Zenobius, a Greek sophist working in Rome in the first half of the second century AD, suggests that Epicharmus' plays were performed as part of a competition among comic playwrights in Syracuse. This line reads: "it lies on the knees of the five judges," (Zenobius vulg. III 64; Hesychius π 1408) and Zenobius explains it as follows:

---

[81] Schol. Pindar *Nemean* 2, 1 c, III 29, 9–18 Drachmann. West (1975) 166, argues in favor of the tradition cited by the scholiast. He notes that this is likely to be simply the first recorded performance of a rhapsode in competition, drawn from the head of a list of names on an inscription.

[82] Burkert (1979) 55.

[83] Janko (1982) 261, n. 88. On the composition of the *Hymn to Delian Apollo*, ascribed to Kynaithos by the scholiast to Pindar, see also Janko (1982) 99–115.

Ἐν πέντε κριτῶν γούνασι κεῖται· παροιμιῶδες, οἷον, ἐν ἀλλοτρίαι ἐξουσίαι εἰσίν. Εἴρηται δὲ ἡ παροιμία, παρόσον πέντε κριταὶ τοὺς κωμικοὺς ἔκρινον, ὥς φησιν Ἐπίχαρμος. Σύγκειται οὖν παρὰ τὸ Ὁμηρικόν, θεῶν ἐν γούνασι κεῖται. Ἐπειδὴ οἱ κριταὶ ἐν τοῖς γόνασιν εἶχον, ἃ νῦν εἰς γραμματεῖα γράφεται. Zenobius, vulg. III 64[84]

The attribution to Epicharmus appears in the Vulgate tradition of Zenobius' collection of proverbs, but Epicharmus' name is left out of other collections of proverbs, where the line appears.[85] Some three centuries after Zenobius, Hesychius seems to confirm the attestation to Epicharmus, explaining the reference to the "five judges" as follows: πέντε κριταί· τοσοῦτοι τοῖς κωμικοῖς ἔκρινον, οὐ μόνον Ἀθήνησιν, ἀλλὰ καὶ ἐν Σικελίαι (Hesychius π 1408).[86]

For a long time, the line was often mentioned in literature on Epicharmus, but was not accepted as useful evidence for a system of judging comedy in early Syracuse. Hesychius' interpretation was rejected, and the modern scholarly consensus was that there was no formal system for judging comedies, like those of Epicharmus, in Syracuse. Instead, the line was added to the complicated evidence for the details of judging in Athens.[87]

As far as Syracuse was concerned, contextual information offered by the ancient commentators, Zenobius or Hesychius, seemed to explain the line away. For example, following Zenobius, Berk noted that Epicharmus is parodying Homer. From this parody, Berk argued that the line is wholly a joke or a pun rather than a reference to something real.[88] Pickard-Cambridge, for his part, noting, like Hesychius, that the custom also occurs in Athens, suggested that the line refers to the tradition at Athens, instead of any similar procedure in Syracuse.[89] The line was treated as a dead end clue, which was duly decided in relevant works, but cannot be relied upon; therefore, it was quoted in many secondary works, but hardly discussed.[90]

---

[84] "It lies on the knees of the five judges. Proverbial, as it means, they are under another's control. The proverb arose because five judges used to judge the comic playwrights, as Epicharmus says. It is composed on the model of the Homeric adage, 'it lies on the knees of the gods', since the judges had on their knees (Crusius proposed a lacuna here, *CPG* Suppl. IV p. 282), those things which are now written on tablets."

[85] Pseudo-Plutarch, Proverbs I 76 and *Suda* e 1425. where the proverb is also cited. This section of the Athos manuscript of Zenobius (Ath. III. 110) is unfortunately lost, and only the title of the proverb is listed.

[86] "So many judged the comic poets, not only in Athens, but also in Sicily."

[87] E.g. Marshall and van Willigenburg (2004).   [88] Berk (1964).

[89] Pickard-Cambridge (1962) 284–5.

[90] Kerkhof (2001) omits the line altogether, and does not discuss it. In fact, it has been bandied about from secondary source to secondary source so cavalierly that the citation Ath. III 110,

It is reasonable to be cautious in using Zenobius' collections of proverbs. He is writing some seven centuries after Epicharmus; and we have noticed that there were texts falsely ascribed to Epicharmus as early as the fourth century BCE. However, since so many of the fragments of Epicharmus are preserved in sources which date later than the fourth century BCE, we cannot afford to dismiss this fragment out of hand.

Zenobius' collection as revealed by the title given in the entry under his name in the *Suda* (Zenobius' epitome of proverbs from Tarraios and Didymos) is drawn from the earlier collections of Lucillus Tarrhaeus and Didymus. Lucillus of Tarrha (in Crete) was a reputable paroemiographer by Miller's account,[91] and Didymus was a renowned scholar of Alexandria, said to have produced 3,500 or 4,000 works. If Zenobius used these respectable sources, his collection may be fairly reliable.

Moreover, the care Zenobius seems to take in citing fragments of Epicharmus suggests both that he may have additional information at his disposal and that he is careful in his quotations and his attributions to Epicharmus. There are six fragments of Epicharmus cited by Zenobius, and of these, two are from identified plays, the *Islands*[92] and the *Trojans*,[93] and four fragments are accompanied by explanations of their Sicilian roots.[94] Zenobius attributes four more fragments to the Sicilian mime-writer of the second half of the fifth century BCE, Sophron, two of which take up a Sicilian theme explicitly.[95] Zenobius' mention of two of Epicharmus' plays by name, and his attention to the Sicilian aspect of both Epicharmus' and Sophron's work, suggest that he, or his sources, is making a fairly careful appraisal of the fragments. Furthermore, the vulgate manuscript tradition, which preserves the full proverb and cites Epicharmus as its source, uses the Doricizing αν, with an "a" sound, for the genitive plural, whereas other citations of the proverb shift to the Attic κριτῶν, with a long "o" sound. Athenaeus, who was writing about the same time as Zenobius, seems likely to have had some complete texts of Epicharmus as his disposal, for he has his characters citing long speeches from the plays, and he records

which refers to the Athos collection of Zenobius, discovered in a monastery on Mount Athos in the mid-nineteenth century is sometimes attributed to Athenaeus.

[91] Miller (1868) 341. Emmanuel Miller traveled from Bucharest to Constantinople, and to Mount Athos, visiting many monasteries in search for editions of ancient texts. He describes his journey and travails in a letter addressed to the Emperor dated February 1865. In the convents of Mount Athos, he reports having investigated about 6,000 manuscripts, and among them, he found a collection of Zenobius' proverbs, known as the Athos Recension, which seems to belong to an earlier stage of the transmission than the "vulgar" text of Zenobius known to that point.

[92] *PCG* 93.   [93] *PCG* 129.   [94] *PCG* 93, 129, 226, and 239.

[95] *PCG*, Sophron frags. 73, 104, 169, 170.

large numbers of obscure words from many different plays. Thus, it is even possible that Zenobius had a text of Epicharmus at his disposal for reference.

The line itself seems to be in anapaests, a meter attested elsewhere in Epicharmus. In 1830, Hermann noted the anapaests, and Crusius, some 50 years later, suggested that the line might belong either to Epicharmus' play *Choreurai* or to his *Epinikon*, both of which are said to have been composed entirely in anapaests. Epicharmus' three regular meters were anapaestic tetrameters, trochaic tetrameters, and iambic trimeters. The exception to this, one line of dactylic hexameter, adds further proof to this argument, for this line seems to be a Homeric parody. As Berk and others have noted, Epicharmus seems to have relied very much on Homeric themes and stories for his plays. So, this proverb – which, as Zenobius so long ago suggested, seems to be modeled on the Homeric line "It lies on the knees of the gods" (repeated four times in the Homeric corpus) – [96] seems very much in character. To these two aspects of the line which are typical of Epicharmus' fragments, meter and Homeric parody, I would like to add a third: metatheatrical reference. There are simple references to current events, and to contemporary Sicilian problems in the plays, for example, references to "Sicily suffering,"[97] "the Sikels,"[98] new citizens, with which the Deinomenid tyrants filled Syracuse, or a play called *Orua*,[99] which Hesychius glosses as a political mixture; but there are also explicit metatheatrical references to poetry and to performance in Epicharmus' fragments. One of these is Epicharmus' reference in his play *Logos kai Logina*, to Aristoxenus of Selinus as the inventor of an iambic meter.[100] In another play, the *Harpagai*, he may have made reference to a training school for choruses, which he called χορηγεῖον, choregeion.[101] If the very fragmentary and erratic remains of Epicharmus' corpus have yielded two such direct metatheatrical references, a comment about judging does not seem out of character.

---

[96] Π 514, Υ 435, α 267, ε3277.   [97] *PCG* 11, ἁ δὲ Σικελία πέποσχε.

[98] *PCG* 207, σικελίζεις; *PCG* I, Epich. fr. 239, Σικελὸς ὀμφακίζεται.   [99] Athen. III p. 94 F.

[100] *PCG* 77, οἱ τοὺς ἰάμβους καὶ τὸν ἄριστον τρόπον, ὃν πρᾶτος εἰσαγήσαθ' ὡριστόξενος.: "[Poets who use] iambics and in the best way, which Aristoxenus was the first to introduce." The title of this comedy seems to refer to male and female personifications of different kinds of speech.

[101] *PCG* 13, Pollux IX.42. ἐκάλουν δὲ τὸ διδασκαλεῖον καὶ χορόν, ὁπότε καὶ τὸν διδάσκαλον χορηγὸν καὶ τὸ διδάσκειν χορηγεῖν, καὶ μάλιστα οἱ Δωριεῖς, ὡς Ἐπίχαρμος ἐν Ὀδυσσεῖ αὐτομόλωι, ἐν δ' Ἁρπαγαῖς χορηγεῖον τὸ διδασκαλεῖον ὠνόμασεν. "They called the training school the choros, as they also called the trainer the choregos and teaching choregein, especially the Dorians, as Epicharmus in *Odysseus the Deserter* and *The Seizures* called the training school the choregeion."

Pickard-Cambridge, though hesitant to attribute Zenobius' fragment to Epicharmus, concedes that it is reasonable to imagine that:

> Tragedy was very probably performed in competition before five judges, this custom, like tragedy itself, being imported from Athens; but the custom may or may not have been adopted for comedy, and the proverb itself may have been imported with the custom.[102]

What is peculiar about this conclusion is that, as Pickard-Cambridge himself demonstrates, there really is not much evidence for fifth-century tragedy in the West, apart from that of Aeschylus, unless Simonides experimented with tragedies, but we have no clear evidence of that. Even the two plays of Aeschylus that we think were performed in Sicily, seem unlikely choices for a competitive festival, I think. One of them, the *Persians*, had already been performed in Athens, and was only reproduced in Syracuse. The other, the *Aitnaian Women*, had been commissioned by Hieron to celebrate his re-founding of the city of Aetna. Surely it would have been peculiar to enter such a piece of propaganda in a competition where it might then lose. Thus we have evidence of only two tragedies performed in the first half of the fifth century in Sicily, neither of which seem likely candidates for a competition, and evidence of only one tragic playwright, Aeschylus. From the second half of the fifth century, we have the uncertain figure of the tragedian Empedocles associated with Syracuse.[103] Much may have been lost over the centuries, but this is slim evidence on which to base a picture of tragic competition in Syracuse.

In the case of comedy, on the other hand, we have the names of three comic playwrights, Epicharmus, Phormis, and Deinolochus, and titles of many of their plays. Indeed each produced many plays, certainly enough for competition among themselves. Moreover, Aelian records explicitly that Deinolochus was Epicharmus' "rival."[104] This tradition is not secure, but it is one more point in favor of comic competition.

The context of the development of comic performance in the West seems also to be very much linked to competitive rivalry. A scholiast on Theocritus reports that a komos was held at the festival of Artemis Lyaia at

---

[102] Pickard-Cambridge (1962) 284–5.

[103] Empedocles appears in several sources and moved to Syracuse at the time of the Athenian expedition. See Todisco (2002) 42. The *Suda* also tells of Carcinus and his four sons, all of them tragedians, who moved to Athens (*Suda*, s.v. Karkinos), although confusion in this *Suda* entry is likely with the theatrical family headed by the Carcinus known to us from Aristophanes' *Wasps* and *Peace*, on which see Rothwell (1994).

[104] *PCG* Din. Test. 2; Aelian, *De Natura Animalium* VI 51. Δεινόλοχος ὁ νταγωνιστὴς Ἐπιχάρμου.

Syracuse, which included songs and costumed revelry, from which a victor emerged.[105]

Athenaeus records that one Diomos was the first to invent the form of rustic song, perhaps similar to those performed at the festival of Artemis just mentioned, and that Epicharmus mentioned Diomos in two of his plays.[106] The anonymous author of the important treatise on comedy found in some of the manuscripts of Aristophanes (see p. 36) reports that Epicharmus "first gathered together the scattered fragments of comedy."[107] Although it is not clear exactly what the ancient writer means, it does suggest that Epicharmus relied on the local Dorian comic tradition to some extent. Perhaps the element of competition, which seems to have been important in this local tradition, was also preserved. Certainly, Epicharmus' plays themselves seem to preserve an agonistic element, as can be seen, for example, in the titles, *Logos kai Logina*, or *Earth and Sea*.

As discussed in the first section of this chapter, other shadowy poets associated with early stages of performance and competition in the archaic period appear in the historical record of Syracuse. Arion may have won prize money through his performances of dithyramb in Syracuse: if Stesichorus wrote for choral performances suitable for large-scale outdoor performance, as Burkert suggests,[108] his poetry may have been performed in the theater; and Kynaithos of Chios may have introduced rhapsodic competition to Syracuse. Thus, Arion, Stesichoros, and Kynaithos associate dithyramb, choral lyric, and rhapsodic competition with Syracuse and, though no single attribution may be completely trusted, in conjunction they suggest that there were public performances, most likely of a competitive kind, very early on in Syracuse.[109]

To these small clues about the context of performance in Syracuse itself there may be added evidence about festivals throughout the island. From fifth-century Gela, for example, comes a lead tablet inscribed on one side with a curse to help the writer's beloved, Eunikos, win an *agōn*.[110] The

---

[105] For passage and translation, see Chapter 3, n. 47.   [106] Athenaeus XIV p. 619 AB; *PCG* 4.

[107] Anon. *De com.* 9, p. 7; *PCG* Test. 6.   [108] Burkert (1987).

[109] In the area of the theater at Syracuse, an inscription was found, which records victors in a theatrical competition of some kind. The fragmentary inscription, which probably dates from a late period, lists a *didaskalos*, a trumpet, and a kithara player (*SEG* XLIX 1330, where it is undated. Rizzo (1989) suggests that it belongs to a pre-imperial period). This eclectic group may point to a more varied set of offerings on the Syracusan stage than were regularly given at, for example, the classical Dionysia in Athens, but without a confirmed date, it is hard to know how to interpret this set of victors. Nevertheless, it reveals a continuing tradition of theatrical competition of some kind.

[110] Dubois (1989); see now Wilson (2007).

curse is directed against the *choregoi* of other competitors. Dubois, who has collected and published these inscriptions, suggests that, although no theater has as yet been unearthed in Gela, there is no reason to discount the possibility that theatrical performances went on in the city as early as the fifth century. In any event, the inscription does seem to confirm that there were very early competitions of some sort of choral performance in Gela.[111]

At Syracuse, however, as discussed more fully in Chapter 6 on theaters, there may have been a public performance space from at least the beginning of the fifth century. Polacco and Anti argue that the remains of this theater can be found in the large theater of Syracuse; others suggest that the small, rectilinear theater nearby, which is very difficult to date, may have served originally as the performance space; in addition, we may imagine, on the model of Athens, for example, that the early performance space was in a completely different place in the city, and only later moved to the area of the monumental theater (see further Chapter 6). The Deinomenid tyrants, rulers of Syracuse in the early fifth century, supported a large number of poets, including tragic and comic playwrights, at their court, and the grand scale and propagandistic nature of their poetry and plays suggest that the tyrants may also have provided a public performance area. Polacco and Anti suggest that Sicilian comedy evolved from the cult of Demeter, as I discuss in Chapter 3, in which cult the Deinomenid tyrants were priests, and they propose an evolution from rough agonistic verses of ribald comedy, to the at least relatively elegant and formal plays of Epicharmus. Whether any direct line of development can be traced from cult to theater or not, the competitive and ribald rivalry in cult traditions would provide a familiar backdrop to comic competition.

In sum, it is not possible to be completely sure about Zenobius' quotation of Epicharmus. We do not have firm evidence that comedy in Syracuse was performed in a competitive format, and certainly not that there were five judges. However, the evidence seems to be at Zenobius' disposal for making a correct diagnosis of the line, and the similarity of the line to the rest of Epicharmus' extant corpus suggests that we should not dismiss the fragment out of hand. In later periods, the monumental theater was ideally arranged to support large-scale productions in front of large audiences, and we may infer that in the golden age of Epicharmus, Deinolochus, Phormis, Aeschylus, and authors of other kinds of public poetry, there was also

---

[111] See now Wilson (2007) for further discussion of the inscription.

a theater of some kind provided for public performance. Moreover, the competitive nature of early sub-literary comedy in Sicily, combined with three named contemporary comic writers, suggests that it is likely that there was some kind of comic competition in early Syracuse, in which Epicharmus took part.

3 | Cult and Circumstance

In recent years, scholars have argued for a profound connection between the cult of Demeter and the early development of theater in Greek Sicily.[1] On close examination, however, the connection appears not to be organic, but an accident of local politics.

3.1 Demeter

In the last pages of his monumental archaeological study of the theater of Syracuse, Luigi Polacco reconstructs the origins of Sicilian drama. He argues that comedy grew out of the cult of Demeter in Sicily, just as tragedy had developed from the cult of Dionysus in Athens.[2] Polacco's argument relies on his analysis of the shifting cults in and near the theater of Syracuse, and his view that the rites of Demeter and her divine mythology and persona nourished the development of drama within the cult. He proves that the cult of Demeter would have been well suited to dramatic rituals,[3] and he argues that the theater itself was part of a sanctuary complex devoted to chthonic cults.[4]

In the last two decades, scholars have begun to agree that Sicilian theater, as a whole, was profoundly connected to the cult of Demeter, rather than

---

[1] I am very grateful to Fiona Macintosh and the Archive of Performances of Greek and Roman Drama at Oxford University, and to Lee Pearcy, Radcliffe Edmonds, Russell Scott, and the Bryn Mawr Classical Colloquium Series for giving me opportunities to present some of the ideas on which this chapter is based. I benefited tremendously from discussion and comments after both talks, and wish to thank in addition Barbara Goff, Lorna Hardwick, Robert Parker, Oliver Taplin, and Bill Tortorelli.

[2] "A Siracusa, nel culto di Demètra, nasce un 'teatro,' esattamente come nel culto di Dionìso esso nacque ad Atene. E come ad Atene nel teatro si forma e si storicizza la 'tragedia,' a Siracusa, terra di Demètra, germina e prende corpo la 'commedia.'" Polacco (1990) 157. On the connection between cult and Athenian drama, see also Sourvinou-Inwood (2003).

[3] Polacco and Anti (1990) 155–9, "III. Perché il teatro."

[4] Polacco and Anti (1990) 119–54. In conclusion (pp. 155–8), they discuss how the cult of Artemis, as well as that of Apollo, would have been linked with that of Demeter, and argue that the combination of all these cults found "nella religione demetriaca la sua più complessa e congrua formulazione."

34

the cult of Dionysus as at Athens.[5] This revisionist movement is a welcome reminder of the particular Sicilian context, where Demeter and Kore were dominant in politics, religion, and daily life. Moreover, it takes part in a more general scholarly revision of Dionysus' dominance in the world of ancient drama.[6] These scholars' views of a connection between theater and Demeter in Sicily draw on the premises articulated by Polacco: that, all over the ancient Greek world, Demeter's cult had theatrical aspects, and, more important, that Sicilian theaters were built in close proximity to cult sites of Demeter.

The first premise is complex but uncontroversial on its face: throughout the Mediterranean, the worship of Demeter included theatrical or performative aspects, broadly understood. Some of her cult sites had seating areas, sometimes called cult theaters or theatral areas, where spectators could gather to watch and perhaps take part in ceremonies. There is reason to believe that her worship included religious performances of her loss of and then reunion with her daughter. Moreover, the myth of Demeter as we have it in the Homeric Hymn, for example, includes burlesque moments that may be associated with early comic forms.

In Sicily, the cult of Demeter and Kore was widespread and enormously important. At Syracuse itself, a hotbed of theater in the West, there were several festivals to Demeter and Kore at which some kind of proto-drama or cult drama may have been practiced, as Diodorus Siculus suggests. The ten-day Thesmophoria, the main festival of Syracuse and "a languid 10-day affair" as Barbara Kowalzig evocatively puts it, was the largest of these. Diodorus describes a practice of ribald speeches and miming of early myth in performance, which is suggestive of some kind of proto-dramatic form:

> τῆς δὲ Δήμητρος τὸν καιρὸν τῆς θυσίας προέκριναν ἐν ὧι τὴν ἀρχὴν ὁ σπόρος τοῦ σίτου λαμβάνει, ἐπὶ δ᾽ἡμέρας δέκα πανήγυριν ἄγουσιν ἐπώνυμον τῆς θεοῦ ταύτης, τῆι τε λαμπρότητι τῆς παρασκευῆς μεγαλοπρεπεστάτην καὶ τῆι διασκευῆι μιμούμενοι τὸν ἀρχαῖον βίον. ἔθος δ᾽ἐστὶν αὐτοῖς ἐν ταύταις ταῖς ἡμέραις αἰσχρολογεῖν κατὰ τὰς πρὸς ἀλλήλους ὁμιλίας διὰ τὸ τὴν θεὸν ἐπὶ τῆι τῆς Κόρης ἁρπαγῆι λυπουμένην γελάσαι διὰ τὴν αἰσχρολογίαν.
> Diodorus Siculus V 4, 7.[7]

---

[5] E.g. Mitens (1988) 20; Todisco (2002) 29; Wilson (2007) 354; Kowalzig (2008) 131.
[6] E.g. Scullion (2002); Nielsen (2002).
[7] "They determine the time of the festival of Demeter, when the seed of the grain starts to sprout; for ten days they hold the festival, which bears the name of this goddess, most magnificent in the brilliance of its preparation and miming the ancient life in a performance. Their custom in these days is to speak obscenities in their associations with one another, because the goddess, grieving at the rape of Kore, laughed because of an obscene speech." The complexity lies in determining if and how these performance events in the context of cult

In this story, grief at the loss of her daughter led Demeter to cast the earth into winter and starve the crops and the people. Obscene jokes provoked the goddess to laughter and to abandon her grief. These jokes, therefore, which suspended Demeter's agony – an agony caused by the descent of Persephone to Hades – take on a pivotal function in the renewing of life after death.[8] As part of the festivities, they mime the ancient life in a performance. It is hard to know if such ribald speeches and mimes were the forebearers of later, formally staged comedies, particularly since, writing in the first century BCE, Diodorus is at some remove from the early period he describes.[9] Nevertheless, this summary does suggest a continuing tradition of performance of some kind in the worship of Demeter, and Malcolm Bell argues that "The rites he [Diodorus] describes should be at least as old as the fourth century."[10]

Polacco and Anti also note five other festivals on a similar theme: the Koreia, in honor of the return of Kore; the Theogamia, celebrating the wedding of Hades and Kore; the Anakalupteria, for the rape of Kore; the Anthesphoria, celebrating the departure of Kore from Sicily to Italy to pick flowers; and the festival in honor of Cyane where Persephone was snatched away by Hades.[11] These frequent popular festivals may have provided occasions for some sort of dramas to be staged. It is not clear, however, whether and how proto-dramatic events, if such these were, at these religious festivals evolved into formal theater. Although a lively theatrical tradition arose at Syracuse as early as the beginning of the fifth century, for example, nothing comparable seems to have occurred at other cities in the Greek world where the cult of Demeter and Kore was important. That the worship of Demeter included performative aspects and that the cult of Demeter was particularly strong in Sicily is uncontroversial, but it remains difficult to determine how religious ceremonies and cult performances related, if at all, to productions of drama in more formal settings.

relate to the development of formal theater. See, e.g., Sourvinou-Inwood (2003); Nielsen (2002); Scullion (2002); Csapo (1997); Redmond (1983); Becker (2003); Hollinshead (2012) and (2015).

[8]   Clinton (2004) examines the importance of epiphanies of the gods in the Eleusinian Mysteries, e.g. Eleusis, Corinth, Pergamum, Cyrene; see Hollinshead (2012); Moretti (2008) 23–52; Becker (2003); Nielsen (2002); Polacco and Anti (1981/1990) 155; and Polacco (1987).

[9]   E.g. Sposito (2004); Polacco (1987) for this and other "drames sacrés."

[10]   Polacco (1987) 9–10 divides the Homeric *Hymn to Demeter* into a series of dramatic tableaux. In the hymn (190–205), Demeter is cheered by the jokes made by Iambe, whose name suggests that she is a female personification of the metre of the ancient verse form of comic abuse in the archaic Greek tradition.

[11]   Polacco and Anti (1981/1990) 26–9.

Map 3.1 Early locations of the cult of Demeter on Sicily

A second argument is therefore often adduced to support a link between the cult of Demeter and theater that focuses the debate more closely on Sicily itself: this is the claim that many ancient theaters in Sicily were built in physical proximity to her cult sites.[12] Although the stone theaters are now mostly thought to have been built in the fourth century and later (see Chapter 6, "Theaters"), physical proximity would nevertheless demonstrate a continuing link between the cult and theater.

A survey of excavated and identified remains of Sicilian theaters, however, suggests that there was no consistent program of building theaters near any single particular cult, including that of Demeter (Map 3.1). In the following very brief survey, I concentrate on theaters which have been excavated and studied within scholarly archaeological memory; those which are known to us from ancient or even more recent (e.g. eighteenth-century travelers') reports but which have not been identified and published, I set to one side.[13]

Two theaters at Helorus and Morgantina and the *ekklesiasterion* at Agrigento are all very near or inside a sanctuary to Demeter. The theater of Helorus, often dated to the fourth or third century BCE, was built adjoining a sanctuary to Demeter, whose temple is dated to

[12] Todisco (2002) 29; Wilson (2007) 354; Kowalzig (2008) 131; MacLachlan (2012) 347 and 352, n. 38.

[13] For discussion of these theater buildings and for bibliographical sources, see Chapter 6.

Figure 3.1 The *ekklesiasterion* at Agrigento. Photo: Clemente Marconi

the second half of the fourth century (see Chapter 6, Table 6.1).[14] Little remains of the cavea, which once may have held as many as 1,250 people, and nothing of the orchestra since a canal now runs through it. Although the theater is, curiously, situated outside the city walls, it is nevertheless thought to have been closely associated with the sanctuary complex to Demeter that lay within the walls as part of a theater/sanctuary complex.[15] At Agrigento, a theater proper has only recently been found, and an *ekklesiasterion* dated to the fourth century was uncovered in the 1960s near to or in a much older chthonic sanctuary (Figure 3.1).

As De Miro notes, the structure of the seating arrangement of the *ekklesiasterion* is not obviously suited to performance: the curve of the cavea extended well beyond a U shape and only just stopped short of forming a closed circle; there is also almost no rake to the seats which were constructed like benches, unlike most formal theaters. Theatrical performers can, of course, overcome such difficulties and formal productions of plays cannot be excluded, but it does not seem that this building was constructed primarily for theatrical performance. Although he does not dismiss the possibility that some cult ceremonies were held here, De Miro argues that the main function of this public edifice (the earliest of its kind found in

---

[14] The results of excavations beginning in 1899 are summarized in Voza (1989) together with bibliography up to that point; for more recent bibliography, see also Marconi (2012) 195–6. See discussion of this theater in Chapter 6. The theater is, curiously, omitted from the surveys of Courtois (1989) and Moretti (1993).

[15] Todisco (2002) 172.

Figure 3.2 Morgantina: theater, chthonic sanctuary, and *ekklesiasterion*. Photo: LaDale Winling

Akragas) was political gatherings.[16] The physical proximity of the *ekklesiasterion* to the chthonic cult is notable, but it is not clear whether this public building was conceived as a theater and whether it regularly, or ever, functioned as one.[17] At Morgantina, as well, there is clear evidence of physical proximity between the sanctuary to the chthonic goddesses and the theater. The theater, dated to the last 30 years of the fourth century, and a rectilinear *ekklesiasterion* flank a sanctuary to Demeter (Figure 3.2).[18] The sanctuary is dated to the mid-fourth century, though it may have been built on an older cult site to Demeter, and it is likely that theater and sanctuary formed part of the same building program.[19] At the sanctuary, moreover, Sposito argues that performances and ceremonies were probably public rather than secret or hidden rituals as so often at the cult of Demeter.[20] Yet, despite the close

---

[16] De Miro (1967) (165–6): "Non e chi non veda che non si tratta di una comoda cavea per spettacoli. Luoghi di riunione per assemblee popolari – quando non sono nello stesso tempo teatri – non hanno preoccupazioni tecnico-estetiche di gradonature, di cui talora sono privi; ed e tutt'altro che improbabile che a tali assemblee si partecipasse stando preferibilmente in piedi." (168) "Certo la connessione con il santuario ctonio sulla platea a nord puo suggerire che in alcune occasioni abbia potuto servire per luogo da cui assistere a particolari cerimonie . . . " "Ma date le notevoli dimensioni della cavea rispetto a quelle, piuttosto modeste, del santuario sulla platea retrostante, riteniamo sottolineare piuttosto certa connessione che si riscontra tra 'ekklesiasteria' e santuari, come ad Atene fra la Pnice e il Thesmophorion." See also De Miro (1963).

[17] Theaters regularly functioned as *ekklesiasteria* (see Chapter 6), but it is not clear whether the reverse happened.

[18] For recent confirmation of a mid-third century date for the monumental phase of the theater, see Bonanno (2008) 72.

[19] Sposito (2004). Cf. Bell (1981) 4–7 for a summary of the foundation and history of the settlement, and the note that the sanctuaries of Demeter and Persephone were no older than the new plan of the city, which may date to the beginning of the fourth century.

[20] Sposito (2004).

physical proximity of the cult site to the theater, the theater itself was formally dedicated to Dionysus, as an inscription at the site reveals.[21]

Indeed, at this point in the survey of Sicilian theaters, the pattern of physical proximity between cult sites to Demeter and theaters breaks down. At several theaters, Aphrodite seems to preside over the nearest cult site and temple (Akrai, Monte Iato, Heraclea Minoa, and perhaps even Segesta and Solunto).[22] At Akrai, evidence of cults to Heracles, Demeter, and Kore have been found in the vicinity of the city, but the temple near the theater is dedicated to Aphrodite and the theater itself is within the sacred ground of this temple.[23] At Monte Iato, inscriptions on small clay acorns found in the vicinity of the theater have led to speculation that there were celebrations in honor of Demeter near the theater, but this cannot be confirmed. Moreover, the nearest excavated temple is to Aphrodite, and from the theater itself come sculpted figures of satyrs and nymphs which must have decorated the *paraskenia* of the theater. Isler has proposed that these figures mark a Dionysiac context.[24] At Heraclea Minoa, a terrace on the hill of the theater yields traces of a sanctuary, but our only secure link there is to Aphrodite; Herakles, Demeter, and Kore are only hypothesized as deities of the cult.[25] In the Punic settlement of Solunto, statues of Zeus-Baal and another of Aphrodite-Astarte have been found north-west of the mid-fourth-century theater.[26] At Segesta, archaeologists are hesitant to associate the theater (mid-fourth century) with the cults of Aphrodite or Artemis found in other areas of the excavation site.[27]

Elsewhere, Dionysus, Zeus, Artemis, Athena, and Heracles (as at Taormina) jostle in the historical record. At other theaters, Pan and the Nymphs (as at Tyndaris, and perhaps Monte Iato and Segesta) seem to come to the fore.[28] At still other theaters, close proximity to cult sites is not claimed or intensively discussed in publications since the excavations are too new (Hippana, Halaesa)

---

[21] Sposito (2004) 286. Cf. Bonanno (2008) 70 on a possible fifth-century cult site to Dionysus in the vicinity of the theater. One may add to these examples the South Building in the main urban sanctuary of Selinunte, currently identified with a rectilinear theater connected with performances mainly associated with Temple R, possibly a cult place of Demeter: Marconi and Scahill (2015). See also p. 41 n. 29 for a possible connection between the theater at Catania and a major sanctuary of Demeter.

[22] Cf. Fountoulakis (2000) on the much later Artists of Aphrodite, who seem to have performed at Syracuse.

[23] Todisco (2002) 168.

[24] Isler (2000) 213; cf. Courtois (1989) 36 for the suggestion that the figures are very similar to ones found at the Lycurgan Theater of Dionysus at Athens.

[25] Todisco (2002) 175; De Miro (1989) 242; De Miro (2014); Diod. Sic. 4.79.3.

[26] Todisco (2002) 188.   [27] Todisco (2002) 183.

[28] Isler (2000) 218 records the possibility that the iconography of Pan in the theater at Segesta might be connected to a local cult (Bulle (1928) 112). See Courtois (1989) 48 on dating the figures of Pan at Segesta to the Hellenistic period.

or the area in which the theater is found is too crowded by the modern city to allow extensive excavation of the ancient city (Catania).[29]

It is on the complex site of Syracuse, however, that Polacco and Anti base their argument for the close connection between Demeter and Sicilian theater. In their analysis of the theater and its associated sanctuaries, Polacco and Anti argue that the archaeological evidence suggests that the cult of Demeter was the most important. They begin with close analysis of the area underlying the theater at Syracuse where they have found evidence of pre-Greek rites associated with water and, probably, the underworld.[30] They then argue that the Greeks superimposed their own rites of Pan and the Nymphs and, ultimately, of Demeter and Kore on native religious rites held in the same sacred spaces. The cult of Demeter seems to have been fairly easily assimilated to pre-Greek, native cults of vegetation and harvest.[31] They argue that the whole theater complex, including a sanctuary above the theater, a high terrace, a sanctuary in the valley, and the theater itself, function as a "topographical, religious and architectonic" unit.[32] A sanctuary west of the theater also shows signs of the cult of Demeter and Kore, and a nearby chthonic altar fits the pattern.[33] Indeed, their findings in the theater led them to the conclusion that the hollow of the theater was itself a *thesmophorion*.[34] Some argue that the nearby remains of a rectilinear theater, which may date to a much earlier period than the large theater, may also have been associated with the cult of Demeter.[35] Thus, Polacco and Anti argue that comedy developed from the cult of Demeter in Sicily, and specifically Syracuse, just as tragedy developed from the cult of Dionysus in Athens.[36] As Polacco summarizes their views, the theater at Syracuse only operated under the auspices of the pagan goddess. With the advent of Christianity, the Madonna took the place of Demeter and the theater was used as a large graveyard.[37]

---

[29] For Catania, however, see more recently Branciforti (2010) 183–209, who suggests that the local theater may have been built in close association with a major sanctuary of Demeter.

[30] Polacco (1990) 139 describes Sikel graves in the area of the theater.   [31] White (1964) 263.

[32] Polacco (1990) 144.   [33] Polacco (1990) 144–50.

[34] Polacco (1990) 142. Cf. Gentili (1959), who proposes that two votive bases with inscriptions to Demeter and Kore, together with many statuettes representing Demeter and Kore, suggest that there was a *thesmophorion* in the Neapolis. For a summary of these and other inscriptions to Demeter and Kore found in the Neapolis, see Dimartino (2005) 92–3.

[35] Cf. Gogos (2008) 30.   [36] Polacco (1990) 155–9.

[37] Polacco (1990) 159: "La fine del teatro coincide con la fine dei culti pagani. [...] Il Temenite torna ad essere soprattutto cimitero, come prima dei Greci. [...] La Madonna prende il posto di Demetra; rimangono le grotte, rimane l'acqua e con l'acqua rimane l'idea della vita che, come quella della morte, non ha fine."

The connection of the theater of Syracuse with the cult of Demeter is not, however, secure. Cicero records two prominent temples to Demeter and Kore (Cic. *Verr.* 2.4.119), but the location of these temples has not been confirmed; a large sanctuary to Demeter and Kore has in fact been unearthed a good 30 minutes' walk away in the Piazza della Vittoria.[38] In a recent excavation and analysis of the site of the great theater, Voza identifies the dominant temple above the theater as belonging to Apollo.[39] As he argues, this temple is not just physically proximate, but truly dominant, with sightlines that position the temple exactly in line with the center of the orchestra. This close connection between the temple and the theater suggests that Apollo played a significant role in the collection of cults in the area, perhaps even the most dominant. In the area of the theater, an inscription to the artists of Dionysus, dating from the second century, is a good reminder that, at the latest by the Hellenistic period, Dionysus had consolidated his role as god of theater even in Sicily.[40] Still later, an inscription recording the artists of Aphrodite, a collection of various performers, suggests that other cults found their footing in the lively dramatic scene of the city.[41]

In sum, cults associated with a number of Sicilian theaters may be summarized in chart form as in Table 3.1.[42]

This rather cavalier survey of theaters does not set out all the more subtle connections between cult and theaters in Sicily, but it is the most accurate general picture of the situation that I am able to draw from secondary sources and excavation reports. In sum, there are two (perhaps three if the *ekklesiasterion* at Agrigento is included) cult sites of Demeter and Kore near which or onto which theaters were built, but there are many more theaters (at least nine, and maybe more) that do not seem to have been built near cult sites of Demeter and Kore, or else the evidence for it is very weak. By the same token, of course, many cult sites of the chthonic goddesses in Sicily boast no formal theater at all.[43] In sum the archaeological evidence for a link between Demeter and theaters in Sicily is not very strong.

---

[38] For a summary and bibliography of recent excavations and interpretations of the archaeological evidence, see Zirone (2005) 176–7. For literary sources about the two temples (or one temple with two cellas) and for literary sources that mention sanctuaries of Demeter, see Facella (2005) 8. For a mid-sixth century inscription to the goddess and her daughter, see Dimartino (2005) 87–8.

[39] Voza (2008).

[40] For a magnificent bibliography of ancient literary sources on the many different cults in ancient Greek Syracuse, see Facella (2005) 35–7 and for an equally thorough summary of epigraphical sources, see Dimartino (2005) 107–12.

[41] Fountoulakis (2000).   [42] Information drawn from Todisco (2002) 167–92.

[43] See Hinz (1998).

Table 3.1 *Cults associated with Sicilian theaters*

Theaters	Associated cult	City or nearby cults
Akrai	Aphrodite (very near by)	Artemis, Demeter, and Kore
Agrigentum (*ekklesiasterion*)	Chthonic gods (rock cuttings suggest festivals in honor of Demeter)	
Helorus	Demeter (sanctuary very near by)	
Heraclea Minoa	Aphrodite	Herakles, Demeter, Kore (hypothesized, not confirmed)
Monte Iato	Statues of Nymph and Satyr decorating the *paraskenia*: Isler suggests Dionysiac context	Demeter? (some inscriptions found nearby suggest that there may have been a cult in the vicinity), Aphrodite
Morgantina	Theater is dedicated to Dionysus	The theater and the *ekklesiasterion* flank a sanctuary to Demeter and Kore
Syracuse	Apollo, evidence of Demeter, Pan and Nymphs	
Soluntum		Zeus-Baal, Aphrodite-Astarte
Tauromenium	Dionysus, Zeus, Athena, Artemis, and Herakles	
Tyndaris	Pan and Nymphs	

One might argue that these theaters, now variously dated to the middle or end of the fourth century and later (with the possible exception of Syracuse), are relatively late edifices and that many had broken with a much older tradition of theater in the cult of Demeter. It is also possible that the Sikeliotes simply thought it unimportant to build a formal temple or cult site to Demeter near theaters, when, as Polacco has argued, it would be perfectly sufficient for the worship of Demeter and Kore to have a big open space, like a theater, in which to celebrate the Thesmophoria rites.[44] Nevertheless, connections between Demeter and theater remain only a possibility: we do not have sustained literary or archaeological evidence of it.

The cult of Demeter, moreover, was not only important in Sicily, but throughout the Greek world,[45] and yet literary comedy, like that of Epicharmus, does not seem to have sprung up in other places devoted to the goddess. This does not preclude a particular connection with the development of theater in Syracuse, but it does require a more precise

[44] Cf. Bell (1981) 102–3 for a caution about different cults requiring different forms of worship.
[45] Among many sources, cf., for example, Guettel Cole (1994).

explanation of the connection between the cult and drama. The archaeological and historical sources admit the possibility of Polacco and Anti's suggestion, but do not prove it.

A messy, but perhaps more likely, interpretation of the evidence is that performances were presented and theaters built under the auspices of a range of gods in Sicily, as elsewhere in the Greek world.[46] Polacco recognizes that even in Syracuse other deities presided over ceremonies that may have fostered cult dramas. One such was a festival in honor of Artemis. A scholiast to Theocritus records that during this festival the participants sang songs and dressed up with wreaths and stags' horns, and hung bread with figures of animals on themselves. A winner was chosen from among them, who took the bread of the losers and stayed in the city. The losers left the city for nearby villages hunting for food. "They sang sportive and ludicrous songs and ended: 'Receive good fortune, receive health, which we bring from the goddess, which she calls down.'"[47] Such competitive performances seem like an early form of

---

[46] On theaters built near cult sites to a range of gods, see Nielsen (2002) 76–80.

[47] Translated by Pickard-Cambridge (1962) 155 from *Scholia in Theocritum vetera, Prolegomena* Ba 17–Bb 14 (Wendel p. 2).

ὁ δὲ ἀληθὴς λόγος οὗτος. ἐν ταῖς Συρακούσαις στάσεώς ποτε γενομένης καὶ πολλῶν πολιτῶν φθαρέντων, εἰς ὁμόνοιαν τοῦ πλήθους ποτὲ εἰσελθόντος ἔδοξεν Ἄρτεμις αἰτία γεγονέναι τῆς διαλλαγῆς. οἱ δὲ ἀγροῖκοι δῶρα ἐκόμισαν καὶ τὴν θεὸν γεγηθότες ἀνύμνησαν, ἔπειτα ταῖς τῶν ἀγροίκων ᾠδαῖς τόπον ἔδωκαν καὶ συνήθειαν. ᾄδειν δέ φασιν αὐτοὺς ἄρτον ἐξηρτημένους θηρίων ἐν ἑαυτῷ πλέονας τύπους ἔχοντα καὶ πήραν πανσπερμίας ἀνάπλεων καὶ οἶνον ἐν αἰγείῳ ἀσκῷ, σπονδὴν νέμοντας τοῖς ὑπαντῶσι, στέφανόν τε περικεῖσθαι καὶ κέρατα ἐλάφων προκεῖσθαι καὶ μετὰ χεῖρας ἔχειν λαγωβόλον. τὸν δὲ νικήσαντα λαμβάνειν τὸν τοῦ νενικημένου ἄρτον· κἀκεῖνον μὲν ἐπὶ τῆς τῶν Συρακουσίων μένειν πόλεως, τοὺς δὲ νενικημένους εἰς τὰς περιοικίδας χωρεῖν ἀγείροντας ἑαυτοῖς τὰς τροφάς· ᾄδειν δὲ ἄλλα τε παιδιᾶς καὶ γέλωτος ἐχόμενα καὶ
   εὐφημοῦντας ἐπιλέγειν
   δέξαι τὰν ἀγαθὰν τύχαν,
   δέξαι τὰν ὑγίειαν,
   ἃν φέρομες παρὰ τᾶς θεοῦ,
   ἃ ἐκελάσκετο τήνα
   ἃν τῶι ἐκαλέσκετο

"The true story is this. In Syracuse, there was once a revolution and many citizens were corrupted and, when finally the mob returned to concord, Artemis seemed to be the cause of the reconciliation. The rustics brought gifts and sang songs to the goddess in their joy. After that they gave a place as a matter of custom to the songs of the rustics. They say they sang, having strung on to them bread with figures of animals, a wallet full of all kinds of seeds, and wine in a goat-skin; they poured libations to those who met them; they wore a wreath and stags' horns in front, and held a throwing-staff in their hands. *The victor took the bread of the vanquished*, and he remained in the city, the vanquished went into the villages collecting sustenance for themselves. They sang sportive and ludicrous songs and ended: 'Receive good fortune, receive health, which we bring from the goddess, which she calls down.'" (Italics mine) Tobias Fischer-Hansen (2009) has examined the evidence for the importance of the cult of Artemis in Sicily and South Italy in the classical period. Terracotta figurines of the goddess, found in very large numbers in South Italian and Sicilian sanctuaries, as far west as Selinous,

theatrical competition, and, as Pickard-Cambridge notes, festivals like this one "at Athens were associated rather with Dionysus."[48] Two other dramatic interludes in honor of Artemis are recorded by Pollux and Athenaeus. The former describes a dance of an Ionic messenger and the latter a dance accompanied by the *aulos,* a reeded pipe, both in honor of Artemis.[49] In his discussion of early theater in Sicily, Christopher Dearden supports the view that Artemis Lyaia may have presided over pre-dramatic cult activities.[50] Although Polacco and Anti argue that Demeter was dominant in the area of the theater at Syracuse, they acknowledge that there were a variety of cults, and, in particular, strong evidence for theatrical rituals in honor of Artemis and for Apollo's pre-eminent position near the theater. Tommaso Guardi, for his part, suggests that theatrical festivals at Syracuse must have been related to Apollo, since the theater was built in a sanctuary dedicated to him[51] and Giuseppe Voza's recent analysis of the relationship of the temple to Apollo and the theater supports this association.

This interpretation of the Sicilian evidence agrees with recent studies on the development of theatrical performances in various cults throughout the Mediterranean and also with the wide variety of gods who presided over theaters elsewhere in the Greek world. Inge Nielsen, for example, has found cult drama associated with the worship of Artemis, Dionysus, Hera, Apollo, and Aphrodite, among others.[52] In her wide-ranging study of cultic theaters throughout the Mediterranean from the Minoan to the Roman period, she concludes that ritual drama developed in many places in the adoration of a wide variety of gods. General trends through space and time, however, emerge, and, in particular, she notes the large number of theaters in cults of gods and goddesses associated with the harvest.[53] She suggests

---

suggest a considerable increase in the popularity of this goddess in the late fifth and fourth centuries.

[48] Pickard-Cambridge (1962) 155.   [49] Pollux IV.103, and Athenaeus XIV 629e.

[50] Dearden (1990b) 155: "The date of these activities is unclear but together they provide a background of choral dance and song suggestive of the pre-dramatic activities from which Attic comedy is conjectured to have arisen."

[51] Guardi (1980) 27: "Che gli agoni siracusani si svolgessero in occasione di festività apolline e reso probabile dal fatto che il teatro era collocato nel *temenos* di Apollo."

[52] Nielsen (2002) 76–80. Nielsen, like Polacco, suggests that cult theater provides the foundation for literary drama, because it contained a "plot and individual actors besides the chorus, and performed as part of a liturgy [. . .]." Therefore, she suggests "[. . .] this kind of drama [. . .] constitutes a kind of missing link between chorus dancing and rituals on one hand, and literary drama on the other." Recent work on theater in the Black Sea area, to be published in Braund, Hall, and Wyles (2019), suggests that Heracles and the divine ancestors of the Argonauts may need to be added to this list.

[53] Nielsen (2002) e.g. 23, 39, 44, 60.

that early ritual plays often dramatized the yearly cycle of life: the loss of life, followed by rebirth.[54]

3.2   Demeter in the Fragments of Epicharmus

The relatively weak relationship between Demeter and theater in Sicily is reflected in her very minor place in the fragments of Doric comedy from the island. Whether or not the religious content of plays reveals information about religious aspects of the performance context is a complicated problem. Nevertheless, as Scullion has shown, scholars have understood the Dionysiac content of Attic tragedy to reflect the Dionysiac performance context of Attic drama. Even Scullion himself, who argues against a tight connection between drama and Dionysus, assumes a logical connection between the text and context.[55] Moreover, if, as discussed above, Sicilian comedy developed out of cult dramas that re-enacted the "ancient tale" of Demeter's suffering at the loss of Persephone and her laughter at obscene jokes, it seems reasonable that traces of this myth may have found their way into early Sicilian comedies or, at least, that Demeter or Persephone were still reference points in the dramas. It may, therefore, be useful to examine the place of Demeter in the early fragments of comedy from Syracuse.

Despite the importance of their cult in Sicily, Demeter and Persephone are rarely mentioned in the remaining fragments of Epicharmus, his Doric contemporaries, or his identified successors.[56] In fact, the only instances that survive of the name of either of these goddesses are preserved in their Latin translation, Ceres and Proserpina, in Ennius' poem on Epicharmus.[57] Although incomplete preservation makes an argument from silence particularly dangerous, the absence of Demeter and Persephone's names in the fragments of Epicharmus does suggest that the goddesses were not prominent in plays performed at Syracuse in the first half of the fifth century. In the remaining fragments of Epicharmus, Demeter and Persephone are

---

[54] See also Moretti (2008) for a summary and discussion of cult theaters in sanctuaries to different gods.

[55] Scullion's argument that ancient Greek theater has been too closely associated with the cult of Dionysus is built on many premises, and one of these is that, statistically, there are few references to Dionysus in the plays and fragments of the Attic tragedians, Scullion (2002) 110–12.

[56] There is, however, one reference to Demeter in an anonymous, undated, Doric fragment, *PCG*, Anonyma Dorica 3, *Pap. Berol.* 21285. Here, however, she appears in a list of other gods, none of whom are particularly connected with the theater.

[57] *PCG* 286 and 287. On Ennius' poem, see Chapter 2, n. 2.

never explicitly celebrated as the deities of the cult from which comedy originally grew; they do not permeate the plays at a deep, unconscious level, such as might have carried over from early cult plays; nor were they studiously left out of comedy on religious grounds.[58] Instead, Epicharmus' very limited treatment of the subject seems circumspect and calculated; his single explicit reference to the cult appears to be an isolated and carefully chosen parallel to the goddesses' role as protectors of Syracuse. This allusion to Demeter, I argue, may have simply supported the Syracusan tyrants' party line that the cult of Demeter was important to the welfare of the city itself.

3.3 *Odysseus Automolos* and Demeter the Savior

The play from which the fragment is drawn, the *Odysseus Automolos* (Odysseus the Deserter), seems to recount a tale, or a parody of a tale, from the epic tradition of the Trojan War. In this passage, someone has accused Odysseus of continued underhanded dealings with the Achaeans, which led him to lose or kill a sacred pig intended for the Eleusinian festivals in honor of Demeter.

> δέλφακά τε τῶν γειτόνων
> τοῖς Ἐλευσινίοις φυλάσσων δαιμονίως ἀπώλεσα,
> οὐχ ἑκών· καὶ ταῦτα δή με συμβολατεύειν ἔφα
> τοῖς Ἀχαιοῖσιν προδιδόμειν τ'ὤμνυέ με τὸν δέλφακα.

> The neighbors' pig for the Eleusinian mysteries, which I was watching, I lost through bad luck, not on purpose. And he now said that I was dealing with the Achaians, and he swore I was selling the pig . . .

> *PCG I*, Epicharmus fr. 99

In piecing together the plot, scholars attempt to reconcile this fragment with another longer passage preserved from the same play. This longer passage, a monologue probably spoken by Odysseus himself, reveals that the play is based on the passage from the *Odyssey* (4.242–58) in which Odysseus, disguised as a beggar, successfully enters Troy, reconnoiters, and returns to the Achaeans.[59] Phillips suggests that Odysseus is also the speaker of fragment 99

---

[58] Cf. Nock (1986) 543, who notes that Demeter was not mocked in Aristophanes: "There are limits, even for Aristophanes: no essential levity touches the Maiden of the Acropolis or Demeter." But cf. Anderson (1995) *passim*, who set out Aristophanes' depiction of Athena, which is, in some cases, humorous.

[59] Willi (2012) 63–73; Phillips (1959) 60; Barigazzi (1955) 121.

cited above,[60] and that, as part of his disguise to infiltrate the city, Odysseus persuaded the Trojans that he was a deserter from the Achaeans and then found employment in Troy as a keeper of the pigs for the Eleusinia. Combining the fragment with other more recently discovered passages from the play, Andreas Willi has argued persuasively that the *Odysseus Automolos* depicts Odysseus' *actual* desertion to the Trojans.[61] In fragment 99, someone seems to have accused Odysseus of continued underhanded dealings with the Achaeans, because of which he lost or killed a sacred pig. Barigazzi and Olivieri suggest that the pig was important because the Trojans were depending on it to win Demeter's goodwill at the Eleusinia and thereby her assistance in the war against the Greeks. As Barigazzi writes: "Si tratta dunque d'un animale d'interesse nazionale;"[62] the city's hope for her divine help is gone with the pig. In this play, therefore, Demeter may have held an important position as the hoped-for savior.

Olson argues that this reference to the Eleusinian festival refers to the Sicilian Thesmophoria – "an anachronistic reference" as Olson writes "which shows that Epicharmus was at least occasionally willing to allow contemporary reality to intrude into his epic settings."[63] All the fragments, however, point to a plot set during the Trojan War, which depended on the fiction of an Eleusinian festival in Troy.[64] To the extent that the reference is to the Syracusan Thesmophoria, it must have been a metatheatrical wink to the audience, a wink that linked the faraway tale of Troy, the Eleusinia, and Odysseus with the modern Syracuse, its Eleusinian festival, and perhaps its political leaders.

In this respect, Demeter's roles in the play and in fifth-century Syracuse are similar. In both, she is cast as a savior to protect a city against a powerful invading force. As she was for the Trojans against the Greeks in the *Odysseus Automolos*, so Demeter was a savior for the Syracusans in their war against the Carthaginians. Diodorus Siculus tells the tale, not only of Gelon's building temples to the goddesses following his great victory over the Carthaginians at Himera, but also of the disasters which befell the

---

[60] Most agree, including Salomone (1981) 67–8. Pickard-Cambridge and Webster (1962) 257 suggest that the speaker is Dolon or another Trojan, but this would not materially change the importance of losing the pig, and therefore the importance of Demeter in the play.

[61] Willi (2008) 176–92 and (2012) 63–73. See Olson (2007) 47–8 for an alternative interpretation.

[62] Barigazzi (1955) 127.

[63] Olson (2007) 51. Contra: Olivieri (1946–1947) 39, who writes that the Eleusinian festival in question is the Athenian one.

[64] Indeed, all the titles and fragments of the five Odyssean plays of Epicharmus seem to be drawn from tales from the epic cycle, and fall into the category of mythological burlesque.

Carthaginians when they had desecrated the temples of Demeter and Persephone in their attack on Syracuse.[65] The Carthaginians are said to have been struck such a blow that they took up the worship of Demeter back in Carthage as well. Just as Aeschylus' *Persians*, the story of Athens' fight against the eastern powers, may have been understood by its Syracusan audience as a parallel to the Sikeliotes' fight against the Carthaginians,[66] so this story of Troy's dependence on Demeter may resonate with the Syracusans, who also held the goddess and her powers in great esteem. This passage suggests that the play might have represented the political importance of worshipping Demeter in the mythical past, as she was politically important in fifth-century Syracuse. The reference to the Eleusinian Mysteries seems less likely, therefore, to be the revelation of deeply rooted, pervasive origins of theater in her cult, than it is a reminder, or a reflection, of the importance of observing her cult in times of military threat.[67] Thus, this reference to the cult of Demeter conformed to the Deinomenid tyrants' party line: the cult of Demeter, in which they were priests, helped defend the city of Syracuse.

3.4 Ideas in the Air: Pythagoras, Prodicus, and Epicharmus' Earth

The other passages that might be understood in connection with the cult of Demeter or chthonic cults more generally are references to Ceres and Proserpina in Ennius' *Epicharmus* and several fragments in the *Pseudepicharmea* about the earth, harvest, and death and renewal. None of these cases reveals a clear link with the cult of Demeter, however, either because of problematic reception of texts or ambiguous meaning. In fact, taken together, the fragments suggest that Epicharmus' views of these subjects (earth, harvest, and death and renewal) may have been, in some ways, similar to popular Pythagorean thought of his day and perhaps, in other ways, akin to the theories of the philosopher Prodicus of Cos.

In the second century BCE, the scholar Varro discussed the Latin names for Demeter and Persephone (Ceres and Proserpina) in a passage which may have been drawn from a poem by the Latin poet Ennius called *Epicharmus*. Ennius' *Epicharmus*, in turn, may have recorded some of Epicharmus' ideas. The evidence of these texts is suspect, because they

---

[65] Diod. Sic. 11.26.7.   [66] Cf. Scodel (2001) and Bremer (1991).
[67] On Epicharmus putting mythical characters in a modern setting, cf. Kerkhof (2001) 128.

are preserved at such a remove from the original, and a number of scholars question their authenticity. Pickard-Cambridge doubts whether Ennius' *Epicharmus* was based on a real text of the poet,[68] rather than on a forgery, and he is also skeptical that these passages come from *Epicharmus* rather than one of Ennius' other works.[69] Collart argues that the Epicharmus recorded is a product of Ennius' imagination.[70] Even if the attribution of the fragments were not in doubt, Ennius' *Epicharmus* seems to have included descriptions of various gods, so that the appearance of Demeter and Persephone here does not signal very much. The first appears to be part of a eulogy of Demeter in her role as the producer of grain:

> Terris gentis omnis peperit et resumit denuo
>
> quae
>
> > Dat cibaria,
>
> ut ait Ennius, quae
>
> > Quod gerit fruges, Ceres[71]
>
> > > > Varro, *De lingua Latina*, V 64; PCG 286

If there is some trace of Epicharmian sentiment left in this fragment, it appears to be generic praise of the goddess.

In the second passage, Varro records some etymological play from Ennius' *Epicharmus*:

> hinc Epicharmus Ennii Proserpinam quoque appellat, quod solet esse
> sub terris, dicta Proserpina, quod haec ut serpens modo in dexteram,
>
> > modo in
>
> sinisteram partem late mouetur.
>
> > > > Varro, *De lingua Latina* V 68; PCG 287[72]

The derivation of the name *Proserpina* from snake, *serpens*, cannot be a translation from the Greek, since the Greek equivalents, "Persephone" or "Kore," have no root that means snake. As Dora Liuzzi notes, however,

---

[68] Kaibel (1899/1958) 134–5 suggests that Ennius took his *Epicharmus* from a single lost poem of Epicharmus, *On Nature*. This theory has been rejected by subsequent scholars, for example, Pickard-Cambridge (1962) 241–5.

[69] Pickard-Cambridge (1962) 242.

[70] Collart (1954) 182: "Il ne s'agit pas ici d'Epicharme lui-même, mais du personage d'Epicharme conçu et présenté par Ennius dans son poème de l' Epicharmus."

[71] "She produces for all people of the earth and takes back in the end she gives food because she produces grain, Ceres."

[72] "Thence the Epicharmus of Ennius also calls her Proserpina, because she is habitually under the ground, she is called Proserpina, because like a serpent, now to the right, now to the left side, far and wide, she moves."

Epicharmus seems to have gathered other etymologies,[73] and Ennius may be imitating the general style of the Greek poet, though not a particular etymology. Liuzzi argues that this passage is some evidence that Ennius tried to adopt a "philosophy of nature," and a Pythagorean pantheism.

In other fragments that include references to the earth, Demeter's domain, Epicharmus makes no allusion to the goddess. Like the quotations from Ennius, these references are problematic, partly because it is not certain that they are genuine fragments of Epicharmus, and partly because, even if they do represent Epicharmus' ideas, their meaning and relevance is not clear. If they can be used to further refine Epicharmus' treatment of Demeter, it is through their avoidance of any direct mention of her. These few fragments discussed below, however, in addition to the three above, are all that remains of Epicharmus' treatment of the earth, and divinity associated with it.

The word gē or its Doric equivalent ga occurs four times in what remains of Epicharmus' work: in two fragments, one play title, and a mocking comment made by a character in one of Menander's comedies. In the most recent editions of Epicharmus' fragments, Kassel and Austin retain one of the fragments as an authentic line from an unidentified play, but Guillén rejects them both, listing them only among the *Pseudepicharmeia*.[74]

> συνεκρίθη καὶ διεκρίθη κἀπῆλθεν ὅθεν ἦλθεν πάλιν,
> γᾶ μὲν εἰς γᾶν, πνεῦμα δ᾽ἄνω· τί τῶνδε χαλεπόν; οὐδὲ ἕν.

There was unification and division and return again to where it had come from, Earth to earth, and air upward. What of these things is difficult? Nothing at all!

> *PCG*, fr. 213, *Incertae Fabulae*;
> Guillén, fr. 386, *Poemas Pseudoepicarmeos*[75]

> Εἰμὶ νεκρός· νεκρὸς δὲ κόπρος, γῆ δ᾽ ἡ κόπρος ἐστίν·
> εἰ δὴ γῆ νεκρός ἐστ᾽, οὐ νεκρὸς ἀλλὰ θεός.

I am a corpse. A corpse is excrement, and excrement is earth. But if earth is a corpse, I'm not a corpse but a god.

> *PCG*, fr. 297, *Pseudepicharmeia*;
> Guillén, fr. 387, *Poemas Pseudoepicarmeos*

---

[73] Servius, *ad Aen.* 1, 8, (*PCG* 229) records Epicharmus' etymologizing of *Musas*. Cf. Liuzzi (1973/1974) 285–6.

[74] Cf. Rodríguez-Noriega Guillén (1996) *ad loc*, who notes that Wilamowitz and Lorenz agree with her, but Schmidt and Gomperz incline towards this being an authentic fragment of Epicharmus.

[75] Cf. Kerkhof (2001) 89–91, who takes up the problem of whether the passage is genuine or not in his discussion of Euripides' emulation of these lines.

Likewise, Kassel and Austin accept Menander's mocking summary of Epicharmus' religious beliefs as a legitimate reflection of Epicharmus' philosophy, whereas Guillén includes it in the *Pseudepicharmeia*:

> ὁ μὲν Ἐπίχαρμος τοὺς θεοὺς εἶναι λέγει
> ἀνέμους, ὕδωρ, γῆν, ἥλιον, πῦρ, ἀστέρας.[76]

> PCG, fr. 199, *Pseudepicharmeia*;
> Guillén, fr. 385, *Poemas Pseudoepicarmeos*

Including these fragments among the *Pseudepicharmeia*, as Guillén has done, is not necessarily an outright rejection of the ideas as un-Epicharmeian, but rather hesitation about the specific text. Although the *Pseudepicharmeia* seem to have been written by later scholars, it seems likely that they adopted Epicharmus' ideas, since his plays, and perhaps other writings were probably still in circulation.[77] It is possible that they even culled quotations and lines from the plays themselves, reorganizing them into collections of proverbs, or inserting them in other texts.[78]

The title *Earth and Sea* is, however, fairly securely attested on a papyrus fragment as well as in Athenaeus' nine references and Aelian's single reference to it. The surviving fragments of this play are mostly fish names, however, and these, preserved as they are for Athenaeus' decadent account of dinner fare, shed little light on the plot or meaning of the play. Thus, individually, these four references to the earth are contested and, even if considered genuine, appear without enough relevant context to understand their import.

Taken all together, however, there are striking similarities among the four references to the word gē, which may help elucidate Epicharmus' general approach. The four passages seem to agree on an interpretation of divinity as an aspect of the natural cycle. This kind of interpretation of the gods is similar to that of the fifth-century sophist Prodicus, who influenced both Euripides and Aristophanes.[79] Prodicus' theories of religion were essentially anthropological; he wrote about how human beings come to revere something, or someone, as divine. Poets writing under tyrants were particularly happy to espouse Prodicus' doctrine of the deification of human beings because it gave them a theoretical foundation from which to advocate revering a tyrant. Although the relative chronology of

---

[76] *PCG* 199. "Epicharmus says that the gods are winds, water, earth, sun, fire, stars."
[77] P. 138: Athenaeus XIV, p. 648 D; Diog. Laert. VIII 78.
[78] Cf., for example, Gigante (1953) 161: "È necessario ribadire che la 'gnome' è alle origini e non ai margini del mondo comico di E. e che nel poeta, pure scarsamente sopravvissuto, e il germe delle ulteriori e numerose falsificazioni."
[79] Henrichs (1984) 145–52.

Prodicus and Epicharmus makes direct influence unlikely, the dispassionate analysis of the concept of divinity reflected in Epicharmus' work seems to accord with the theological questioning of his century. Epicharmus' references to the earth certainly do not suggest a spiritual concept of earth and cult activity, which might be linked to Demeter, but rather an explanation of the divine as a natural force.

The fragments also espouse Pythagorean ideas of the four elements, fire, water, earth and air, as the basis for all things. Vitruvius lists Epicharmus in company with Pythagoras and Empedocles, noting that they all believe there are four principal substances: air, fire, water, and earth.[80] Plutarch calls him "an old man taking part in a Pythagorean way of life."[81] To what extent Epicharmus' own plays actively promoted Pythagorean ideas and to what extent Epicharmus himself espoused Pythagorean philosophies is unknown. The political disruption the Pythagoreans seem to have caused, and their consequent ousting from Sicily, have not left a clear historical record.[82] Whether Iamblichus is right that Epicharmus presented Pythagorean ideas, but guardedly so as not to offend Hieron, cannot be confirmed.[83] Gigante suggests that Epicharmus' plays were built on a foundation of critical examination of humanity, which led him to absorb and interact with the ideas of philosophers of his day. Epicharmus' plays, according to Gigante, were built on his shrewd, witty, and open-minded observations of life.[84] In sum, the extant fragments do not reveal anything more substantial than a cursory knowledge of Pythagoras' work, which might be expected of any intellectual of the age. A fascination with the underworld and the dominance of Persephone, and in part her mother Demeter, seems also to be apparent in the poems of Pindar, for example. In *Olympian* 2, dedicated to Theron, ruler of Akragas, Pindar alludes to mysteries of the afterlife. Zuntz discusses how the poem reveals the "devotion and eschatological persuasion" of the tyrant, and records the note by

---

[80] Vitruvius, *De arch.* VIII, praef. I.   [81] Plutarch, *Vit. Num.* 8, 16 f. (*PCG* 296).

[82] Whether and to what extent Pythagoras was involved in politics at all is also a controversial question. De Vogel (1966) suggests that it is difficult, if not impossible, to distinguish the religious and political leader from the philosopher. On the possible presence of Pythagorean ideas in Epicharmus' work, see also Battezzato (2008).

[83] Iamblichus (250–325 CE) wrote that Epicharmus covertly propagated Pythagorean ideas, of which Hieron disapproved, in his comic verse (Iambl. *VP* 266).

[84] Gigante (1953) 161–2: "Spirito aperto alle esperienze concrete della vita ed alle ansie degli indagatori della natura e della gnoseologia, egli attinse e rimuginò e ricreò nell'artificio elegante e squisito i motivi fondamentali di quel tormentato cammino del pensiero: egli non fu filosofo; partecipazione al movimento ideologico si risolse, per lui, sempre sul piano ed a servizio dell'arte; adesione o polemica non avevano valore assoluto e determinante, erano moduli della fantasia, stimoli della creazione." See also ibid. 169 f.

the scholiast on *Olympian* 2.123 (Drachmann), "Pindar here follows Pythagoras."[85] From this poem alone we have evidence both of the strong influence of Pythagoras in the region, and particularly on its ruling classes, and of public discussion of the mysteries of the afterlife.

In some particulars, Epicharmus seems to disregard the Pythagorean tradition altogether. Many fragments preserved from *Earth and Sea* and a substantial number of others consist of strings of fish names, many peculiar and unattested elsewhere. Pythagoras, it appears, disapproved of fish, and banned the eating of many varieties.[86] Since in a number of cases these lists seem to be the wedding presents of the gods for the wedding feast of the goddess Hebe, it seems unlikely that Epicharmus strictly propagated Pythagorean ideas in every respect. Moreover, Pythagoras, who set about inspiring a "love of freedom" among his followers, seems to have "saved [cities] from the oppression of tyranny." In particular, for example, he "persuaded the tyrant Simichus to abdicate his throne and was critical of the totalitarian Phalaris."[87] Since Epicharmus seems to have accepted the patronage of Hieron, and perhaps Gelon before him, and seems to have thrived under their rule and also written at least some congratulatory passages about them in his plays, he also seems to have ignored this aspect of Pythagoreanism. At a superficial level, Pythagoras' system for living seems to have involved communal living, or at least regular and frequent gathering – neither of which Epicharmus is likely to have done in a city where Pythagoreanism was banned.

On the other hand, as Nancy Demand has suggested, all fragments need to be considered not only for their information, but also for their value as the lines of some lost comic character. She takes two different sections of the *Pseudepicharmeia,* which have been generally considered imitations. In the first (*PCG* 280), the speaker declares that a later philosopher will take the speaker's ideas, strip them of metrics, and present them as his own thoughts. This is often thought to have been a late imitator, playing on the idea that Plato took some of his ideas from Epicharmus. In the second (*PCG* 277), two people discuss what "the good" is, by comparing it to aulos-playing and an aulos-player. This has frequently been rejected as spurious, because it seemed so emphatically to take up the Socratic style. Demand, however, demonstrates that the first passage might well be the comic speech of a pompous, self-important fool, and that the second seems to hark back to Gorgias. She argues that both are spoken by the same character, who is meant to be a caricature of

---

[85] Zuntz (1971) 84 f.   [86] Gorman (1979) 126, and cf. 129.   [87] Gorman (1979) 131.

Gorgias, and suggests that these fragments come from the lost play, *Logos kai Logina*.[88] Her premise that a character's, rather than Epicharmus', voice is expressed in a fragment might well be applied to the Pythagorean sentiments: whether or not Epicharmus was a proponent of Pythagoreanism, his characters might have voiced some Pythagorian ideas in jest.

If the chthonic cult of Demeter and Persephone was at the root of Sicilian comedy, there seems to be little evidence of it in the writing of its first major exponent, Epicharmus. Their names are only mentioned in the much-debated poem of Ennius, and their rites are mentioned only once in the fragments, where they serve a clear political purpose. When the subject of the earth and the cycle of life, which might lead Epicharmus to mention Demeter, are brought up, the fragments seem to reveal philosophical and sophistic interests, rather than religious ones. Although this absence of significant references to the two goddesses in the fragmentary remains of Epicharmus' plays does not prove that the cult of Demeter was not at the heart of Sicilian comedy, it does suggest that neither the goddess nor her cult was commemorated in formal comedies.[89]

3.5 Dionysus, the God from the East

Dionysus is revered as the god of theater in Sicily in poetry from the Hellenistic period. These sources are particularly interesting because they explicitly set out an association between the god and the early development of theater in Sicily. Moreover, from the beginning of the fourth century, comic vases, probably influenced or painted by Sicilian vase-painters, show Dionysus in conjunction with comic actors. In this chapter, I examine still earlier literary sources, particularly the fragments of Epicharmus from the beginning of the fifth century, and argue that they support the Hellenistic and art-historical testimony for a very early association between drama and Dionysus in Sicily. The interesting and difficult question is whether the presence of Dionysus in Sicilian theatrical records points to the influence of Athenian drama at an early period, as his presence in the fourth century and later seems to do. In this chapter, I suggest that Epicharmus' comic and lighthearted treatment of Aeschylus' plays may extend to an equally lighthearted spoof of Attic theatrical social and cult contexts. What we can glean from his comedies does not suggest that Dionysus presided over performance in Syracuse as he did in

[88] Demand (1971) 453–63. She suggests the two were contemporaries, citing the dates of Gorgias as 500/497–391/388, following Wilamowitz (ibid. 456, n. 15).
[89] Contra: MacLachlan (2012) 343–64.

Athens, but rather that Epicharmus and his Sicilian audiences were keenly aware of Dionysus' association with theater in Athens and were both entertained by the thematic links between the characteristics of the god and the nature of dramatic performance and curious about his formal role in Athens.

3.6   Dionysus' Precarious Position

In his highly original argument for Demeter's role in the origins of Sicilian comedy, Polacco takes a stand against a prevailing view that Dionysus was the god of theater, and particularly well suited to be the god of comedy. He demonstrates that the cult of Dionysus did not have much hold in Sicily in the early fifth century, as there is evidence of only one festival to Dionysus in this period.[90] Even this festival, he argues, celebrated an earlier version of the god, the demon Morychos, who did not come with all the attributes normally associated with Dionysus as god of the theater.[91] He rejects the evidence normally thought to prove the connection between Dionysus and theater in the West, i.e., the rich iconographic and literary presence of the satyrs, Pan and Silenus, arguing that they "had an independent meaning and a separate existence from Dionysus in the Archaic period. Only later, especially in Attica, did they become companions of Dionysus."[92]

This questioning of Dionysus' right to the title of god of theater finds support in a number of more recent, general treatments of the subject. Scullion, for example, suggests that the link made between Dionysus and tragedy has grown from too narrow an interpretation of Aristotle's treatment of the subject (Arist. *Poet.* 1449a–b). He argues that the link between Dionysiac cult and theater is an unimportant piece of history for Aristotle, and that, in fact, Aristotle *begins* with the assumption that the two are linked, and does not bother to prove it, or even discuss it at any length.[93] Scullion then takes up six additional arguments that modern scholars have

---

[90]   Cf. Dearden (1988) 37, who also notes: "Particular dramatic festivals with which performances might be connected are not known for Magna Graecia." He notes, however, that Dionysus appears on many phlyax vases, "and performances in honour of that god are reported on the occasion of a visit of Roman envoys to Tarentum in 282 B.C. where all the citizens were found to be in the theatre, and drunk."

[91]   Polacco and Anti (1990) 156.

[92]   Polacco and Anti (1990) 157: "Pan è presente nel teatro di Siracusa in un rilievo ed i Satiri in sculture architettoniche, come li ritroviamo anche nei teatri di Segesta, Morgantina, Iato, e fuori della Sicilia nell'affine ambiente magno-greco, a Locri e a Pompei. Se non che tutti questi demoni in età arcaica avevano un significato proprio e una vita indipendente. Solo in un secondo tempo, soprattutto in ambiente attico, faranno compagnia con Dioniso [...]."

[93]   Scullion (2002) 102–10.

used to prove the association, and dismisses them all: Dionysus is not mentioned more frequently than other gods in the extant plays; the festival connection is mainly Athenian; masks are not exclusively Dionysiac; Dionysiac ecstasy is less about stepping into a role on stage as an actor, than it is about stepping out of oneself to accept the god; the billygoat prize, even if it was the prize for early dramatic competition, was not particularly Dionysiac, but a common sacrificial animal for many gods; and, finally, the chorus, a feature of every god's cult, sings odes about life, rather than cult.[94]

Scullion, Nielsen, and others like them,[95] have shaken Dionysus from his stranglehold on theater in the popular and scholarly imagination, and allow us to interpret what evidence there is of a connection between Dionysus and theater with fewer preconceptions than before. Nevertheless, Dionysus remains an important divinity in early Greek theater. The vast body of work on the role of Dionysus in the origins of theater in general, against which Scullion in particular is reacting, is too large to be examined here, and not altogether apposite in its details. Suffice it to say that Dionysus is clearly the god of Athenian theater, and that by the later Hellenistic period he is associated with theater throughout the Greek world.[96]

Despite Polacco's specific refutation of the role of Dionysus in early Sicilian theater, there is some literary evidence in Sicily to the contrary. These sources tell a more complicated story about the role of Dionysus in fifth-century Syracuse than the archaeological sources admit.

3.7 Commemorating Sicilian Theater

Later Sicilian sources not only uphold Dionysus as god of theater, but also associate him with early traditions of Sicilian theater as far back as

---

[94] Scullion (2002) 110–37.

[95] These are not the first attempts to question the primacy of Dionysus in early Greek theater. Even in antiquity the argument may have been voiced, if the infamous proverb, "nothing to do with Dionysus," can be interpreted in this way. Arguments for a general human instinct for mimicry and ultimately drama are well supported by anthropological studies, as well as comparative literature. (In fact, the source which preserves this Athenian proverb, Zenobius, also preserves a tradition recorded in Chamaeleon which says that it functioned as a protest against theater which had too little connection with its ancestral tutelary deity, Dionysus. See Seaford (1984) 12). But cf. Miller (1961), who notes that: "There is no evidence for the existence of e.g., Chinese, Indian, or Japanese drama as early as the fifth century B.C.; and Egyptian ritual did not develop into drama proper."

[96] Most recently, Sourvinou-Inwood (2003) has argued for connections between ritual and tragedy. On phallic processions of Dionysus turning into comedy, cf. Csapo (1997). On the festival of Dionysus and the theater of Dionysus at Athens, cf. Pickard-Cambridge (1968, 2nd ed. and 1946).

Epicharmus. Sources dating to the fourth century and later neither celebrate nor remember Demeter as an important deity in the history of Sicilian
theater. Indeed, the later ancient Sicilian tradition gives Dionysus pride of
place in the history of theater in Sicily. This is notable because the Dorians
fiercely maintained their own primacy in the development of theater.[97]
They do not, at least in recorded texts, acknowledge the influence of
Athenian drama, but explicitly pronounce themselves to be the originators
and jealously guard their own tradition of theater, most markedly in their
continued use of Doric dialect.[98] In this climate of defensive self-
promotion, distinguishing features of the early development of theater
are more likely to have been preserved in the social memory and in the
ancient scholarly tradition than they might otherwise be. That is, if
Dionysus was not the god of theater in Sicily, but rather Demeter or
some other set of gods, we might expect this to be remembered in
a scholarly tradition concerned with identifying the original and important
theater of the island. These later records cannot provide trustworthy
evidence for Epicharmus himself or for the early period of Sicilian theater
that they celebrate, but they do show how the memory of that famous early
time was celebrated and evoked by later generations. These records are,
moreover, roughly contemporary with the dates given for many Sicilian
theaters, which, as discussed above, are often used to support the argument
for a fundamental and organic link between the cult of Demeter and
theater. If late theaters can reveal information about much earlier developments in drama, then the comments of Hellenistic scholars and poets may
also yield precious evidence.

Aristotle famously reports that the Dorians claim both tragedy and
comedy as their own invention, and does not mention a presiding deity
in this Doric tradition:

> διὸ καὶ ἀντιποιοῦνται τῆς τε τραγωιδίας καὶ τῆς κωμωιδίας οἱ Δωριεῖς (τῆς
> μὲν γὰρ κωμωιδίας οἱ Μεγαρεῖς οἵ τε ἐνταῦθα ὡς ἐπὶ τῆς παρ᾽ αὐτοῖς
> δημοκρατίας γενομένης καὶ οἱ ἐκ Σικελίας, ἐκεῖθεν γὰρ ἦν Ἐπίχαρμος {ὁ
> ποιητὴς}[99] πολλῶι πρότερος ὢν Χιωνίδου καὶ Μάγνητος· καὶ τῆς
> τραγωιδίας ἔνιοτῶν ἐν Πελοποννήσωι) ποιούμενοι τὰ ὀνόματα σημεῖον·
> αὐτοὶ μὲν γὰρ κώμας τὰς περιοικίδας καλεῖν φασιν, Ἀθηναίους δὲ δήμους,
> ὡς κωμωιδοὺς οὐκ ἀπὸ τοῦ κωμάζειν λεχθέντας ἀλλὰ τῆι κατὰ κώμας

---

[97] See Bosher (2013a).

[98] Cf. Hordern (2004) 11 on Sophron's defiant choice to use Doric prose, though other fellow
Sikeliotes wrote in Ionic or Attic dialects.

[99] See Janko (1987) 73, who omits ὁ ποιητής, arguing that it is a gloss "made by a copyist when
Epicharmus had ceased to be a household name."

πλάνηι ἀτιμαζομένους ἐκ τοῦ ἄστεως· καὶ τὸ ποιεῖν αὐτοὶ μὲν δρᾶν,
Ἀθηναίους δὲ πράττειν προσαγορεύειν. Aristotle, *Poetics* 3, 1448a 30[100]

Since Sicily and Epicharmus are specifically mentioned here, it might not
have been out of place to mention the Syracusan cult of Demeter, if Sicilian
theater was closely tied to it. Indeed, since Syracuse is directly compared
with Athens by way of the Athenian comic playwrights, Chionides and
Magnes, and since the aim here is, above all, to show that the Dorians
developed theater *before the Athenians*, claiming that comedy in Syracuse
developed under completely different divine auspices from theater in
Athens might have strengthened their case. Although the absence of
Demeter does not prove that she did not preside over early Sicilian comedy,
it suggests that, if she did, she was no longer important by the end of the
fourth century.

An epigram by Theocritus some 70 years after Aristotle confirms that
Demeter was no longer important in the historical tradition of the Dorian's
invention of comedy. In this poem, inscribed perhaps on the base of
a bronze statue to be set up in the theater of Syracuse,[101] Theocritus is
particularly concerned to glorify Epicharmus as the originator of comedy,
and to emphasize that comedy was originally written in Doric. Despite this
preoccupation with things local and Doric, Theocritus does not mention
the goddess Demeter. Instead, he associates drama, the theater of Syracuse,
Epicharmus and Dionysus without apology:

> ἅ τε φωνὰ Δώριος χὠνὴρ ὁ τὰν κωμωιδίαν
>   εὑρὼν Ἐπίχαρμος.
> ὦ Βάκχε, χάλκεόν νιν ἀντ' ἀλαθινοῦ
>   τὶν ὧδ' ἀνέθηκαν
> τοὶ Συρακούσσαις ἐνίδρυνται, πελωρίσται πόλει,
>   οἷ' ἄνδρὶ πολῖται.
> σοφῶν ἔοικε ῥημάτων μεμναμένους
>   τελεῖν ἐπίχειρα·

---

[100] "The Dorians lay claim to both tragedy and comedy. Both the Megarians, from the time when
democracy was developing among them, and those in Sicily, for the poet Epicharmus was there
long before Chionides and Magnes, lay claim to comedy. Some of those in the Peloponese lay
claim to tragedy. They make the name out to be significant, for they say that they call the
surrounding villages, 'kōmas,' whereas the Athenians call them 'demes.' Thus the word
comedy comes, not from the verb 'kōmazein,' but from wandering about in the 'kōmas' having
been dishonored by the city, and for the verb 'to do' they use 'dran,' whereas the Athenians use
'prattein'."

[101] Rossi (2001) 252–3 is less certain than previous scholars that this epigram was meant to be
inscribed on a statue set up in the theater.

πολλὰ γὰρ ποττὰν ζόαν τοῖς παισὶν[102] εἶπε χρήσιμα.
μεγάλα χάρις αὐτῶι.[103]

Theocritus, *Epigrammata* 18

Although the Dorians of Aristotle's report make a very general claim to the invention of theater, the Syracusan citizens of Theocritus' epigram are celebrating their own local, literary hero, emphatically described as a citizen of Syracuse. The site of the bronze statue seems to have been the theater of Syracuse itself, and they are grateful to Epicharmus for his education of their own citizens. Yet it is Bacchus (Dionysus) whom they hail as the patron god of the theater of Syracuse, and perhaps even as the patron god of the great Syracusan comic playwright Epicharmus himself.

A second epigram, dedicated to Epicharmus, and preserved in the Palatine Anthology, even more explicitly associates Epicharmus with Dionysus:

Δωρίδος ἐκ Μούσης κεκορυθμένον ἀνέρα **Βάκχωι**
καὶ Σατύροις Σικελὸν τῆιδ' Ἐπίχαρμον ἔχω.

PCG I, Epicharmus Test. 19, *AP* 7.82[104]

Much may have been lost in the two centuries that separate Epicharmus and Theocritus, and it may be that other gods including Demeter were aspects of the early theatrical tradition that was overlooked and, by the early third century, forgotten or deemed unimportant. In the intervening years, many Athenian influences were brought to bear on Sicilian theater. Euripides and, if we accept the arguments of Csapo, Taplin, and Webster,[105] Aristophanes, were popular in the West by the late fifth century. Certainly, by the early third century, Dionysus' hold on theater had spread throughout the Greek world. The poems of Theocritus and from the Palatine Anthology reflect contemporary associations between theater and the god Dionysus, and they might simply project this

---

[102] The παισὶν of the original is often reasonably emended to πᾶσιν. See Handley (2003) 142–8 for a discussion of the epigram and a summary of the argument (146–7). I added the phrase 'for all men' to my translation to try to catch the ambiguity of the word.

[103] "The voice is Doric, so's the man, who founded comedy:
    Epicharmus, here in bronze and not reality.
    Hail Bacchus! What they've set up here, inside the giant city,
    Syracusans put him here – this man, this citizen –
    Remembering wise precepts that he set out for the children,
    Advice for ordering their lives and useful words for all men.
    'Tis fitting that they pay him back, and honor him they should,
    Greatest thanks to him, therefore, who did them so much good."

[104] "From the Dorian Muse, a man crested with Bacchus
    And with Satyrs, I have here Epicharmus the Sicilian."   [105] See Chapter 5.

association back onto their commemorations of Epicharmus. Thus, one might imagine that the Athenian god had first traveled west with the Hellenistic troupes,[106] supplanting the range of gods and goddesses under whose auspices theater was performed in Sicily, were it not for the striking presence of Dionysus in the fragments of Epicharmus.

3.8 Dionysus and Comic Actors

Before turning to Epicharmus, a second category of evidence brings the association made in the Hellenistic sources between Dionysus and theater back to at least the beginning of the fourth century. A set of vase paintings depicting comedies in performance (once called phlyax vases), which are found almost always in the West, often show actors together with Dionysus.[107] On most of the comic vases that are classified as Sicilian, most dating to the third quarter of the fourth century, however, Dionysus does not, in fact, appear.[108] Nevertheless, a strong argument has been made by Trendall and Green among others that Paestan comic vases were directly influenced by early Sicilian comedy, and so the many Paestan vases that show Dionysus may shed some light on the relationship of Dionysus to fourth-century Sicilian theater. Moreover, a large vase from Lipari attributed to the Painter of Louvre K 240 (who is thought to have brought his art from Sicily to Paestum) shows Dionysus with comic actors (Figure 5.4).[109] This vase takes us back to 360–350 BCE. Another proto-Paestan vase, found in Albania, and dating to the second quarter of the fourth century, further confirms this association.[110] J. R. Green writes: "It is possible that this is a local Paestan vase made by a Sicilian migrant."[111] In this way, the comic vases may take us back to the first half of the fourth with Dionysus as a god associated with comic performance in Sicily. Earlier than this, we do find images of Dionysus on vases together with satyrs, nymphs in South Italy and Sicily, but not in explicitly theatrical situations.

---

[106] Cf. Taplin (2012) on traveling actors from an early period in the West.

[107] The phlyax vases are discussed at length in Chapter 5.

[108] With many thanks to J. R. Green who kindly sent me his preliminary list of Sicilian comic vases for his revised catalogue of *Phlyax Vases* for the *Bulletin of the Institute of Classical Studies*.

[109] Lipari 927, from Lipari t. 367. Sicilian/Paestan calyx-krater, Lipari, Museo Archeologico Regionale Luigi Bernabò Brea 927, from Lipari, t. 367: Trendall (1987) 46, num. 99, pl. 12f (Painter of Louvre K 240); U. Spigo in Lyons, Bennett, and Marconi (2013) 117, fig. 67.

[110] Apollonia 325.

[111] From J. R. Green's draft notes on his forthcoming revision of the *Phlyax Vases*.

Is this a meeting point? Does Dionysus come into the theatrical picture in the fourth century together with, as Oliver Taplin and Eric Csapo have now demonstrated, the rapid dissemination of Attic drama throughout South Italy and Sicily from the beginning of the fourth, and perhaps even the end of the fifth century?

The answer to this question has implications not just for understanding theater in the West, but might also shed some light on the relationship of Attic theater to that of the West. If theater in the West came to be associated with the cult of Dionysus only at the beginning of the fourth century, then this might suggest that Athenian influence brought about this change.

3.9   Dionysus in the Fragments of Epicharmus

Apart from Hephaestus, Dionysus is the only Olympian god whose name figures in an extant title of the Epicharmian corpus.[112] Indeed, among the few surviving fragments of Epicharmus' work, there are four titles suggestive of Dionysiac subjects: *Bacchae, Dionysoi, Dionys*[, and *Komasts or Hephaestus*.[113] A papyrus list of the plays in alphabetical order stops at eta, and only lists the plays *Dionysoi* and *Dionys*[. The title *Bacchae*, though it falls within the alphabetical scope of the papyrus list, only survives to us in citations by Athenaeus and Hesychius, and is not recorded on the papyrus, though perhaps it was listed under a different name (one of the *Dionys-* ?). The *Komasts or Hephaestus*, which falls too late in the alphabet to have survived on the fragment of papyrus, is likewise recorded by Photius, Athenaeus, Apollonius Dyscolus, and Hesychius.[114] Though the preservation of titles appears to have been largely haphazard, that Dionysiac material appears in three or four plays may be significant.

From the *Bacchae*, one line and one word survive. Athenaeus quotes the single surviving line as an example of the word "epiplous," apparently a delicacy:

---

[112] As discussed below, even the title that includes Hephaestus, "Κωμασταὶ ἢ Ἅφαιστος," *Komasts or Hephaestus*, most likely belonged to a play with a Dionysiac theme (*PCG* p. 51; Phot. η 230 = *Suda* η 481). On the fragmentary Homeric *Hymn to Dionysus* and sources for the myth in which Dionysus persuades Hephaestus to return to heaven to free Hera, see West (2001).

[113] Conversely, the papyrus records no play with the name Demeter, though of course the truncated list does not allow us to reject the possibility of another name referring to her cult, for example, some cognate of Kore or Thesmophoria.

[114] *PCG* 73 (Athen. IX, p. 388F) 74; (Apoll. *Dysc. Pron.*, GrGr II 1,1 p. 75, 3) 75 (Hesych. φ 930); and page 51 (Phot. η 230 = Sud. η 481).

ὁ μὲν ἐπίπλους παρ' Ἐπιχάρμωι ἐν Βάκχαις "καὶ τὸν ἀρχὸν ἐπικαλύψας
ἐπιπλόωι" καὶ ἐν Θεαροῖς· *PCG I*, Epicharmus fr. 16; Athenaeus III 106 e–f

Epicharmus uses the word "epiplous" in his play the *Bacchae* and in the
Thearoi: "having hidden the leader (or the bum) in the fat membrane."

Guillén, like Olivieri before her,[115] notes that this play, though written at
least a half-century before, may have been on the same theme as the
Bacchae of Euripides. She suggests that the double meaning of archon in
this line might signal a plot similar to that of Euripides' famous play.
Pentheus might have been dressed like a woman so ridiculously, that the
archon (both the leader and his bum) resembled a sausage. The play would
then, presumably, have followed the same general plot as Euripides' play,
with Pentheus, as the leader of the Theban forces, dressed up as a woman in
order to spy on the Bacchants.[116]

The other fragment, a single word surviving from the play in a citation of
Hesychius, is consonant with this story line: αἴγλη (*aigle*) is the word for
handcuffs in the *Bacchae* by Epicharmus.[117] Like the cross-dressing of
Pentheus, the chaining of Dionysus is used to great dramatic effect in the
plot of Euripides' *Bacchae*. The restraints prove unable to restrain
Dionysus, and, by breaking free of his prison and his chains in the dramatic
earthquake scene, he proves his divinity. Did the handcuffs in Epicharmus'
Bacchae serve a similar function of restraining the god? Or someone else,
perhaps a Bacchant, inspired by the god's rites?

Much of the appeal, and perhaps the point, of Euripides' *Bacchae*, and in
particular Pentheus' disguise, rest in the recurring theme of appearance,
deception, and make-believe, which is the province of theater, no less than
of Dionysus himself. Even if Dionysus and theater are not to be ubiqui-
tously and unthinkingly associated, they are inextricably linked in the plot
of Euripides' *Bacchae*, and perhaps also in Epicharmus' *Bacchae*.
A metatheatrical plot, like that of Euripides' *Bacchae*, would have suited
what we can glean of the style of Epicharmus' plays, which often seem to
have been metatheatrical and self-referential.

The title, *Bacchae*, is familiar, not only from Euripides' play, but also
from the later comedies of Antiphanes, Diocles, and Lysippus, and the
tragedies of Aeschylus, Sophocles, Iophon, Xenocles, and Cleophon. These,
like Euripides' play, are all later than Epicharmus' comedy, with the

---

[115] Olivieri (1946–1947) 13.   [116] Rodríguez-Noriega Guillén (1996) 24.

[117] (Hesychius a 1730) αἴγλη· χλιδών, Σοφοκλῆς Τηρεῖ [χιτών]. καὶ πέδη παρὰ Ἐπιχάρμωι ἐν
Βάκχαις (*aigle*: "of luxurious things, as in Sophocles' Tereus (*chiton*). And also handcuffs in
Epicharmus in his *Bacchae*").

possible exception of Aeschylus' tragedy. Epicharmus may have written a spoof on another Aeschylean play, the *Persai*, performed in Sicily. Perhaps Epicharmus' *Bacchae* also played on Aeschylus' original. We have no independent record of any performance of Aeschylus' *Bacchae* in Sicily, but two playwrights working in the small inner circle of Hieron's court might well have exchanged ideas.[118] One fragment survives from Aeschylus' play:

> τό τοι κακὸν ποδῶκες ἔρχεται βροτοῖς
> καὶ τἀμπλάκημα τῶι περῶντι τὴν θέμιν
>
> Fr. 22, Radt.[119]

This sort of gnomic statement would be appropriate in any number of Greek tragic plots, and it is also suited to the story of the *Bacchae*, in which Pentheus oversteps the bounds. That Aeschylus took up the story of Pentheus and Dionysus is made more likely by two other play titles of his that survive in the record, *Pentheus* and *Semele* (Radt. frags. 183, 221–4).

Epicharmus may also have been interested in the full myth of Dionysus, as a fragment from the comedy, *Periallos*, suggests:

> Σεμέλα δὲ χορεύει· καὶ ὑπαυλεῖ σφιν ~ σοφὸς κιθάραι παριαμβίδας· ἁ δὲ
> γεγάθει πυκινῶν ἀκροαζομένα
>
> PCG I Epicharmus fr. 108; Athenaeus IV 183[120]

In myth, Semele, daughter of Cadmus and Harmonia, was impregnated by Zeus and their child was Dionysus. The fragment above seems to belong to the part of the story which precedes the *Bacchae*, in which Semele is courted by Zeus. The depiction of Semele's carefree life, with its suggestion that she is young, beautiful, and altogether the sort of young woman who might catch the fancy of the god, sets the tone for the advent of Zeus and the sudden changes in her life that ensue. The puzzling title of the comedy, *Periallos*, does not help to define the plot,[121] and it has been

---

[118] Cf. Svarlien (1990–1991); Guardi (1980).

[119] "Swift-footed evil comes to humans
   And error to one transgressing what is customary and lawful."

[120] "Semele dances and a skilled poet plays on the pipe for her † accompanying airs on the harp. She rejoices listening to the rapid strumming. . ." PCG fr. 108.

[121] A second possible line from the same play is cited by Athenaeus who says that it appears both in the *Periallos* and in the *Hope*: "Dinner among the Dorians is called αἶκλον. Epicharmus, for example, in the *Hope* says: 'Someone invites you to dinner (αἶκλον) unwillingly, and you, most willingly, rushing, go there.' He said these same things in the *Periallos*." (Ath. IV 139) ἐκάλεσε γάρ τύ τις ἐπ' αἶκλον ἀέκων· τὺ δὲ ἑκὼν ᾤχεο τρέχων. τὰ αὐτὰ εἴρηκε καὶ ἐν Περιάλλωι. (PCG fr. 34). The line does not help with the broader outlines of the play, but it suggests that the tone was caustic and that some of the actions of the play were

variously interpreted as a reference to the hip, or perhaps a sensual dance moving the hips,[122] as a reference to someone arrogant and boastful,[123] and as a proper name.[124] It is possible, of course, that this description of Semele is just an aside in the play, rather than central to the plot. A full play setting out the parentage and birth of Dionysus would prove that Epicharmus was interested in the story itself, but even an aside shows that Epicharmus knew and used the myth, and that his audience was familiar with it as well.

If, in his *Bacchae,* Epicharmus took up a similar plot to that of Euripides, then he put on stage not only a chorus of Bacchants but also the complex problem of reconciling wild Bacchic religion with city law. Since an audience unfamiliar with Bacchic rites and Dionysus could not be expected to appreciate such a play, we may presume that the early fifth-century Syracusan audience had a basic familiarity with Dionysiac religion. Indeed, in yet another play, Epicharmus takes up at least one of the social problems central to the story of the *Bacchae* and considers it in a local context. This is the problem of marginal (or apparently marginal) religions or cults exerting an influence on the people and leading them astray. In Epicharmus' play, *Harpagai* (Robberies), as in Euripides' *Bacchae,* the targets of these manipulative religious mystics are women.

> ὥσπεραὶ πονηραὶ μάντιες,
> αἵ θ'ὑπονέμονται γυναῖκας μωρὰς ἂμ πεντόγκιον
> ἀργύριον, ἄλλαι δὲ λίτραν, ταὶ δ' ἀν' ἡμιλίτριον
> δεχόμεναι, καὶ πάντα γινώσκοντι τῶι ... λόγωι.

Just like the knavish prophetesses
Who trick the foolish women out of a "fiver" of silver,
Others taking a pound, and still others a half-pound, and they know
  everything.

PCG fr. 9; Pollux IX 81

---

rather mundane. This kind of local plot does not correspond to the overarching story of Semele and Zeus, and I am inclined to agree with Kaibel who notes that he is not sure whether Epicharmus used the whole line in both the *Hope* and the *Periallos.* Athenaeus may just have meant that the Doric word for "dinner" turned up in both plays.

[122] Meineke (1853) defends this possibility in his commentary on Alciphron I 39 (IV 14) from a definition given by Hesychius p. 1572. See Rodríguez-Noriega Guillén (1996) 94.

[123] Lorenz (1864) 147; Olivieri (1946–7) 71; Welcker (1835) 304. Rodríguez-Noriega Guillén (1996) 93–4.

[124] Kaibel (1899/1958) q.v.

From elsewhere in the *Harpagai*, a single line is preserved which suggests that the troubles described in the play are both local and widespread: ἁ δὲ Σικελία πέποσχε. (And Sicily has suffered.) (*PCG* fr. 11; Et. Gen. AB). Dislike of marginal religious prophets and new gods is too widespread to draw a close connection between the problem of the women who run wild in adoration of the god, Dionysus, in a play like Euripides' *Bacchae*, and the problem of foolish women duped by prophetesses in the *Harpagai*. The choice of presenting this issue in a play, however, suggests that Epicharmus, and presumably his audience, were concerned with some of the social questions presented in Euripides' *Bacchae*. These two additional plays, therefore, both the *Periallos*, with its reference to Semele and the early stages of the myth of Dionysus, and the *Harpagai* with its criticism of gullible women and the prophets who cheat them, suggest that the story of Dionysus and the *Bacchae* would have been readily comprehensible and relevant to the fifth-century audience of Epicharmus' plays.

As in the line quoted from Epicharmus' *Bacchae* (Athenaeus III 106 e–f), an irreverent treatment of Dionysus may be implied in the title of Epicharmus' play *Dionysoi*. Although a play mocking Dionysus falls comfortably into the type made famous and preserved for posterity in Aristophanes' *Frogs,* for example, a play about Dionysuses is more problematic. Webster notes the strangeness of the title, suggesting that it, like the three other Dionysiac play titles listed above, refers to a chorus, who act as supporters of their leader Dionysus.[125] Thus, he preserves the single god, and subordinates the crowd announced in the title as the god's supporters. Guillén, likewise, translates the title as the companions of Dionysus,[126] and Walker, in his relatively free translations of the fragments of Epicharmus into French, limits the number of gods, calling the play "Les Deux Bacchus."[127] Richard Janko and Ruth Scodel have both suggested to me that it might refer to a real Dionysus and a false Dionysus, on the analogy of Aristophanes' *Frogs*. But what if Epicharmus actually put *Dionysoi* on stage?[128]

---

[125] "[…]it is tempting to explain the curious title *Dionysoi* on the analogy of similar titles in Attic comedy, as a chorus of padded dancers with a leader *Dionysus* […]" Webster (1956) 100. Cratinus wrote a play by the same name, and Magnes, Alexandros, and Timocles wrote comedies called *Dionysus*. Pickard-Cambridge and Webster (1962) 280 and 160 notes that Cratinus' *Odyssies* had a chorus of Odysseus' sailors.

[126] Rodríguez-Noriega Guillén (1996) 32, "Los compañeros de Dioniso."

[127] Walker (1930) 20.

[128] It is perhaps interesting to note that one play for which two alternative titles are given, *Komasts* or *Hephaistos*, preserves the singular form of the god's name, and does not confuse it with the plural "Hephaistoi" to represent, for example, "the companions of Hephaistos."

The inherently comic effect of a dozen round-bellied gods is perhaps reason enough for such a play, but the ironic and metatheatrical tone of much of Epicharmus' work (see Chapter 2) suggests that this effect might also be put to critical use. Multiplying the god reduces his individuality and his stature; he becomes himself the chorus, no longer an active player in the comedy, but the supporting role. He is no longer possessed of an individual personality, but is reduced to a stereotype. If Dionysus is above all the god of Athenian theater, then this presentation in Syracuse might be a joke at the expense of Athenian theater.[129] This kind of jab at an Athenian institution may also appear on a comic vase of some 80 or 100 years later. The "*Choregoi*," first published by Kossatz-Deissmann, and then reinterpreted by Taplin, depicts an unlikely pair of *choregoi*, which Taplin identifies as exponents of that peculiarly Athenian institution, the *choregia* (Figure 5.1).[130] If, as Taplin argues, these two figures are members of the chorus, then they too seem to be reduced and stereotyped versions of the people they represent, that is to say, wealthy benefactors of the theater, members of the Athenian upper class. Another fragment of a South Italian vase, dating to the first quarter of the fourth century, may also show this sort of joke (Figure 3.3).[131]

On this fragment, we see Dionysus as a character in a comic play. This is unusual: on the comic phlyax vases, he normally appears as a god in the company of actors, not as a character himself. The central figure is Dionysus, identified by his thyrsus; the figure to his left has been identified as Zeus because of his scepter; and the suggestion has been made that the half figure to his right is Apollo. Despite these specific identifications, what is most striking about the fragment is, I think, the extraordinary similarity of the masks and the costumes of these characters: the clothing has the same trim, these two characters seem to have the same, or very similar, masks,[132] and the characters are proportioned similarly and seem to be the same size. Could this vase have recorded a play that made a similar joke? Could these characters be Dionysuses? Or at least replicated gods of some kind?

Preposterous numbers and long lists are perhaps generic comic material, but they certainly play a very large role in Epicharmus' comic repertory, as

---

[129] For Epicharmus' mockery of Aeschylus, recorded by the scholiast to the *Eumenides*, see Chapter 4.

[130] See Chapter 4 for a discussion of the "*Choregoi*" vase.

[131] Apulian bell-krater fragment, Museo Archeologico di Taranto 121613: Trendall (1967b) *PhV* 45, num. 61, pl. 5c.

[132] The masks are, however, identified as different in the *PhV*.

Figure 3.3 Apulian bell-krater fragment depicting Zeus and Dionysus. Taranto, Museo Archeologico Nazionale, 121613. First quarter of the fourth century BCE. Su concessione del Museo Archeologico Nazionale di Taranto

best we can determine it from the fragments. Ridiculously long lists of obscure fish names, for example, loom large in the fragments. Certain classes and professions are criticized through stereotyping, and Epicharmus is credited with the presentation of the first drunk as a stereotype, and perhaps with the first parasite.[133] Whether this play, *Dionysoi*, actually attempted to reduce Dionysus, the Athenian theater god, to a stereotype we will probably never know,[134] but this solution conforms to the tone of much of his work, and preserves the originality, which the title so strikingly implies.

This brief review of Dionysiac elements in the fragments and play titles of Epicharmus suggests that the god turns up relatively frequently in Epicharmus' plays. Unlike Euripides' (and perhaps Aeschylus')

[133] Pickard-Cambridge and Webster (1962) 273. *PCG* 31, 32, 33, 34.
[134] The one surviving line from the play, a note about cooking lentils, does not add much to the debate. Athenaeus IV, p. 158 C (*PCG* 30).

tragedies that presented Dionysus as all-powerful, if vindictive and violent, we must assume that Epicharmus' *Bacchae* was a comedy and had a lighter touch. It is very likely that Dionysus, and perhaps the whole story of Pentheus in Epicharmus' *Bacchae*, was represented comically. Likewise, in the *Dionysoi*, he may turn up as a replicated, stereotypical version of himself in the form of a crowd of chorus members. Why was Dionysus such a frequent character in these early Sicilian comic dramas?

As Scullion, Nielsen, and Polacco argue, Dionysus is not always associated with theater, and other gods can take his place as theatrical patron at theaters outside Athens. Moreover, as Polacco and Anti have argued, Dionysus does not appear to have been identified as the god of theater in Sicily in the archaic and classical periods, including the period in which Epicharmus was at work. In Athens, however, Dionysus was pre-eminently the god of theater. Is his presence in the early theatrical tradition of Sicilian theater a sign of Athenian influence?

The Deinomenids' support of literary genius was certainly not limited to local, Doric, literary fare; indeed, the most flamboyant act of Hieron's theatrical sponsorship seems to have been the commissioning of a play by Aeschylus.[135] To what extent Aeschylus influenced Doric plays (or the reverse) is a subject of great debate.[136] The evidence of Dionysus in Epicharmus' plays, combined with the absence of any significant cult activity on the island in honor of Dionysus, may reflect engagement with Athens and Athenian drama. That this was an Athenian association must have been all the more clearly demarcated in Syracuse, where Demeter, and not Dionysus, held such an important place in the city. The mocking tone we can trace in Epicharmus' treatment of Dionysus may indicate a rivalry with Attic drama, but it may also derive more straightforwardly from the comic nature of Epicharmus' work.

The exiguous remains of Epicharmus' comedies suggest that Dionysus was introduced to the theatrical landscape at least as early as the fifth century (and perhaps before, though we have no record of it). Evidence drawn from comic dramas alone is not enough to suggest that early Sicilian theater was performed under the auspices of Dionysus, as it was in this period at Athens; however, in conjunction with the later tradition, in particular Theocritus' memorial to

---

[135] For discussion of this play, *Women of Aetna*, see Chapter 4.
[136] E.g. Griffith (1978); Herington (1967).

Epicharmus invoking Dionysus, the balance of evidence points to an early interest in Dionysus, rather than Demeter or any other god. Even if Epicharmus mocked Dionysus as the god of Athenian theater, as he appears to have mocked Aeschylus himself, Dionysus like Aeschylus may, at the same time, have been admired and been welcomed into the cultural and artistic melting-pot of the Sicilian west.

3.10   Demeter's Island and Sicilian Tyrants

If the evidence for Demeter is so thin, why has the theory of a connection between Sicilian theater and Demeter proven so resilient in the last two decades? One of the difficulties in examining connections between Demeter and the theater is that her cult became so widespread on the island that it dominated many others and permeated many aspects of Sicilian life. Therefore, evidence of her cult in association with a theater may simply be a result of her enormous importance, rather than a specific connection with theater.

In 70 BCE, Cicero, who had been quaestor in Sicily five years earlier, wrote that mother and daughter held unchallenged sway in the spiritual life of the Sicilians:[137]

> Vetus est haec opinio, iudices, quae constat ex antiquissimis Graecorum litteris ac monumentis, insulam Siciliam totam esse Cereri et Liberae consecratam. Hoc cum ceterae gentes sic arbitrantur, tum ipsis Siculis ita persuasum est ut in animis eorum insitum atque innatum esse uideatur. Nam et natas esse has in his locis deas et fruges in ea terra primum repertas esse arbitrantur, et raptam esse Liberam, quam eandem Proserpinam uocant, ex Hennensium nemore, qui locus, quod in media est insula situs, umbilicus Siciliae nominatur. Quam cum inuestigare et conquirere Ceres uellet, dicitur inflammasse taedas iis ignibus qui ex Aetnae uertice erumpunt ... Cicero, *In Verrem* 4.106[138]

---

[137] Orlandini (1968–1969) 334.

[138] "It is old, this opinion, judges, which concludes from the most ancient literature and monuments of the Greeks, that the island of Sicily is completely consecrated to Ceres and Libera. Although other peoples think this, the Sicilians themselves are so persuaded of it that it seems to be rooted in their souls, and even innate. For the goddesses are thought to have been born in these places and the harvest to have been found on this earth first, and Libera, whom they call Persephone, was stolen away, from the grove of Enna. This place, because it is situated in the middle of the island, is called the navel of Sicily. When Ceres wanted to search and investigate, she is said to have lit torches from those fires which pour forth from Etna...."

Cicero, Diodorus Siculus,[139] and modern archaeologists agree[140] on the tremendous importance of the two goddesses on the island. After the classical period, the cult is ubiquitous and so enmeshed in all aspects of Sicilian life, that it is difficult to isolate its relationship to drama or any other particular activity.[141] This pervasive presence on the island does not, of course, preclude Demeter from having a particular connection to theater, but it does make it difficult to determine exactly what the connection was.

Although the cult quickly swept the island as Greek civilization gained a firmer footing, its early presence in the Orientalizing and Early Archaic periods was much more localized, archaeological evidence being available only from Gela, Selinus, and Acragas. In particular, the earliest documented site of the cult on the island is the sanctuary of Demeter Thesmophoros at Bitalemi, Gela.[142]

Whether the cult actually began in Gela or not, early tradition associates the Deinomenids, rulers of Gela, with its early presence on the island. Donald White argues that, from an early period, the cult of Demeter was a useful political tool for the Greeks to spread their culture as part of a political assimilation of the island. He cites Herodotus, who describes how Telines, the ancestor of the Deinomenids, won control of Gela with the help of the goddess.[143] Thereafter, members of the Deinomenid family held the ruling priesthood of the cult (Herodotus 7.153). Diodorus (11.26.7),

---

[139] οἱ ταύτην οὖν κατοικοῦντες Σικελιῶται παρειλήφασι παρὰ τῶν προγόνων, ἀεὶ τῆς φήμης ἐξ αἰῶνος παραδεδομένης τοῖς ἐκγόνοις, ἱερὰν ὑπάρχειν τὴν νῆσον Δήμητρος καὶ Κόρης· ἔνιοι δὲ τῶν ποιητῶν μυθολογοῦσι κατὰ τὸν τοῦ Πλούτωνος καὶ Φερσεφόνης γάμον ὑπὸ Διὸς ἀνακάλυπτρα τῆι νύμφηι δεδόσθαι ταύτην τὴν νῆσον. τοὺς δὲ κατοικοῦντας αὐτὴν τὸ παλαιὸν Σικανοὺς αὐτόχθονας εἶναί· φασιν οἱ νομιμώτατοι τῶν συγγραφέων, καὶ τάς τε προειρημένας θεὰς ἐν ταύτηι τῆι νησωι πρώτως φανῆναι καὶ τὸν τοῦ σίτου καρπὸν ταύτην πρώτην ἀνεῖναι διὰ τὴν ἀρετὴν τῆς χώρας (Diod. Sic. 5.2.3–4).

   "The Siceliotae who live in this island have received from their forefathers the tradition (word of which has been transmitted over the years from each generation to the next in succession), that the island is sacred to Demeter and Kore. Some poets, however, narrate the myth that, at the wedding of Pluto and Persephone, the island was given as a marriage gift to the bride by Zeus. The notion that the primeval inhabitants of the island, the Sicani, were indigenous, is found in the most respected of the historians, and also that the above mentioned goddesses first appeared on this island, and that it was the first because of the excellence of its soil in producing the fruit of the corn."

[140] Polacco (1986); Brelich (1964–1965); Curbera (1997).

[141] Cf. White (1964), who argues that the political function of Demeter's cult in Sicily can be traced particularly clearly in the Hellenistic period, just before Roman rule: "At this time Demeter's fate becomes closely identified with that of the island."

[142] Hinz (1998), in particular 56–64.

[143] As a resident of the Athenian settlement of Thurii in South Italy (founded ca 443 BCE), Herodotus may have had particularly good access to information and stories about Sicily.

and Cicero (*Verr.* II, 4.53.119) report that Gelon built twin temples in honor of Demeter and Persephone following his victory at Himera.[144] White notes that this support of the cult would have benefited Gelon in two ways. First, he had a mixed population made up in part of Geloans, who had worshiped Demeter in Gela, where the cult was very strong. Moreover, Demeter presented an alternative to the traditional deities of the Syracusan aristocracy: Zeus, Athena, Artemis, and Apollo. Thus, the cult provided a popular focus, already familiar to some, and distinct from the deities of the previous rulers. Secondly, as a priest of the cult, Gelon "was invested with a kind of holy sanctity" and thus he was able to "fortify his domestic position with Syracuse's polymorphic citizenry at the same time as he weakened the stance of its discredited aristocracy."[145]

The truth of these theories is much debated, however. Recently, Valentina Hinz has argued that the tyrants were not the driving force behind the growing cult, and, at the most, simply benefited from it where they could. She acknowledges that the *communis opinio* holds that the cult had a political function, but argues that its growth and popularity was simply the effect of the spread of Greek settlement through the island, rather than a tool used by the conquerors to consolidate their military conquests.[146] Hinz brings up a number of archaeological and historical problems to undermine the idea that the cult of Demeter was a particularly important means of cultural expansion, deliberately used by the tyrants. She points out that Gelon set up memorials to other gods (namely, Apollo and Zeus, and one temple to all the gods) following his victory at Himera, not only a temple for Demeter and Kore in Syracuse. She also notes that the chronology of the scholiast, who attributes the origin of the cult to the early Deinomenids, is wrong.[147] She demonstrates, moreover, that the cult was already popular in some areas before the rise to power of the Deinomenids.

For our purposes, however, the sheer existence of Herodotus' story as early as the fifth century BCE is the most important point. Gelon's attention to other gods does not demonstrate that he did not foster the cult of

---

[144] Diod. Sic. 14.70.4. Diodorus also writes that when the Carthaginians pillaged the Syracusan sanctuary of Demeter in 386, and were struck by various disasters, they decided to introduce the cult of the goddess in Carthage in order to expiate their sacrilege (Loicq-Berger (1967) 220–1).

[145] White (1964) 265. The Deinomenid control of the cult in Sicily might be compared to the significant role of the Eumolpidai and the Kerykes in Attica, on whom cf. Burkert (1985) 285. White sets out the case for the tyrants' political use of theater, both at length in his thesis (1963) and in an article (1964).

[146] Hinz (1998) 22: "Seine Ausbreitung in diesen Landstrichen ist daher nicht Mittel, sondern Ergebnis der Hellenisierung."

[147] Hinz (1998) 22.

Demeter and Kore in order to win more popular approval. Whether the Deinomenids actually had ancestral rights to the priesthood is immaterial: they behaved as if they did; they promoted the cult; and they seem to have used it to further their own ends. Even if the literary sources are not entirely accurate, they do point to the political advantages that the cult afforded the tyrants, and they suggest that this was a popular perception of the events. Since, inevitably, the spread of Greek culture coincides with the spread of the cult, it is difficult to make the fine temporal distinctions to determine which led to the growth of the other. Hinz does, in fact, agree that the cult must have had some political importance for the rulers, simply because it was so widespread. This is sufficient for this argument: just as the Deinomenids need not have single-handedly invented and supported theater on the island in order to use it for political ends, so they need not have been the sole supporters of the cult, or solely supporters of this cult, in order to make use of it for their own political purposes. In my view, the ancient record of the origins of the cult, written shortly after the heyday of the tyrants, is a strong indication that the cult was manipulated in the fifth century by the tyrants in some fashion. This is true even if they also worshiped and built temples to other gods; it is even more true if they do not have a real ancestral link to the cult, but made it up.

The cult may even have been officially linked with the state and with democracy.[148] Hinz agrees that the archaeological evidence for the cult suggests that its widespread popularity was a unifying element among the populations uprooted and moved at will by the tyrants.[149] A 'Great Oath' of allegiance was sworn to Persephone and Demeter to ensure loyalty to the state. In one case, Agathocles had to swear to the goddesses that he would not harm the democracy; in another, Callippus swore that he would not plot against the tyrant Dion.[150] "It was no accident that Demeter should have been so employed," writes White, " since the oath must have evolved out of a situation in which Gelon and his brother both embodied the state and served as the chief priests of the goddesses."[151]

The lack of clear archaeological evidence tying theater to Demeter in Sicily and the dominance of Dionysus rather than Demeter in the fragments of Epicharmus suggest that the notion of Sicilian theater developing out of the cult of Demeter should be set aside. Instead, the evidence for the Deinomenid tyrants' support both of the cult of Demeter and of the theater suggests that any relationship between the two was circumstantial and

---

[148] For the tyrants' assumption of democratic appearances, see Chapter 4.   [149] Hinz (1998).
[150] Diod. Sic. 19.5.4; Plut., *Dion* 57. Drawn from White (1964) 265–6.   [151] White (1964) 266.

contingent. Thus, as in the fragment of *Odysseus Automolos* discussed above, the tyrants' message of the importance of Demeter might often have echoed in the plays, which were, in turn, financed by the Deinomenids. The range of cult sanctuaries near which later stone theaters were built further supports the view that no single god or goddess was exclusively associated with theater in Sicily, until, in the later Hellenistic period, Dionysus came to dominate theater throughout the Greek world.

In sum, the Deinomenid tyrants, high-ranking priests in the cult of Demeter, seem to have used the cult as a state religion during their tenure as rulers of Syracuse in the early fifth century, whether or not they were entirely responsible for its continuing popularity. Likewise, as I shall show in subsequent chapters, the tyrants backed early theatrical development, funded large-scale productions, and reaped the benefits of this public forum for the expression of ideas, and, more crudely, propaganda. The development of both the cult and the theater were bids to win immediate popular approval and to establish an infrastructure to disseminate the ideology of the new regime – in essence, to create a state religion and a state theater. Thus, at times, these two projects of the tyrants seem to cross paths, feed into one another, and, indeed, develop together. The essential dramatic properties of the Demeter myth and cult, which I have discussed above, are important, but their link to the sudden growth and popularity of the theater in early fifth-century Syracuse, an early theatrical tradition unparalleled anywhere in the Greek world except in Athens, was ultimately circumstantial.

3.11 Burlesque and the Grave

Nevertheless, as Demeter permeated so much of life in Sicily, so she became enmeshed in some aspects of theater, particularly the shadowy links between Dionysus, theater, and the afterlife. In wider Greek religion, moreover, thematic similarities between the cults of Dionysus and Demeter seem to link the two, and some of these similarities, in turn, associate them both with comedy. As deities of the vine and wheat, respectively, both seem to have a connection with liminal rites, and particularly the transition into life. Likewise, both are connected with ribald and obscene jokes, *aischrologia*. In Attica, in a procession to Eleusis, celebrants shouted Ιακχ᾽, ὦ Ιακχε; *Iakchos* is believed to be both a daimon of Demeter and an epithet of Dionysus.[152] Along this route, ribald and obscene jokes are made, much

[152] Burkert (1985) 287.

like the ones described by Diodorus in Syracuse, and, as at Syracuse, with a view to celebrating the laughter of Demeter at the lewd jokes of Baubo. Luigi Todisco also notes that the connection between burlesque and chthonic cults is also demonstrated by burlesque performances possibly held in the sanctuary of the Megaloi Theoi at Samothrace and in the sanctuary of the Cabiri at Thebes.[153] As Bonnie MacLachlan demonstrates, evidence from women's cult rites at Locri Epyzephiri ties worship of Demeter and burlesque with the afterlife.[154]

Moreover, in the Pythagorean tradition, with which, as we have seen, Epicharmus is sometimes associated, the myths of Demeter and of Dionysus sometimes overlap. One god particularly revered in their cult was Dionysus Zagreus, who was said to be the son of Persephone.[155] He was a daemonic incarnation of the god, and particularly associated with the underworld. The worship of Demeter and Dionysus intersects with Pythagoreanism in, among other places, the underworld.

Thus it seems likely that Epicharmus was working in a tradition of cult rites and reverence for the gods of the underworld. Indeed, much of the archaeological evidence for theater in Sicily is circumstantially associated with death, for it has been found in graves. One such body of evidence is made up of terracotta figurines of comic actors.[156]

Comic figurines and miniature comic masks have been discovered all over the Greek world, but in greatest quantity on the island of Lipari, off the northern coast of Sicily. On Lipari, as elsewhere, the figurines have been found in three main places: graves, votive deposits, and garbage dumps. Although both masks and figurines seem to have been made on the island, Cavalier and Bernabò Brea have identified many of them as representations of characters in Athenian plays. Other masks they have identified as characters drawn from myth[157] and still others, though clearly comic or

---

[153] Todisco (2002) 181. Cf. Nielsen (2002) 133–7, who also notes the burlesque character of the performances depicted on vases in the sanctuary of the Cabiri, and describes some of the early cult performances in the sanctuary of the Megaloi Theoi. Cf. Burkert (1985) 282 on burlesque in the cult of the Cabiri at Thebes. He suggests, however, that the theater built beside the sanctuary of the Great Gods at Samothrace "is unlikely to have had cultic functions" (283). See also Polacco (1987) 15–16; Marconi (2010) 106–35.

[154] MacLachlan (2012) 343–64.   [155] Gorman (1979) 91; Burkert (1985) 298.

[156] These are generally later than the fifth century, though Luigi Bernabò Brea and Madeleine Cavalier have identified two figurines found in Lipari, as possibly dating to the fifth century. They associate these figurines with the comedy of Epicharmus, though there is no proof of this other than the early date of the figurines and the popularity of Epicharmus in the period. Bernabò Brea and Cavalier (2001) 23–5.

[157] For example, the Heracles and Hades masks which have been associated with a passage in the *Iliad* 5.395–404. Bernabò Brea (1998) 12. U. Spigo in Lyons, Bennett, and Marconi (2013) 110–11, figs. 61–2.

tragic, have not been associated with a particular play or myth. Bernabò Brea and Cavalier, among others, speculate that the terracotta masks were precise copies of masks used for theatrical production. Some of the larger terracotta pieces may, they suggest, have even been used as models for the stage masks, since the terracotta versions were probably more easily transported.[158] The latter case is very much the exception, however, since most of the masks are 8–10 cm in size.[159] The many basic similarities among the terracottas probably reflected similarities among actual masks. Thus the terracottas seem to confirm that, on stage, generic masks were used for the various temperamental types and basic characters, and that slight details were added to distinguish one character from another when necessary.[160]

Terracotta versions of the masks of Old Comedy which had rough, crudely comic features can be distinguished from those of New Comedy where the features seemed to express distinct emotions and finer gradations of character. Using the classification of masks in Pollux's *Onomasticon*, Bernabò Brea and Cavalier divide up the masks and show how they could be roughly grouped under those ancient categories. The work of these two archaeologists has culminated in fine classification and description of the various character and mask types. Knowledge of costume and mask design has been hugely enriched by the detailed comparisons and analyses done from the finds at Lipari.

Collections of masks or figurines are often identified with a certain play. Thus they suggest that at least six tragedians are represented by these masks: Astydamas (*Hector*), Aeschylus (*Philoctetes*), Euphorion (*Philoctetes*), Euripides (*Alcestis, Alexandros, Chrysippos, Hekabe, Philoctetes*), Philokles (*Philoctetes*), Sophocles (*Philoctetes*), and five comedians: Aristophanes (*Ecclesiazusae, Frogs*), Diphilus, Epicharmus, Philemon, and Menander. Other collections of figurines and masks are imagined to represent plays, which we simply do not have enough information to identify.

The careful assemblages of dramatic pieces in these graves is remarkable. No other type of artifact seems to be placed with as much precision. Pots and jewelry, combs and mirrors are included in the tombs, but do not seem to be put together in any united fashion. For instance, bowls do not seem to form a set, nor is there a marked variety of vessels as if the dead might need a range of pottery. Moreover, the pottery seems to range from elaborately

---

[158] Bernabò Brea and Cavalier (2002) 29–30.   [159] Bernabò Brea and Cavalier (1991) 57.
[160] Bernabò Brea and Cavalier (1991) 164.

painted larger pots to very simple functional cups. Thus, the care taken to include a cohesive group of masks seems fairly unique in the grave arrangements.

Figurines and masks are not all modeled on theatrical characters, however. Many of the statuettes represent divinities, or simply women or men without any precise function. The masks also sometimes represent a key political or artistic figure, rather than a character from a play. Since the theatrical characters share the medium with these other types of figures, how similar are the functions they perform? Many, though not all, of the divinities represented in figurines might be easily linked to a function with the underworld (for example, Demeter, Hermes, Persephone, Hades, Aphrodite), but there are many that do not seem connected to the afterlife (for example, Gorgon, Hera, Nike). That these statuettes were included merely because they were beautiful can never be entirely discounted. Even if their inclusion had something specific to do with the god represented, this is too disparate a group to trace a general theme, and each may have been chosen for private reasons.

Despite the large number of theatrical masks and figures from the site as a whole, the greater proportion of graves (more than 2,200 have been uncovered to date) do not seem to have them. Two graves (1986 and 1988) are particularly interesting because they both have masks or a figurine and both were the graves of small children. Of all the graves unearthed in this section (which dates from the first half of the fourth century to the first decade of the third century), only three contain dramatic material: two of these are children's graves and the third is not identified. The other seven graves, all of adults, contain many grave goods including painted pots and jewelry, but no theatrical terracottas. Possibly the masks and figurines were meant to entertain the children after death.

The two chief excavators at Lipari, Cavalier and Bernabò Brea, concluded that the many figurines with dramatic associations found in graves were evidence of the strong influence of Dionysism, especially the link between the cult of Dionysus and the underworld, on the island. They associate the cult of Dionysus with the figurines partly because Dionysism was widespread by the fourth century in Sicily and Magna Graecia,[161] and partly because of the Dionysiac revels depicted on some associated pots, but primarily because of

---

[161] Bernabò Brea and Cavalier (2001) 19 note simply that Dionysism seems to have been widely diffused in all of Magna Graecia and Sicily from the beginning of the fourth century. But cf. Zuntz (1971) 86, n. 3, who argues that there is very little evidence for any cult of Dionysus in Sicily before the fourth century. There is, however, a significant body of visual evidence from the island reflecting the local significance of this god, since the Late Archaic period: see more recently De Cesare (2013) 76–7.

Figure 3.4 Sicilian calyx-krater from Gibil Gabib showing a comic Dionysus
followed by Demeter. Gibil Gabib Group. Caltanisetta, Museo Civico Archeologico,
258. Second half of the fourth century BCE. Su concessione del Polo Regionale
di Gela e Caltanissetta e per i siti culturali

the much-studied association between Dionysus and the theater. On this
theory, the two domains of the god (theater and the liminal crossing to the
underworld) merge when theatrical figurines become grave goods.[162]

Since Demeter was the main chthonic goddess of the island, the appearance of the comic figurines in graves may have derived from (or perhaps
themselves created) a more general association between chthonic cults and
burlesque comedy in Sicily. Although there is no explicit evidence that
associates the cult of Demeter with the origin of literary comedy in
Syracuse, drama in Syracuse might well have been influenced by this familiar
association between *aischrologia* and rituals pertaining to the afterlife.

Dating to the second half of the fourth century, a vase uncovered near
Caltanissetta further suggests a connection between the two gods (see
Figure 3.4).[163]

---

[162] Bernabò Brea and Cavalier (2001) 19–22, 275–7.
[163] Sicilian calyx-krater, Caltanissetta, Museo Archeologico 258, from Gibil Gabib: Trendall
(1967a) 600–1, num. 95, pl. 235.1 (Gibil Gabib Group); Panvini (2003) 33.

On this vase, Demeter, carrying her familiar torch, follows a theatrical Dionysus, complete with thyrsus and cothurnoi, the shoes of an actor. This scene of two gods frolicking together cannot confirm an original derivation of theater from the cult of either of them, but it does show that by the fourth-century Demeter was sometimes linked to a theatrical Dionysus. This window into the chaotic world of burlesque and devotion to the gods probably suggests, as Bonnie MacLachlan proposes, that "a ritual encounter with the Underworld was an experience that invited a parodying of the mythical and dramatic tradition."[164]

---

[164] MacLachlan (2012). For a connection between the Lipari masks, their funerary context, and the associated cults of Dionysus and Demeter, see Schwarzmaier (2011) 201–18.

4 | Politics and Propaganda

The plays of Epicharmus are often described as mythological burlesques without political relevance.[1] The accidents of preservation[2] and the scholarly assumption that Athens was unique in its encouragement of real social dialogue through theater have contributed to a widely held view that Syracusan playwrights were entertainers without serious social concerns or roles. Pickard-Cambridge, for example, describes the apolitical nature of Epicharmus' plays in his *Dithyramb, Tragedy, Comedy* of 1927 (revised by Webster 1962) which remains an important comprehensive summary of Epicharmus' work in English:

> If we ask why there was no political comedy in Sicily, we need not have recourse to Hieron's temper or to the dangers of life under a monarch for an explanation. The simple reason seems to be that the earlier kinds of performance out of which Sicilian comedy developed were entirely non-political, and that political comedy was a special extravagance peculiar to Athens and does not lie in the main stream of the development of the art.[3]

Plays imported from Athens, which have survived whole and whose political content is unmistakable, have sometimes been assimilated to this picture of Sicilian theater by using the argument that they were understood differently in Sicily. For example, Oliver Taplin, acknowledging recent studies that interpret Attic drama within the specific social and political context of fifth-century Athens, has argued that non-Athenian audiences could appreciate Athenian plays at a more general or different level.[4] Other scholars argue that plays retained political power, but of a different sort in

---

[1] Norwood (1931); Pickard-Cambridge (1962); Kerkhof (2001).

[2] Many fragments of Epicharmus, for example, are found in Athenaeus as proof of obscure grammatical points or to fill out his lists of rare fish. Cf. Wilkins (2000).

[3] Pickard-Cambridge (1962) 239. Cf. Millino (2000) 129–30; Csapo (2010) 40 on Epicharmus' sophistication.

[4] Taplin (2007) 6: "This dissemination must have been thanks less to its Athenianness and more to its 'universality,' or – if that notion is too problematic – to its potential for adaptability."

Magna Graecia.[5] In sum, the tragedies may have been promoting democratic values in their original circumstances of performance, but non-
democratic audiences could well have ignored the democratic features.

Subjective interpretations of the plays must account for much of the
popularity that Athenian drama has enjoyed in many ages and centuries,
and the cleverness and sheer entertainment value of the plays of
Epicharmus and his peers no doubt did much to popularize their work.
The force of theater in the West and particularly in Sicily, however, may
have been coherent and deliberate enough to leave evidence of a sustained
political role in the political and social world of fifth-century Sicily. Studies
on isolated plays performed in fifth-century Sicily have begun to demonstrate that the theater was more than popular entertainment. In particular,
Carol Dougherty has situated Aeschylus' *Women of Aetna* in the literary
framework of foundation and colonization poetry. The play has always
been recognized as propaganda for Hieron, but Dougherty presents
a subtle analysis of its form and political function.[6] Moreover, Giovanni
Millino has made a convincing argument that one of Epicharmus' plays is
a mythical parody of the battle of Himera.[7] Could these plays have been
part of a more comprehensive attempt on the part of the tyrants to develop
the theater for their own political purposes?

Although the evidence is as sparse as it is for most questions of theatrical
history in fifth-century Sicily, what little we can tell about the social and
political context of performances and about the subjects of the plays
suggests that Gelon and Hieron used the theater to further their own
political aims. Aeschylus' and Epicharmus' plays have often been treated
separately, perhaps because the former are more easily analyzed with the
wealth of evidence for his plays in Athens, whereas the latter are fragmentary and rooted in Syracuse, about which we have far less knowledge.
However, the political and social purposes of theater in Syracuse are easier
to trace if the two genres performed in Syracuse – Athenian tragedy and
Sicilian comedy – are considered together. Since the question has often
been bypassed in scholarly works, I have begun with a brief review of the
overtly topical aspects of the imported tragedies and local comedies. Some

---

[5] Allan (2001) 81 argues that plays, like *Children of Herakles*, retained political power, though of
a different sort in Magna Graecia, because "[. . .] even this most 'Attic' and 'political' of tragedies
confronted issues, such as the conflict between self-interest and justice or the proper treatment of
refugees, which were of interest to audiences well beyond Athens [. . .]" and 80: "This is not to say
that the play's political content is effaced or overshadowed by its representation of myth, but
rather to stress that the play's political impact in Megale Hellas will be different from its impact in
Athens."

[6] Dougherty (1993) 83–102. Cf. Dearden (1999) 231.   [7] Millino (2000).

of these fragments and themes are discussed in greater detail later in the chapter, which takes up some of the social and political purposes that the plays might have served. In general, the plays seem to have promoted a sense of community among the uprooted and mixed populations of the Sicilian cities, marked the dominance of Syracuse over the eastern side of the island, and glorified the tyrants. The political role of theater in Sicily may not have been to provide a democratic rallying point and forum to identify with fellow citizens, as many scholars believe was true in Athens; but I shall argue that even this aspect of the theater was appropriated by the tyrants into their self-glorifying propaganda.

4.1   Plays about Current Affairs and Local Settings

Hitherto, Epicharmus' plays have been thought to consist mainly of mythological burlesque, jokes about food and other coarse humor, clever word play, and the development of character types.[8] The philosophical fragments are generally rejected as spurious, or, at most, are thought to have been derived from clever jokes in the plays, and to be meant, above all, for entertainment.[9] Most scholars acknowledge the existence of a few fragments suggesting topical political subjects, but they relegate these to the category of rare exceptions.[10]

The fragmentary state of his work, however, makes a general appreciation of it difficult, and it is hard to distinguish what is representative. The fragments about food, for example, a topic probably common in all comedy, are almost all preserved in Athenaeus, whose particular interest in obscure food names makes this a very idiosyncratic collection and not therefore necessarily representative. Apart from the lists of fish, the fragments about eating suggest a rough humor,[11] which, since it is also found in Aristophanes, need not preclude the kind of topical political comedy that Aristophanes made famous. This rough humor, moreover, is mixed with jokes and references that seem to assume a sophisticated and attentive

---

[8] Norwood (1931) 97–113 adds the conflict of abstractions, such as land and sea, to burlesque and comedy of manners. Pickard-Cambridge (1962) 282 ff. lays stress on Epicharmus' development of character types. Kerkhof (2001) notes the parody of myth, and also the invention of character types in his discussion of Epicharmus' influence on Attic poets.

[9] Cf. Pickard-Cambridge (1962) 247 f.

[10] E.g. Norwood (1931) 104; Pickard-Cambridge (1962) 271; Kerkhof (2001) 132–3.

[11] "[…] the kind of farce and horseplay that is always an element of popular comedy of a not very advanced type […]" Pickard-Cambridge (1962) 281–2.

audience.[12] Strong character types do seem to dominate the fragments, but it is difficult to tell what role they played in the plot or theme of the plays, since we rarely have more than a few lines indicating their behavior. The mythological burlesque, for which there is quite a lot of evidence, is not necessarily devoid of political import, as Millino's article shows.[13] When the fragments are considered alone, however, it is difficult to paint a very complete picture of Epicharmus' work, and so it seems safer to conclude, as many scholars have done, that the plays were clever mythological burlesque without particular social or political import.

The literary and historical circumstances of Epicharmus' productions, however, point in a different direction. The plays of his contemporary Aeschylus, the only other surviving dramas of any length from early fifth-century Sicily, provide an important context. Both Aeschylean tragedies known to have been imported by Hieron suggest that the Syracusans, or their tyrant, favored topical subjects in their theater.[14] One, the *Persians*, is about the Persian Wars of a few years before;[15] the other, *The Women of Aetna*, seems to have been written as an aetion in conjunction with a celebration of Hieron's refounding of the city of Catania in 476. These recent events are remarkable subjects for tragedy, because in Athens explicitly current subjects seem to have been discouraged.[16] Phrynichus, for example, seems to have been fined for his troubling portrayal of the recent Persian capture of Miletus.[17] In Syracuse, on the other hand, the only two tragedies we know of took a recent event for subject matter, and the tyrants seem to have funded both productions. Apart from the later ancient authorities who write that Hieron hired Aeschylus to write a play, the subject of *The Women of Aetna* is fairly good evidence that Aeschylus was writing to Hieron's specifications.

[12] E.g. *PCG* 221, mockery of Aeschylus; *PCG* 77, noting the meter first brought in by Aristoxenus.

[13] Millino (2000). Likewise, although explicit references to contemporary politics are rare in Athenian tragedy, implicit and veiled references to current events abound. The political relevance of mythological burlesque was familiar in Athens as well, as the argument to Cratinus' *Dionysalexandros* makes clear by noting that Pericles and his role in the war were satirized by the play (*POxy.*, IV, 69–72). See further Bakola (2010) 181–3.

[14] For the possible connection of Aeschylus' satyr play, *Theoroi or Isthmiastai*, with Sicily, particularly as it can be deduced from the Silenos antefixes of Naxos, see Marconi (2005).

[15] On the question of whether *Persians* was performed in Syracuse, cf. Herington (1967) 75 f., who has also collected the primary evidence on pages 82–3 and Griffith (1978) 106 and n. 5.

[16] Cf. Goldhill (1988) 189–93, who notes that the *Persians* "fits uneasily into many general arguments about Athenian theatre" (189). But Bremer (1991) 59 suggests that "it is probable that in the early days of tragedy there have been more tragedies dealing with historical events that happened in Attica or were related to the fate or glory of Athens than we are inclined to assume."

[17] Hdt. 6.21.10. Cf. Pickard-Cambridge (1962) 64.

It is likely that the tyrants supported Epicharmus in the same sort of way, and for similar reasons, that they did Aeschylus (and the other poets of the court such as Simonides, Pindar, and Bacchylides).[18] Both playwrights produced plays under Hieron, and Epicharmus seems to have been a familiar at court as two anecdotes about Epicharmus being invited for dinner and engaging in familiar conversation with the tyrant suggest.[19] Epicharmus knew Aeschylus' work (Schol. on Aesch. *Eum.* 626: Kaibel (1958) 214), and his near contemporary, Phormis, seems also to have been intimately associated with the Deinomenids as tutor for their children (*Suda* 609).

If Epicharmus' plays are considered together with those of Aeschylus, it seems reasonable to search the fragments for evidence of contemporary, topical subjects. Indeed, some of Epicharmus' comedies, like the tragedies of Aeschylus, seem to be about current events. One play title, *Persians*, suggests a reworking of Aeschylus' play of the same name, and perhaps, therefore, taking as its subject the Persian Wars (*PCG* 110 and 111). That Epicharmus made Aeschylus the butt of jokes is suggested in a scholiast's note on the *Eumenides*, which relates that Epicharmus mocked Aeschylus for his excessive use of the word "τιμαλφούμενον" (*PCG* 221).[20] A few details from the fragments also suggest an interest in current affairs and daily life. For instance, a scholiast to Pindar's first *Pythian* records that in the *Islands* Epicharmus described Hieron preventing Anaxilas of Rhegium from destroying the Locrians.[21] Elsewhere, Epicharmus puts a parasite sycophant on stage, a figure who, as Pickard-Cambridge notes, must be contemporary with the democracy.[22] Many of Epicharmus' plays seem to be set in Sicily; others include both local and contemporary references to modern coins and current religious festivals.

If both the comedies and the tragedies (to say nothing of the lyric poetry being performed at the same time) presented contemporary subjects, set in recognizable and local places, the next, and more interesting, question is whether the plays took up identifiable political themes.

---

[18] Svarlien (1990–1991). Cf. Bremer (1991) on the payment of tragic poets both in Athens and elsewhere.

[19] *PCG* Test. 14 (Plut., *Quomodo adul. ab amico internoscatur* = *Mor.* 68A); *PCG* Test. 15 (*Apophth. reg. et imp.* 175 B (Hiero 5)). For further discussion, see Novokhatko (2015).

[20] This translates to "honored."

[21] *PCG* 96 (Scholiast (DEFGQ) Pind. *Pyth.* 1, 99a, II p. 18, 21 Dr.).

[22] Pickard-Cambridge (1962) 233 and 258: "the reference to sycophants excludes a date before the establishment of the democracy in 466 B.C."

4.2 Creating a Community of Greeks

The early Syracusan tyrants, Gelon (485–478) and his brother Hieron (478–467) consolidated control over their territory in two ways which were particularly disruptive to society: they moved populations to ensure that there were loyal citizens in the right places and they gave loyal mercenaries citizenship and land. This was a technique used by many of the Sicilian rulers. Hippocrates, tyrant of Gela (498–491), under whom Gelon was a lieutenant, worked the first complete ethnic reorganization of a polis at Camarina. Although Camarina capitulated peacefully, the real allegiance of the citizens was in question, and therefore Hippocrates ordered their removal and the settling of the town by new citizens of his own.[23] When Gelon took over power in Syracuse, he adopted the same methods, settling the richest citizens in Syracusan territory, thereby bringing wealth to the city, and also settling his mercenaries, who formed the basis of a loyal hoplite class.[24] Theron, tyrant of Akragas (ca 488–472), Gelon's contemporary and ally, also violently shifted populations to remove potential pockets of rebellion.[25] Following the same policy, Hieron famously resettled the inhabitants of Aetna, thereby assuming the title of founder. This frequent resettling of populations seems to have been a technique peculiar to the Sicilian tyrants, and distinguished them from their counterparts on mainland Greece.

These methods, effective as they may have been militarily and politically, created social confusion. One step in repairing the torn social fabric of southeastern Sicily was to recreate a sense of identity and communal cohesion. The threat of barbarian invasion was useful; a more controllable method was the hiring of poets to sing the praises of the Sicilian tyrannies and to inspire a sense of pride in the new communities.[26] As Bruno Gentili and others have noted, tyrants' use of art to consolidate their political position is a well-known phenomenon, and the Deinomenids are in no way exceptional. What is interesting here is how the same plays which seem to tell a democratic and anti-tyrannical story to scholars of Athenian social history helped the tyrants of Sicily.

If the main aim of resettling citizens was to ensure a unified front against the Carthaginian threat, or, at least, if this aim, rather than the safeguarding of the tyrant's control, could be claimed, then the common Greek heritage

---

[23] Consolo Langher (1996) 211.   [24] Consolo Langher (1996) 218 f.

[25] Consolo Langher (1996) 210.

[26] This seems to be a well-accepted truism. Cf. for example, Gentili (1988) 115: "For the rich nobleman or city aristocrat and, above all, for the tyrant, the artist's work was a means of increasing status and consolidating political position." Cf. also Guardi (1980) 26.

of the newly settled cities could provide unity among them. Poetry which celebrated the Greek roots of the people involved might help smooth over differences of uprooted and newly mixed colonies. Lyric poetry seems frequently to have been harnessed to this cause. Pindar's epinicians in praise of Hieron do seem to point to Syracuse's connection with the wider Greek world, as, for example, in the famous association of the battle of Himera with that of Salamis in *Pythian* 1.[27] Celebration of Olympic or other sporting victories also positioned the tyrants and by extension their populations in the framework of the larger Greek world.[28] In the same way, Athenian tragedies can have appealed to the Sikeliotes' sense of a common mythical background. William Allan has shown that the central Greek myths of the plays served to unite the audience by reminding them of their common heritage.[29] This was useful both in the larger political framework of 'establishing hellenicity' to impress other Greek states, as Oliver Taplin has pointed out, and also to foster unity among the Syracusans and the Sicilians.[30]

In defining the patchwork society of Sicily as above all Greek, Athens, as a cultural center, was a useful touchstone. Aeschylus, among the famous poets whom Hieron hired to celebrate his reign, might have helped the Sicilian audiences put Greek heritage above city state, not only through the subjects of his plays, but through his own roots in Athens, and his fame throughout the Greek world. As with most events of this period in Sicily, we cannot be absolutely certain of the timing and number of Aeschylus' voyages; however, it seems most likely that the *Life of Aeschylus* is right in its statement that Aeschylus did visit at Hieron's invitation.[31] Aeschylus would have lent not only sophistication to the tyrant's court, but also a direct connection with the Attic world of which he was a part.

The generation which followed Epicharmus considered him, likewise, as part of the wider Greek tradition, for they identified him as one of the great dramatists and philosophers of the fifth-century Greek world. As early as

---

[27] *Pyth.* 1.75–80. Aristotle also suggests that this connection was intended (*Poet.* 1459a25) as does Herodotus 7, 165–6. Cf. Bremer (1991) 41.

[28] Cf. Larmour (1999).   [29] Allan (2001).   [30] Taplin (1993) 1.

[31] The debate about how often, and exactly when, Aeschylus came to Sicily has been going on for more than a century. Classical sources suggest at least twice, and possibly as often as five times. For a summary of the arguments to date, see Herington (1967), especially pages 82–3 for a collection of the pertinent ancient sources. The tragedian Phrynichus may have made a voyage to Sicily (although the source for this, the anonymous treatise *On Comedy* found in some manuscripts of Aristophanes, seems to have confused him with the somewhat later poet of Old Comedy of the same name (*De com.* p. 8, 36 K)). If he did so, he may possibly, like Aeschylus, have died there. Guardi (1980) 35. In Bosher (2012b) I argue that Aeschylus developed the extant version of *Persians* for Syracuse.

Plato and Aristotle, he is listed in the canon of major Greek writers. Plato compares him with Homer (*Tht.* 152 E), for example, and Aristotle with Magnes, Kratinos, Krates, Pherecrates, Phrynichos, Eupolis, and Aristophanes (*Poet.* 5 1449b 5).[32] Although this is in large part a tribute to the quality of his work, which we are less able to appreciate since so little has survived, it is also a sign that the plays were works which, like those of Aeschylus, could appeal to many other audiences in the Greek world, besides that of his own town, Syracuse.

The titles of Epicharmus' plays also suggest that he frequently took up subjects similar to those of his Athenian contemporaries. For example, like Sophocles, he wrote an *Amycus*, like Euripides, a *Bacchae* and a *Heracles*, like Cratinus, a *Bousiris*, like Aristophanes a *Geraia* (Aristophanes, *Geras*), a *Dionysoi* (Aristophanes, *Dionyson Nauagon*), and *Elpis* or *Ploutos* (Aristophanes wrote two plays called *Ploutos*), etc. That he took up subjects central to the Greek mythological tradition may seem inevitable, given his cultural heritage, until one looks at the plays of the following century when myths seem to have been pushed into the background and comic plots on common social foibles and concerns became popular. Menander and his Roman followers, Plautus, Caecilius Statius, and Terence, hardly ever used central Greek mythological themes as did Epicharmus and most Athenian tragedians. This change to more generic plots with human interest coincides with the changing political use of theater.[33] Although Pickard-Cambridge and others suggest that Epicharmus' plays are forerunners of this later comedy, his titles and subjects do, at least, and unlike the later new comedies, seem aimed at opening a forum for promotion or discussion of Greekness, among other things.

Epicharmus' plays seem to have been so similar to those of his Attic contemporaries that most of the scholarship on him deals with the problem of how much and whether Epicharmus influenced the Attic poets or they him.[34] This question was raised early in the ancient world, perhaps by the obscure figure of Alcimus who claimed that Plato borrowed many of his ideas from Epicharmus.[35] Without rehashing the debate, which has

---

[32] Cf. also Alexis fr. 140 with Athenaeus IV 164 B–C, which gives a reference to a collected works of Greek poets which includes Epicharmus along with Hesiod, Choerilus, and Homer. See also Diogenes Laertes I 42; and Apuleius *Flor.* 20, p. 41, 5.

[33] See Csapo (2010) 168–204 for a discussion of the hiring or buying of theater companies in the Roman period in the service of political campaigns.

[34] E.g. Kerkhof (2001); Svarlien (1990–1991); François (1978); Henderson (1975) 223–8; Demand (1971); Herington (1967); Gigante (1953).

[35] Diogenes Laertius, quoting Alcimus *To Amyntas*, 264. Cf. Pickard-Cambridge (1962) 247 f.; Henderson (1975) 223–8.

thoroughly explored many possibilities for cross-pollination between the early Attic playwrights and Epicharmus, it is possible to conclude that, even in the unlikely event that there was no direct influence in either direction, Epicharmus' work was almost certainly similar in enough ways to that of his Athenian counterparts to make his plays, and the exercise of going to see them, be a nod to the greater Greek culture of the day.

There is general agreement that Athenian plays were imported by tyrants on the fringes of the Greek world to mark their hellenicity and to distinguish their people from the barbarians who surrounded them.[36] Although the exportation of Athenian plays to Sicily was no doubt helped by Athens' wish for self-promotion and that of its playwrights,[37] the key to its success in the West was the patronage and encouragement it received from the local tyrants and the local population. The Sicilians may have wanted to emulate Athens, the cultural center of the Greek world at the time, but this emulation served specific and local purposes in Sicily in general, and in Syracuse in particular.

4.3   Controlling the Island: Establishing Greek Dominance

Many scholars are willing to acknowledge that Athenian plays overseas promoted and reaffirmed Hellenic identity; I have argued that Sicilian theater performed a similar function. But this is only the backdrop for more specific political roles for the theater in Sicily, which the tyrant Hieron, and perhaps Gelon before him, seem to have developed. The first of these, on the largest scale, was to support and encourage Syracuse's hegemony on the eastern side of Sicily.

Local "barbarians," the Sikels, natives of the island itself, figured in the plays of both Aeschylus and Epicharmus. They occupied a peculiar place in the social make-up of fifth-century Sicily, for the tyrants had bought many of them as mercenaries and subsequently settled them as citizens. Other Sikels, however, kept their distance, and their difficulties with the colonizing Greeks came to a head during the rebellion of Ducetius shortly after Hieron's death.

In 476, Hieron made himself the founder of a new city. He founded this city by driving the citizens out of Catania and Naxos and settling them in Leontini and then repopulating the city of Catania, under the new name

---

[36] Cf. Kurke (2000) 84; cf. Aristoxenus fr. 24; Scodel (2001) 215–27; Hall (1989).

[37] Scodel (2001).

Etna, with immigrants from the Peloponnese. Catania, or Etna as he renamed it, was situated in a key location at the crossroads of a number of major thoroughfares, in hitherto Chalcidian territory and at a cultural center for the indigenous Sikels. By taking over this pivotal spot, Hieron was setting a Dorian outpost in Chalcidian territory and asserting the power of Syracuse deep within the native Sikel heartland.[38]

Aeschylus then seems to write a play celebrating Hieron's "founding" of the city. It is very likely, though impossible to prove, that Hieron paid for the production and, likely, paid Aeschylus for writing the play. Like Pindar's first *Pythian* following the founding of the city, Aeschylus' play seems to join in the general praise of the event.[39] Only two significant fragments and a number of single words survive from Aeschylus' *Women of Aetna*. The first excerpt is quoted by Macrobius because it demonstrates Aeschylus' etymologizing of the name *Palici* from the phrase: πάλιν γὰρ ἵκουσα.[40] The Palici were gods of the region who had been worshiped for a long time by the natives of the place. Aeschylus' etymology seems to have been false for, as Croon points out, the name actually derives from Italic roots.[41] Croon dismisses this as simply a mistake on Aeschylus' part.[42] However, given the context of the composition, Carol Dougherty's suggestion that Aeschylus was deliberately imposing the Greek myth on the native site to help support Hieron's resettlement of the city seems a likely explanation. Hieron could then be presented, not as the brutal invader of the sacred lake of the Palici, but as its Greek protector.[43]

The second excerpt, discovered on a papyrus from Oxyrhynchus, describes changes of scene uncharacteristic for Aeschylus[44] and other fifth-century

---

[38] Adamesteanu (1962) 167–83.

[39] For a recent discussion of Pindar's *Pythian* 1 in this context, see Morgan (2012) 52–4; Morgan (2015) 300–58.

[40] Α τί δῆτ᾽ ἐπ᾽ αὐτοῖς ὄνομα θήσονται βροτοί;
Β σεμνοὺς Παλικοὺς Ζεὺς ἐφίεται καλεῖν.
Α ἦ καὶ Παλικῶν εὐλόγως μενεῖ φάτις;
Β πάλιν γὰρ ἵκουσ᾽ ἐκ σ<κό>τους τόδ᾽ εἰς φάος
A. What name, then, shall mortals put upon them?
B. Zeus commandeth that they be called the holy Palici.
A. And shall the name "Palici" abide as rightly given?
B. Aye, for they shall "come back" from darkness to this light.
Macrobius, *Saturnalia* V 19, 17f. 24 (trans. Herbert Weir Smith)

[41] Croon (1952) 119–20.

[42] Croon (1952) 119: "The Greeks attached a myth to the Twin Brethren which may be passed over here; it was merely an aetiological story to explain the name Palici which they derived wrongly."

[43] Dougherty (1991) 119–32; (1993) 83–102.

[44] The only other certain example of this is in *Eumenides*, where there is a scene change between Delphi and Athens, although there may be another change in *Eumenides* from the Acropolis to the Areopagus, and one from outside Ajax's tent to the seashore in Sophocles' *Ajax*.

tragedians. In trying to reconcile these peculiar scene changes with Aeschylus' other work, scholars have generally assumed that, since he was not restricted by conventions governing tragedy in Athens, Aeschylus was following Hieron's wishes. Bremer suggests that this very unusual aspect of the play ("so absolutely deviating from the normal practice of tragedy") was due to Hieron's wish that it "emphasize the unity of the territory dominated by King Hiero."[45] The changes of scene, from Etna to Xuthia to Etna to Leontini to Syracuse to Temenite, suggest that the play may have actually dealt with the resettling of the population itself. The ending of the play in Syracuse may perhaps be linked to a triumphant finale in the home city. In its celebration of the founding of the colony, the play leaves little doubt that the tyrant saw poetry and plays as political tools to reinforce his status and methods.

However, the *Persians*, like the *Women of Aetna*, also presents Greek versus barbarian in the recent story of the Persian War. This is a reason for the tyrants' allowing, or indeed inviting, the play.[46] As we saw, Bremer suggests more specifically that the *Persians* may be another attempt to connect the battle of Salamis with Himera.[47] There are, likewise, occasional references to the East in Epicharmus' fragments. Nowhere in the sparse collection that survives is there an explicit contrast made between East and West, but the kinds of references which do occur might easily have belonged in such a dichotomy. Two play titles in particular are perhaps the most telling examples: *Persians* and *Medea*. Even a comic send-up of the Athenian tragedies, as these may have been, must have incorporated the Persian/Greek divide as a central theme.

Other plays of Epicharmus also seem to have taken up topics celebrating Greek mastery over the barbarian. Millino has argued that a fragment in which Heracles battles the Pygmies represents the Greeks against the Carthaginians.[48] The play *Bousiris*, in which Heracles fights the Egyptian tyrant, tells the same story of Greek overcoming barbarian.[49] Another

---

[45] Bremer (1991) 40. On the other hand, it is interesting to note how many Athenian Greek tragedies are centered on a plot which emphasizes the travel of the hero, or other characters, to other places, and which depends on their return home for the resolution of the story. Certainly, the place of dramatic action does not shift about much, but the audience is frequently taken on imaginative excursions to distant lands. For example, *Agamemnon*, *Iphigeneia in Tauris*, *Heracles Furens*, *Helen*, and *Andromache*. Taplin (1977) 416–18 doubts the attribution of the fragment.

[46] Cf. Scodel (2001).   [47] Bremer (1991) 41.   [48] *PCG* 65. Millino (2000).

[49] The Greek view of Egyptians was particularly ambivalent, however, as Livingstone notes, because of the antiquity of Egypt, and its "conspicuous literate culture." Livingstone (2001) 73. Isocrates offered an argument to redeem Bousiris' good name by noting that, despite his brutality, he was the founder of the Egyptian civilization. This is not unlike Hieron's ploy to improve his reputation by making himself founder of Etna. Cf. Livingstone (2001) 2. Vasunia (2001) has much enriched our understanding of the way Egypt is imagined in ancient Greek

mythological play, *Amycus*, seems to have taken up a similar topic. The myth involves the subduing of the brutal giant Amycus by the sophisticated Pollux, who then, according to Theocritus, seems to have spared Amycus' life.[50]

Epicharmus seems to have targeted the local Sikels specifically as well. For example, a native Sikel is described as, literally, "stealing green grapes" (ὀμφακίζεται) or, figuratively, being eager to steal even things of no value.[51] Whether the native Sikels were a regular butt of his jokes is not possible to determine from the very fragmentary remains of his plays, but he does seem to have juxtaposed cultivated and rougher social groups in a few plays.[52] This is not peculiar in ancient comedy, as can be seen in Aristophanes and later Menander. However, given the mixed communities in the cities that the tyrants created by their wholesale resettling of populations, such broad divisions, between Greek and Easterner, Greek and Sikel, or sophisticated and unsophisticated, might have helped to unify the citizens who, although originally from various cities, could think of themselves as, collectively, sophisticated Greeks in opposition to the unsophisticated Easterners and Sikels.[53]

4.4 Theater and Democracy

An important premise for the political significance of theater in Athens is its role in democratic government. As Christian Meier points out, the very earliest place for citizens to meet, the agora, was "not merely a place for meeting, but also the original site for theatre."[54] Later, Athenian citizens, as they sat in the same building in which they met for the assembly, saw plays which took up topical issues.[55] But could such a system develop under tyrants such as the Deinomenids?

---

drama and literature more widely. On barbarians including Egyptians in Greek comedy, see Long (1986).

[50] In Apollonius of Rhodes 2, 1–97, Amycus was killed.   [51] Cf. *PCG* 239 and 207.

[52] *PCG* 1–3 and 219.

[53] The position of the Sikel mercenaries who had been given citizenship is a complicated one. After Hieron's death, when Thrasybulus was ousted, the citizens of Syracuse revoked the citizenship of the Sikels living in their city. How uneasy the relationship between Greeks and Sikels had been under the rule of the tyrants is difficult to ascertain. That they identified, at least overtly, with the Greeks seems likely because of their willingness to fight as mercenaries for the tyrants.

[54] Meier (1993) 21.

[55] When the Pnyx proved too small a venue for the meetings of the citizen body, the *ekklesia*, they moved the meetings of the *ekklesia* to the Theater of Dionysus. On the very few *ekklesiasteria* built in the Greek world, and the correspondingly frequent use of the theater for meetings of the citizen body, see Chapter 7.

The link between theater and democracy in Athens has been studied extensively in the past 30 years.[56] Earlier critical approaches, which explained the plays in philosophical, humanizing, and universalizing ways, have been replaced with very context-specific studies of theater in fifth-century Athens.[57] Several kinds of argument are regularly adduced: for example, that the festival was a celebration of democracy;[58] that the audience represented the citizen body;[59] that the plays represented marginalized groups in society[60] or, conversely, that mainstream values of Athenian democracy were sometimes contrasted with non-Athenian systems of government;[61] and that peculiarly democratic institutions were developed to support the theater.[62] It is difficult to know whether the ancients themselves saw this connection. That Athens was the center of the theatrical world may have been reason for fifth-century Greeks to associate it with the Athenian form of government.[63] The Old Oligarch seems to confirm the association in his *Constitution of the Athenians*.[64] That the western Greeks also associated the two is suggested in Aristotle's note about a Dorian claim to have developed both tragedy and comedy, the former when the city was becoming democratic.[65]

An argument against finding a democratic subtext and purpose in Athenian theater has been made by Jasper Griffin,[66] and, as he argues, the psychological and emotional appeal of tragedy, in particular, is an important

---

[56] Cf. for example, Easterling (1997); Pelling (1997).   [57] Cf. Hall (1997) 94.

[58] Cartledge (1997).

[59] For various views on the plays being written for the democratic audience of Athens, see Goldhill (1997); Taplin (1999); Sommerstein (1997).

[60] Hall (1997).

[61] Hall (1997); Sommerstein (1997) 79: "Aeschylus was using tragedy as a political weapon, and using it in the name of that *demokratia* which may have been coined as a political catchword about this very time..."

[62] Wilson (1997) 82–108; Halliwell (1997) 121–41.

[63] Cf. Scodel (2001) on the Athenian dramatists' conscious effort to write for a wider audience.

[64] 2.18: "They do not permit anyone to ridicule the demos in comedy..." Cf. also the indignation of the character Canus in Cicero's *On the State* 4.11, that Greek comedy was allowed to ridicule important politicians such as Pericles. *Both* are cited and discussed in Csapo and Slater (1995) 171 and 165 f.

[65] Aristotle, *Poetics* 1448a 28–40, Csapo and Slater (1995) 174: "The assumption that comedy must have developed out of a democratic state is at least as old as the Megarian claim to comedy on the basis of the fact that Megara had a democracy long before Athens."

[66] Griffin (1998) 39–61. Cf. also Taplin (1999) and (1993); and Dearden (1999) 1 and 2. Further important arguments challenging the relationship at least of tragedy to democracy have also been made by Carter (2004) and especially Rhodes (2003), but the discussions often confuse the idea of a democratic origin with a democratic function during the period from which our extant Athenian tragedies derive: see Hall (2006) 188.

reason for its popularity both in ancient and modern times. But the psychological, emotional, and philosophical appeal of the plays needs not preclude a political one. In the case of Syracuse, in particular, the Aeschylean play brought in for reperformance, *The Persians*, is particularly emphatic about the advantages that accrue to citizens of a democracy.[67] Perhaps the Syracusans and their tyrant overlooked or dismissed any democratic elements in the play, as Oliver Taplin and Ruth Scodel,[68] for example, suggest. Following this line of thought, imported Athenian plays seem to shed their democratic overtones in Syracuse, but kept their prestige value as a cosmopolitan Athenian art form. Though this might have been the case, it is worthwhile, I think, also to consider what an association between democracy and theater might have meant to the *demos* of Syracuse and why Hieron would have been willing, even eager, to have such plays performed.[69] A brief analysis of the social and historical circumstances of Gelon's rise to power and the Deinomenids' reign suggests, I think, that democratic propaganda would not have been entirely out of place in the city.

4.5 Defining Tyranny

Although the distinction between tyranny and kingship had not been drawn as clearly in the fifth century as it was in the fourth, the problems associated with individual autocratic rule had already come under scathing attack by the lyric poets. By the fourth century, the word τύραννος had come to assume all the negative characteristics of kingship and had become an insult in itself.[70] When it first came into use, it was not necessarily a damning term,[71] but the aspects which came to be so closely associated with it in later centuries were already condemned by lyric poets: hubris (Alcaeus fr. 306 LP); greed (Theognis 824–5; Archilochos,

---

[67] Hall (1997).   [68] Taplin (1999) and Scodel (2001).

[69] For less controversial reasons for the appeal of the play, see Scodel (2001) and Bremer (1991), who note that the Deinomenids tried to associate Himera and Marathon, and that this play helped recall the moment. The Syracusans, then, could associate with the Greeks and interpret the Persians as Carthaginians.

[70] J-P. Liou (1991), although the terms are somewhat ambivalent in Isocrates as well.

[71] Lévy (1993) 7: βασιλεύς is an old word already found in Linear B, whereas τύραννος is a fairly recent one, which according to Hippias (DK 11 6 B9) did not get spread about in Greece until the first half of the seventh century with the poetry of Archilochos. If this is so, then the word must have started out with fairly unsavory overtones, since Archilochos does not seem to be much in favor of tyranny.

fr. 15); violence and oppression (Theognis 1181–2; Solon 14, 8); and self-interest (Theognis, 1203–6).[72]

Herodotus does not seem to have presented a systematic opposition between good king and bad tyrant, as Plato and Aristotle did later. Rather the concepts of kingship and tyranny were fairly interchangeable and both types are described as good and bad in different passages. Negative images of bad tyrants abound, however, and even if the term was not formally pejorative it can be distinguished from *basileus*, Lévy argues, in that it is "absolute and arbitrary."[73]

A key lyric text which seems to present tyranny in a favorable light is that of Pindar in an ode to the glory of Hieron himself (*Pythian* 3, 85). This ode, however, like many others, is emphatic in its warning not to exceed the role allotted by the gods (Koronis, 20–3) and in its praise of those who do not (Chiron, 63). Most importantly, the ode stresses the tyrant's role as caretaker of the people. Chiron, the great healer, is given as an example in his assiduous care of other human beings; likewise Hieron, a great ruler, takes care of his people (70–1). When Hieron is called a tyrant (the first word in the line, and the word which qualifies the title), here too, his duties to the people are stressed.[74] That βασιλεύς and τύραννος (*basileus* and *turannos*) seem interchangeable in the poem suggests that good and bad characteristics had not necessarily come to be associated exclusively with one or the other.[75] But the insistence on a measured and moderate approach to life, combined with the emphasis on the tyrant king's duties to his people, suggest that the ambivalent and potentially dangerous nature of solitary rule, as king or as tyrant, were issues of central importance in a poem to the glory of Hieron.

Elsewhere Pindar reveals that he was not always a supporter of kingship or tyranny: "I condemn the condition of tyrant" (*Pythian* 11, 53).[76] He does not even support a popular tyrant, for he praises the hero Euxantios for refusing to rule over Crete when the people offered it to him (*Paean* 4, 7).[77]

---

[72] Casevitz (1991), who notes that "solitude" was already a suspect condition for Homer, and who discusses the lyric passages noted here in more detail. Lévy (1993) 7–8.

[73] Lévy (1993) *passim*.

[74] Tyranny, so often the object of "eros," seems here to be comparable not only to Chiron's gift of healing, but also to Koronis' love affair with the god Apollo and to Peleus and Cadmus' winning of their divine wives. But with this well-loved power, as with a loved god, or goddess, the mortal must not "desire what is not there" (20) and fall victim to hubris. Tyranny is as seductive and dangerous as the object of romantic love.

[75] Casevitz (1991) 209 also notes that in the lyric poets *monarchos* can represent the sort of autocratic ruler later described as tyrant.

[76] Gentili (1988) 134 and 149 f.   [77] Casevitz (1991) 204–5.

Although "tyranny" may not have become a buzzword for despotism and unethical behaviour as early as the fifth century,[78] the idea of a despotic and unethical tyrant was certainly fully conceived.

The interesting question is whether being a good tyrant or king, rather than a bad one, was sufficient. It is possible, for example, to interpret the *Persians* as a presentation of a good king, Darius, compared with Xerxes, a bad king.[79]

4.6   Aeschylus' *Persians*

Sara Forsdyke has demonstrated that the democratic polis associated civic strength with political freedom.[80] She uses the *Persians*, in conjunction with Herodotus' tale of Demaratus, as evidence for a democratic trope that tyranny creates a weak people whereas democracy, in which the population is free, becomes strong.[81] A central point of comparison is the weakness of Xerxes' army, which, though huge, does not stand a chance against the smaller army of the Athenians. The messenger strikingly juxtaposes the valiant band of Athenians who are fighting for freedom with the barbarians, a term the Persians use of themselves in the play.

The second half of the play, however, seems to set up a different opposition. In line 640, the chorus begins to call for the ghost of their old king, Darius, a tyrant like his son Xerxes. In this ode, the chorus recalls the tragic failure of Xerxes by describing the successful and just reign of his predecessor Darius (*Persians,* 652–6). Xerxes is described as the opposite, not of the moderate democrats of Athens, but of another tyrant, his father. His real crimes are revealed in the discussion between the chorus and the dead king: Xerxes had had the hubris to "yoke" the Bosporus (722, 746–9); he had acted through naïveté in the rashness of youth (744); he had challenged the gods (749–50). Excuses are, moreover, offered: perhaps he was sick (750); certainly he was egged on by bad advisors (753–8). Indeed, Darius goes to great lengths to point out how many successful tyrants ruled Asia before him (759–86). He concludes that it was Xerxes' youth which brought on the disaster, not the form of government (782), because no other who held the scepter before ever brought such a calamity on the people:

---

[78] Though Casevitz (1991) 208–9 argues that it had already from the time of Theognis.

[79] On Sicilian interest in Persia and the Near East, particularly at the beginning of the fifth century, see Marconi (1994) 268–74.

[80] Forsdyke (2001).

[81] Forsdyke (2001) 342: "I am arguing first that the dramatic presentation of certain political values in Aeschylus' *Persians* reflects and itself helped to construct some of the ways that the Athenian democratic culture represented its political values to itself."

ἅπαντες ἡμεῖς, οἳ κράτη τάδ' ἔσχομεν,
οὐκ ἂν φανεῖμεν πήματ' ἔρξαντες τόσα.

Take all of us together who have held this kingship, and we will not be
   found to have caused this much suffering.

Aeschylus, *Persians*, 785–6

Such protestations on Darius' part, might, it is true, be taken as the vain
excuses of a losing power. Perhaps an audience should see through this
speech and, understanding the characterization of the elderly tyrant, be
unimpressed by his excuses. But why does Aeschylus go to such lengths to
present an argument that the failure of the Persians was not due to the system
of government, but to the youthful hubris of their new leader? Xerxes, we
understand from the second half of the play, was not typical, and even if the
Athenian spirit was particularly fierce, it was not the sheer fact of the tyranny
that led to the Persians' downfall, but the arrogance of one man, Xerxes.

One particularly strong argument that tyranny is unfavorably compared
to democracy is that the Persians are represented as longing for, and not
having, free speech. Two instances are adduced to prove this point: first, the
Persian elders fear that the people will no longer be silent but will speak
freely (591–7), and secondly, the chorus and the queen hesitate to speak
freely in front of their old king Darius (694–706).[82] A slightly different
interpretation might be put on these passages, if one wanted to absolve the
play of setting up stark oppositions between democracy and tyranny. In
the first case, the first verb of the previous stasimon, περσονομοῦνται,
personomountai (585) is translated in LSJ as "are under Persian law or
governed by Persians." The elders fear that "those who live throughout Asia
will no longer be under Persian law." It is these same people whom they fear
will no longer keep their thoughts to themselves, but will be free to utter
them. Who are these people who "live throughout Asia governed by Persian
laws"? If they are not themselves Persians (which would explain the emphasis
Aeschylus places on their subordination to Persian laws),[83] then perhaps
they are the myriad other peoples who were ruled by the Persians in Asia
Minor (including the insubordinate Ionian Greeks). This description of
subject peoples throwing off Persian domination need not then be
a reference to the beginning of democracy, but a description of
a conquered people regaining their freedom (and it would still be freedom

---

[82] Forsdyke (2001) 344.
[83] He seems to have made the verb up for this play. It allows an aural connection to be drawn
between the proper name Persai and the aorist stem, pers-, of the verb *perthein*, sack or conquer.
This use and the instance at 919 are the only examples of the verb cited at all in LSJ.

if a king of their own took their own throne). One might imagine that peoples subject to the will of the democratic state of Athens (such as, for example, Mytilene) might have experienced the same sense of relief and freedom had their rebellion succeeded, and they had been freed from the control of Athens, a democratic city.

The second example of restricted speech occurs in the dialogue between Darius, the Persian Queen, and the chorus. However, the reluctance of the chorus to tell Darius that his kingdom has been completely destroyed is not necessarily caused by fear of the tyrant, but natural dislike of bringing bad news. Their second excuse, that they really do not like telling the people they love bad news, further supports this characterization of a chorus just desperately not wanting to be the bearer of bad tidings.[84]

For an audience unwilling to accept that the Athenians won because of the strength derived from democracy, Aeschylus offers another interpretation of their success. In line 346, the messenger says that it is the gods who preserve Athens. The chorus, too, early in the play makes reference to the inscrutability of the gods who bring unexpected twists of fate (107–19). This reference to the whims of fate, which lurk in the background to most tragedies, combined with the clear depiction of Xerxes' youthful hubris, would, I think, provide a sufficient explanation for the tragedy depicted here.

Like the *Persians,* which presents the wise, capable character of Darius in contrast with his foolhardy, hapless son, Xerxes, many of the plays performed in Syracuse seem to promote the idea of a great leader. Hieron's commissioning of *The Women of Etna* to celebrate his "founding" of the city of Etna is the most straightforward use of theater to celebrate the tyrant as city founder. Epicharmus' portrayal of heroic Greeks overcoming brutal barbarians and wicked enemies is most explicit in *The Islands,* in which he reported Hieron saving the Locrians from the tyrant Anaxilas of Rhegium. This plot was preserved in a note by the scholiast to Pindar's first *Pythian* near a line disparaging the brutal tyranny of Phalaris, the earlier Sicilian tyrant who was said to have roasted his enemies in a bronze bull.[85] Hieron was clearly distinguishing himself from these brutal rulers; he was a good tyrant.

---

[84] Such ineffectual hesitation on the part of a chorus occurs elsewhere, most notably perhaps in the chorus' ditherings in the scene of the death of Agamemnon in Aeschylus' trilogy 14 years later, the *Oresteia* (*Ag.* 1344–71).

[85] *PCG* 96 (Scholiast (DEFGQ) Pindar, *Pythian* 1, 99a, II p. 18, 21 Dr.).

4.7   A Good Tyrant

That the tyrants were keen to impress upon the population that they were good rulers is also suggested by Pindar's odes. One of the conditions of being a good ruler was, it seems, to be suited to the role.[86] Gelon was successful in war, twice an Olympic victor,[87] and a priest in the cult of Demeter. Hieron, like him, was an Olympic victor, conducted successful military campaigns, and was a priest of Demeter. He more actively sought legitimacy by making himself a founder of the city of Aetna. Jacquemin suggests that Hieron was, above all, trying to outdo his brother, Gelon, who had been so successful in winning the approval of his people. Hieron does seem to have sought legitimacy by turning himself into the founder of a city, though the superficiality of this gesture is marked by the Catanians, who, returning to the city after the Deinomenids were ousted from power, destroyed Hieron's founder-tomb.[88] Proving themselves worthy rulers with suitable personal characteristics seems to have been a central concern for the tyrants. Even more important, however, as Pindar's odes suggest, was the establishment of a desirable relationship with the citizen body.

The corollary to a truly tyrannical leader is a subservient population, as Edith Hall, among others, has pointed out. Much of the Athenian propaganda about freedom, for example, centres on the ability of citizens to make judgments for themselves, rather than on the absence of a tyrannical leader, *per se*.[89] This is the rhetoric of much of Greek tragedy, including the *Persians* brought to Syracuse by the tyrants.[90] The defeat of the Persians seems to be attributed at least as much to the mismanagement of Xerxes as to the monarchical system, as was noted above. However, the stark contrast between barbarian other and Greek, must mean, as so many have argued, that the Syracusans were meant to identify with their fellow Greeks, albeit Athenians, against the Persian barbarians. Thus the references to the freedom and independence of the Greeks, in opposition to the subservient masses of the Persian king's army, must have been a crucial aspect of the play even in Hieron's Syracuse.

---

[86]   Casevitz (1991) 206: "La ville idéale, c'est celle où les bons ont le pouvoir, les méchants le dessous. Ce qui est condamné, c'est le retournement *qui amène* ceux du dessous à avoir le dessus, l'injuste à devenir juste par la force, un méchant à devenir tyran, *monarchos*."

[87]   On the connection between sporting victories and success as a tyrant, see Luraghi (1994) 276 and 240–1; Larmour (1999).

[88]   Jacquemin (1993) 24.

[89]   Pericles for example. Forsdyke (2001) has argued that the polis associated political freedom with civic strength.

[90]   Cf. Hall (1997).

The circumstances of the Deinomenids' accession to power and their actions thereafter suggest that they wished to create the impression that the citizens had a real role in government. Both Gelon and Hieron seem to have given, at the very least, the illusion of some form of involvement of the civic body. Perhaps precisely because the terms of tyranny and even democracy were not yet fully defined, it was possible for these tyrants to attempt to mix the two, at least in appearance, without seeming as hypocritical as they might have, and indeed as Dionysius did, in the fourth century, when, in a play of his own, he is reputed to have written "Tyranny is the mother of injustice."[91]

4.8 Tyranny and Democracy in Syracuse, 490–466

The period of 30 years in Syracuse from the expulsion of the *gamoroi* some time before 485[92] to the expulsion of the tyrant Thrasybulus in 467 saw rapid changes of government from one extreme, democracy, to the other, tyranny. In the early fifth century, the *demos* of Syracuse rose up, threw out their aristocratic overlords, and established a democracy.[93] When this failed, they accepted Gelon in 485/4 as head of the city and tyrant.[94] His rule was the start of the short Deinomenid dynasty, which continued through the reign of his brother, Hieron, but was abruptly terminated when his third brother, Thrasybulus, was thrown out shortly after he came to power on Hieron's death in 467. In 466, another democracy was established, along with a festival to Zeus Eleutherios to celebrate the city's freedom from tyrannical rule.[95]

That democratic uprisings framed the tyrants' 20-year hegemony suggests that the Syracusans were interested in the possibility of self-rule. Although Gelon and Hieron did control Syracuse and other cities that fell under their power, they also seem to have catered to the Syracusans' wish for political involvement. The importance Gelon placed on the role of the

---

[91] Cf. Xanthakis-Karamanos (1980) 159–60, who suggests that since Dionysius was "a tyrant notorious for his injustice, [the fragment] would *appear* to be mere irony."

[92] The date of the expulsion of the *gamoroi* is uncertain. Cf. Ghinatti (1996) 57, who sets the expulsion date at 491/490; Consolo Langher (1969–1970) 130; Consolo Langher (1988–1989) 242; Berger (1992) 35; Luraghi (1994) 281 ff., especially n. 37, who notes that the account of Herodotus suggests that not much time passed between the expulsion and Gelon's accession to power in 485. Huttl (1929), 54 and n. 3, puts the date of the expulsion as early as 520.

[93] Arist. *Pol.* 5.1302b 30 f.; Herodotus 7.155.2; Mafodda (1996) 68; Ghinatti (1996) 57.

[94] Luraghi (1994) 273; Diod. Sic. 11.38.7; Arist. *Pol.* 5.1315b 34.

[95] Karlsson (1995) 15: "It can be assumed that the Syracusans regarded Zeus Eleutherios both as a symbol of democracy and as a symbol of freedom from tyranny...."

citizen body in Syracuse is revealed, ironically, by one of his most typically tyrannical actions: the shifting of populations. The injection of a thousand *neapolitai* (entirely new citizens) into the citizen body from various places and from various social classes, and especially of mercenaries in his debt,[96] allowed him to keep up the appearance of involvement by the *demos*, without worrying about one party becoming too powerful.[97] Upon coming to power, he seems to have brought nearly half the population of Gela, the entire population of Camarina, which he had destroyed, and the wealthy citizens of Megara Hyblaea and Euboea to Syracuse and made them all citizens.[98] This restructuring of the citizen body gave him a solid, if short-lived, power base.[99] To this population, he added mercenaries, who, owing their citizenship entirely to him, could be counted upon to support him. The old aristocracy of Syracuse had come back into the city with his help and might also, therefore, have been allies. His complete reworking of the citizen body seems to have been an effort to maintain an equal balance between the different parts, so that none became strong enough to rule all the others. This balancing of citizen groups is not democratic *per se*, but it lays the groundwork for some aspects of ancient direct, non-representative democracy by ensuring fairly equal representation from groups with different agendas.

Perhaps it was this careful combining of different social and political groups within the citizenry which gave Gelon the latitude to allow a popular assembly.[100] He agreed to keep the constitutional arrangements of the democracy, which had been tried in the years before he came to power.[101] Mafodda describes the situation thus: "Gelon esercitò la propria

---

[96] That these last did not fit with the other citizens is strongly suggested by the removal of their citizenship when the tyrants were ousted in 467. Diod. Sic. 11.72.2–3; 73; 76.1–2. Mafodda (1996) 79. Krasilnikoff (1995), which is a discussion primarily of the rule of Dionysius I, makes the general comment that the main leverage a tyrant had was centralized military force, and that "the employment of mercenaries in Sicily was almost entirely in those periods and in those poleis where tyrants held power." This is no doubt true, but it does not mean that some tyrants, namely Gelon and Hieron, did not *also* attempt to win over the citizen body by maintaining the appearance of popular involvement in government.

[97] Mafodda (1996) 71f.   [98] Cf. Luraghi (1994) 288–9.

[99] Such is the view of Luraghi (1994) 288. Mafodda (1996) 71 f. agrees and adds that the aristocrats who had been granted citizenship would not only be in his debt for this, but also keenly aware of the alternative fate of being sold into slavery which befell the citizens comprising the *demoi* of their cities.

[100] Finley (1968) 56 dismisses the popular assembly as farce. Ghinatti (1996) 58 notes that it is hard to judge what role the assembly played.

[101] Diod. Sic. 11.26.5; Polyaen. 1.27.1; Ael. *VH* 13.37. Mafodda (1996) 69 and 71: "il garante del mantenimento in Siracusa dell'ordinamento costituzionale democratico, nel cui ambito l'ekklesia conservava le fondamentali prerogative decisionali contro possibili tentativi di

arché in un contesto instituzionale di tipo democratico senza privilegiare l'adesione politica ad una componente cittadina piuttosto che all'altra."[102] Although these institutions may have had little real power, their existence alone suggests that Gelon was willing, if not actually eager, to give the impression of political involvement on the part of the *demos*. The circumstances of his accession to power may have led him in this direction, for he was received by the people as a mediator between them and the exiled *gamoroi* whom he brought back with him. As Luraghi points out, this was simply a role it suited him to play, for his power was in fact neither revocable nor within the city's control.[103] Nevertheless, to play this role properly required that he foster the notion that the citizenry played a political role.[104]

The tyrants' eagerness to downplay their tyrannical position has long been recognized in two specific categories of evidence: their inscriptions and their coins.[105] On neither of these did they mark their positions as rulers of the city, and on the coins they seem to have made no reference to themselves at all. This reticence, as Finley describes it, has sometimes been explained as an attempt to be accepted by the rest of the Greek world, which had, by this point, developed some antipathy to tyrants.[106] Although this was no doubt one reason, another may have been their wish to be accepted by their own citizens. At the very least, it may have made their rule more palatable and the fiction, if such it was, of political influence on the part of the *demos* more credible.

Without doubt, the tyrants were brutal and despotic in their treatment of many hapless people who fell under their control. The example of Megara Hyblaea and Euboea illustrates this well, for although only the upper classes had made war on Syracuse, Gelon sold the innocent populations of

---

restaurazione da parte dei *gamoroi*". Ghinatti (1996) 58, "un regime che si delinea con qualche principio di ordinamenti democratici."

[102] Mafodda (1996) 6: "Gelon exercised his power (arché) in an institutional context of democratic character, without privileging one political group of the citizenry over the other."

[103] Luraghi (1994) 287, whom I have paraphrased in the sentence to which this footnote belongs; Mafodda (1996) 82–3.

[104] For the contrary view that the tyrants simply crushed the population through military force, and that the assemblies were reduced to a farce, see Krasilnikoff's (1995) study of the rule of Dionysius I. Although many of his arguments may apply generally to the earlier periods of Gelon and Hieron, his argument rests on details and facts culled from evidence about Dionysius I, not from evidence about the Deinomenids of some 60 years before.

[105] Finley (1968) 56.

[106] Finley (1968) 56. However, some argue that the damning of the concept of tyrant did not come into full force until the fourth century.

ordinary people from these two cities into slavery.[107] The aristocrats he made citizens of Syracuse, to their great surprise as Herodotus reports it (7.156). But brutality in some domains does not necessarily preclude the assumption of a veneer of democratic values in others. When the citizens of Acragas, after forcing their tyrant Thrasydaeus into exile, established a democracy and sent an embassy to Hieron, for example, he granted them autonomy, although he could have conquered and controlled Acragas at far less risk and greater profit to himself. McGlew notes how peculiar it is that Hieron was a champion of democracy in the case of Acragas. Apart from some possible benefits in allowing a city like Acragas to rule itself, it may be that Hieron aimed to present himself as more than an autocratic ruler. McGlew describes the close link between the concepts of tyranny and *eleutheria*, comparing this to the link between democracy and *autonomia*.[108] Likewise, he notes that one of the most powerful attributes of a tyrant was a judicious use of what the Greeks called *preumeneia* or *praotes* and the Romans *clementia*.[109] Allowing the people to make some choices and to feel that they had some say in the social workings and political decisions of the city seemed to be a popular and sensible approach used by both Gelon and Hieron. There is no real evidence that Gelon treated his own citizens with undue harshness; and even if he was harsh or irrational to individuals or isolated groups, this would not necessarily have upset the image he seems to have been trying to present to the city at large.[110]

Perhaps the most explicit proof that Hieron was attempting to foster the idea that the people were real participants in the government of the city can be found in an incident recorded by Diodorus in the aftermath of the battle of Himera. Having won the battle, and defeated the Carthaginians, he is reported to have appeared before the assembled citizen body of Syracuse, dressed only in his *himation*, without arms or *chiton* and to have pronounced the victory theirs. This was a splendidly engineered appearance, for the people unanimously acclaimed him king and savior.[111]

The introduction of large-scale theatrical performances by his brother Hieron[112] may have been a similar effort in the greater project of winning

---

[107] Herodotus 7.156: see Luraghi (1994) 288–9.   [108] McGlew (1993) 141.

[109] McGlew (1993) 43.

[110] Cf. Finley (1968) on the brutality; on the inconsistency of democratic and tyrannical positions, see Morgan (2003) in which, for example, the "tyranny" of democratic Athens over her subject cities is discussed.

[111] Cf. Mafodda (1996) 86; Diod. Sic. 11.26.5–6.

[112] Supported by ancient anecdotes, admittedly unreliable (see n. 31 above) about Phrynichus.

over and keeping the goodwill of the citizens. Large, well-funded spectacles were not only popular entertainment, but also provided a forum for current issues to be raised. This citizen gathering was, if not technically democratic, at least strongly suggestive of popular political involvement.[113] Moreover, the Athenian democratic model, in place some 30 or 40 years before and celebrated in their own theater of Dionysus, must have been brought vividly to mind by the importation of some of these Athenian plays. If Hieron did not literally step in front of the people in his tunic, he did seek to convince the population of his success by commissioning the *Women of Aetna* to celebrate his recent victory over the city of Catania and to strengthen his position further by celebrating his new role as city founder. Rush Rehm, puzzled that Aeschylus agreed to write a play celebrating such a tyrannical act as Hieron's wholesale removal of the citizens of Aetna, points out the incongruity of such a theme with the pro-democratic ideals presented in the *Persians*,[114] which was also performed at Syracuse. However, if Hieron was aiming both to present himself as a successful ruler and to encourage the belief that the people of Syracuse enjoyed a share of freedom and political power, the themes of the two plays do not seem so incompatible.

4.9   Epicharmus

Thus the people were interested in the possibility of self-rule; the tyrants' propaganda tactics included at least the appearance of a kind of democratic involvement on the part of the people; the *Persians* of Aeschylus suggests that Hieron was not excessively worried about presenting a powerful and free *demos* on stage. If these historical and literary pieces of evidence are taken together, a politically conscious and controversial theater of the kind we associate with the Athenian democracy does not seem impossible in Hieron's Syracuse.

Did Epicharmus use the theater for more than entertainment and straightforward promotion of the tyrants as described in the sections above? Plutarch records two exchanges between Epicharmus and Hieron which suggest that Epicharmus was, at least by reputation, able to tease, and perhaps even chastise, the tyrant in his jokes.[115] In one of these exchanges, Epicharmus is reprimanded for saying something indecent in front of Hieron's wife (Plut. *On the Sayings of Kings and Emperors*, *Mor.* 175b–c).

---

[113] Taplin (1999).   [114] Rehm (1989).   [115] See p. 126 above.

Far from revealing that the poet was unduly repressed by the tyrant, this anecdote suggests that normally Epicharmus felt himself able to speak freely. In the second fragment, Plutarch cites Epicharmus as making a very sharp remark about Hieron's recent execution of some other citizens (Plut. *How to Tell a Flatterer from a Friend, Mor.* 68a). It is impossible to determine how much truth there is in these tales from Plutarch; however, they do suggest a tradition that Epicharmus was able to speak fairly freely. Since these biographical traditions often seem to have been drawn from author's poetry by scholars in antiquity, this may suggest that Epicharmus was able to present controversial themes in his plays during the tyrant's reign. Iamblichus notes that Epicharmus took the cover of comedy to make statements of which Hieron would not otherwise have approved (*On the Pythagorean Life* 226). This further suggests that Epicharmus' comedies did, although perhaps elliptically, make political points and engage in topical debates. At least in the ancient world, Epicharmus seems to have been viewed as a politically conscious, and perhaps controversial, writer.

Some of the titles of his plays and the few fragments associated with them do seem to take up subjects of civic interest. Some of these have been viewed as evidence of a preoccupation with particular character-types. Pickard-Cambridge, for example, writes that Epicharmus' innovation or excellence was in the portrayal of various sorts of characters. These types, however, can also be understood as part of a broader concern with social groups and also the divide between city and country. Some of the comic stereotypes such as credulous women, conmen magicians, and boorish mythological heroes seem to be digs at popular myths and religions, an angle which is made more plausible by the number of plays which seem to be about a contemporary religious rite, rather, one might imagine, in the vein of Aristophanes' *Thesmophoriazusae*. More serious approaches are suggested by the title *Politai* from which, unfortunately, no fragment remains, and the title *Orua*, glossed by Hesychius as a political mixture, which may have been a satirical approach to contemporary events.[116] A reference to the word νέοικος (*neoikos*) in the play *Harpagai* (noted by Pollux in his comparison of different words used to describe a new citizen from Plato, Eupolis, and Epicharmus) suggests that the play dealt with the complications of the newly mixed society that Gelon and Hieron had created.[117] There were indeed many new citizens and this play seems to

---

[116] Hesychius s.v. "oroua." He glosses this noun thus: "Pig-tripe-sausage. Or a political mish-mash (*suntrimma politikon*), a drama of Epicharmus."

[117] Pollux, *Onom.* IX.27, p. 125 in Dindorf (1824).

have taken up some of the issues that this influx of people brought about. Perhaps one of them was a breakdown in old world, standard religion, carefully controlled and shielded, and the growing prominence of the quack doctrines of various prophets or seers (*PCG* 9). There is perhaps a self-referential undertone to his use of the word *choregos* or *didaskalos* in the same play; at any rate, it suggests a discussion of the process of preparing for a celebration, if not, indeed, a play. Epicharmus' general interpretation of the situation may have been depressing or at least skeptical if his line "Sicily suffered" (*PCG* 11) had any sort of central meaning.

4.10 Conclusion

Allowing the theater to be a moderately controversial arena for political and social criticism may have operated in the same way as the calculated refusal of absolute power by the tyrant. In both cases, the tyrant creates the appearance of some democratic involvement, but he is never in any real danger of losing absolute control. Whether one needs to posit the extreme reversals of a "carnival" atmosphere is difficult to determine from the evidence. However, the few pieces of evidence remaining do point not only in the direction of a light touch from the tyrants and the provision of a forum for public entertainment, but also for the expression of political and social ideas. The image of Epicharmus as a teacher and leader in philosophical and moral matters supports this picture as well. Not only did later generations erect a statue to his memory as having effected a large amount of social good, but the ancient critical tradition allowed him to be a great thinker and philosopher and to have had a significant effect on his contemporaries.

Bremer notes that the playwrights in Athens, like those of Syracuse, were originally supported by the tyrant Peisistratus to "heighten his popularity."[118] He concludes that the great difference in democratic Athens was that the poets were made to feel "proud servants of their own proud community."[119] Whether Aeschylus felt that he retained some dignity in his Sicilian works by complicating the issues presented in his plays, and by tempering praise with warnings, advice, and moral tales, is difficult to determine. It is, however, instructive to note that poets such as these are first mentioned in the tyrannies of Gelon and Hieron in which an effort was made to give the *demos* a voice

---

[118] Bremer (1991) 55.   [119] Bremer (1991) 60.

following their revolt against the *gamoroi*. Can the interest in public enter-tainment be explained in part by the growing and more formalized role of the *demos* in the cities? Public spirit and indeed democracy may have grown hand in hand with the rise of the theater in Syracuse, as Meier suggests it did in the case of Athens.

5 | Taking Theater Home

Images of Comedy and Tragedy on Vases

Although the first 100 years of the history of theater in Sicily can be roughly sketched by following scattered references in texts and piecemeal archaeological clues, as I have tried to do in the first four chapters of this book, the most important and well-known pieces of evidence for Sicilian theater, and perhaps for much of early Greek theater in general, come from the fourth century. It was at this juncture of the classical and Hellenistic periods that both theaters and theatrical vases began to be produced in great number.

Many theaters were built and theatrical vases produced in the Greek West, but these are regularly understood by way of Attic drama and the conventions of Athenian theater and theater-building. South Italian and Sicilian vases painted with tragic myth are thought to represent Attic tragedy.[1] Likewise, although the comic phlyax vases were long thought to represent a rough burlesque comedy native to South Italy and Sicily, in recent years, these too have been traced to Attic comedy.[2] Athenian influence and leadership in theater is well known and it is certain that Athenian plays were introduced to Sicily and South Italy and may sometimes be represented on western vases. This focus on Athens, however, leaves the picture of the history of theater in Sicily incomplete, for it implies that theater in fourth-century Sicily was suddenly sparked into life by the introduction of Athenian plays. Although the Sicilian theater scene was no doubt boosted by the introduction of new plays and Athenian models, there is evidence of considerable theatrical activity beforehand, as I have argued in the first four chapters of this book. Moreover, quite apart from the problem of the referent of the vases (that is, whether they represent Attic or western Greek drama), the sheer number of South Italian and Sicilian comic and tragic vases, a collection unparalleled anywhere in the ancient Greek world, suggests

---

[1] E.g. Taplin (2007).

[2] Hughes (1996); Taplin (1993); Csapo (1986); Webster (1948). This is part of a larger century-long debate about where South Italian red-figure vases come from – are they mostly Attic-inspired or Attic pieces? See Lippolis (1996) 357–61 for a summary of the debate.

something distinctive about the interests of the western Greeks and the native populations of South Italy and Sicily.

From South Italy and Sicily, hundreds of representations of ancient theater on vases, terracotta figurines, and other materials produced between the last decades of the fifth century and the first decades of the third are still extant. From Sicily alone, we now have at least thirty-seven vases, whole and fragmentary, which explicitly represent theatrical performance, of which some thirty-five are comic and two are tragic.[3] The Paestan tradition of comic vase-painting, which is thought to be significantly influenced by Sicilian vase-painters who emigrated to Paestum, gives us another seventy-nine vases and fragments. All the comic images show costumes and masks with great vividness, including lines at wrist and ankle where the "naked" costume met the actual skin of the wearer. Several of them show performances taking place on stage, with the stage itself sketched in on the vase. A tragic vase from Capodarso, a few miles south west of Enna, shows a performance of tragedy on a raised wooden stage and another, also attributed to the Capodarso Painter, shows characters, apparently on a stage, listening to an elderly messenger figure.[4] The collections of South Italian and Sicilian images related to the theater are extraordinary, both for the explicit depiction of performance on individual vases and for the sheer number of vases. By contrast, Attic vase-painters painted very few scenes of performance; the iconographic material related to theater from Attica is, with a few exceptions, of an entirely different sort, concentrating mainly on the festival and choral aspect of productions and, more often than not, representing actors offstage and together with the key cult figure of drama, Dionysus.[5] Since the nineteenth century, therefore, scholars have puzzled over what the huge and still growing assortment of explicitly dramatic images from the West represents: local western Greek traditions of theater, native Italian traditions, imported Athenian plays, or some combination?

---

[3] For statistics on comic vases, see Green (2012) 342; for estimates of tragic vases, see Taplin (2007) 15; for theaters, see Chapter 6 and Map 6.1. With thanks to J. R. Green for generously letting me see his updated lists of vases for Sicily and Paestum for his forthcoming revised version of the *BICS Phlyax Vases* volume.

[4] Sicilian calyx-krater by the Capodarso painter (Gibil Gabib Group), ca 330s (Caltanissetta, Museo Civico 1301 bis) (Figure 5.8); Sicilian calyx-krater attributed to the Gibil Gabib Group, probably the Capodarso painter, ca 330s (Syracuse Museo Archeologico Regionale "Paolo Orsi" 66557) (Figure 5.9). See below pp. 150 and 151. Though most other tragic vases seem to represent the myth itself rather than performance of a play, Taplin (2007) has identified more subtle markers of performance on many of these vases.

[5] Csapo (2010) 1–37.

5.1   Viewers and Settings

Before turning to the difficult problem of what the vases represent, I briefly explore the corollary to this question: why are there so many explicitly theatrical vases from the West? Several general solutions to the problem of why so many theatrical images were produced in and for the West have been proposed and these offer necessary but not entirely sufficient explanations, at least from the point of view of understanding the history of theater in Sicily. Chief among them is the now familiar comment that the western Greeks were crazy about theater. This we know to be true, and we have traced the history of this enjoyment of the stage in the preceding chapters. We also know, however, that the Athenians were crazy about theater, and we might attribute similar excitement to the eastern Greeks whose enormous Hellenistic theaters rival those of the Mainland and the Greek West. Why did equivalent traditions of comic vase-painting not spring up for the first audiences of Aristophanes, Eupolis, and others in Athens, the acknowledged center and hotbed of Greek theatrical activity? Csapo notes that Attic vase-painting was in decline by the last decade of the fifth and in the fourth century, precisely when vase production and painting were on the rise in the West. Had the Athenians maintained their dominance in pottery production in this later period, when popular tastes for actors and representations of performance proper were on the rise, the Athenians would have produced more comic vases celebrating the actor.[6] Thus, South Italian and Sicilian comic vases can be seen as tokens of a growing obsession with the craft of acting and performance throughout the Mediterranean world in general, Athens included. A difficulty with this explanation is that Athens was still producing a large quantity of red-figure pottery, but selling most of it to export markets to the north, south and further west than Italy.[7] Why did other markets, including Athenian, not clamor for such images on vases in the first three-quarters of the fourth century, as they appear to have done in the fourth quarter of the century and later, when they drove an international market in theatrical figurines from Athens as well as production centers in the West and elsewhere? We

---

[6] Csapo (2010) 72. Csapo's main thesis is that if all kinds of iconographic representation of theater are taken into consideration, Athens did not produce less theater-related material than Sicily and South Italy, and this argument about chronology is just by way of supporting the main premise.

[7] Trendall (1987) 9, new markets for Attic vases included Southern Russia, the western coast of the Black Sea, North Africa (Cyrene), and Spain (Ampurias). On the implications of the fragment of a late fifth-century Athenian vase depicting tragic chorusmen and musicians found at Olbia Pontica, see Braund and Hall (2014a).

may still ask why the western Greek market was so important in the creation of theater-related images.

Postcolonial attitudes together with rigorous archaeological method have allowed us to begin to take account of the fact that many comic and tragic vases were not found in the Greek centers of the West, but on their periphery and often in Italic centers and Italic graves. Some scholars, for example, Todisco, Giuliani, and Green, have been hesitant to assume Italic interest in seeing the plays, or the ability or opportunity to do so or to fully appreciate the comedies, tragedies, and myths represented on the vases; they suggest that the vases may often have been curiosities and luxury goods.[8] Others, including Robinson, Carpenter and, most recently, Taplin, argue that the evidence suggests that Italic interest in and exposure to Greek theater was substantial and that there is no reason to believe that they had only a superficial or confused understanding of the images.[9] In either case, however, the presence of strong native markets for explicitly theatrical vases is a key distinguishing feature of the context in which they were produced.

As Michael Shanks demonstrated in his study of the life of Corinthian perfume jars, we ought not to think of painted pottery as pebbles in the wood of ancient history, but as a window into a culture, and into the reactions to and the desire for images of this kind.[10] In the case of the comic phlyax vases, the culture in question is a complex and varied medley that might in shorthand be called western, and the reactions and desires under investigation are those of the Italiotes and Italics, Sikeliotes and natives of Sicily. Without denying that Panhellenic enjoyment of theater might be part of the explanation for the trove of vases in the West, I look here for more local conditions that, in my view, must have played a role in the demand for and creation of this unique group of vases over the course of the first three quarters of the fourth century.

But what counts as local? Is the distinction between vases painted by recent immigrants from Athens or other parts of mainland Greece, or by colonial Greeks, Italics, or natives of Sicily? Or does it mostly matter whether the symbols and scenes themselves echo regional painting styles or speak specifically to regional viewers or not? And at what level of

---

[8] Todisco (2012); Giuliani (1995); Green (1986).

[9] Taplin (2012); Robinson (2004); Carpenter (2009). The relationship between certain theatrical images – especially those depicting recognition scenes – and the ritual context of the funeral is increasingly the focus of attention: see Giuliani (1995) and Hall's response in Hall (2013) ch. 4.

[10] Shanks (1999).

specificity must we identify the audiences of the vases: is it reasonable to examine all together in the context of a broad colonial and perhaps postcolonial world in the West? Should we distinguish between the Daunian and the Tarentine Greek each buried together with a phlyax vase? Or between the viewers of an Apulian phlyax scene in the 490s, a Paestan vase in the 460s, or a Sicilian vase from Manfria in the 430s?[11] Or, from a different angle, are we evaluating the possibility that the images evoke sub-literary dramas regularly viewed or created by western Greek or even Italic or native Sicilian festivalgoers to the exclusion of literary plays – or plays by local Greek Sikeliote playwrights? Or might parody or adaptation of imported Athenian dramas qualify as local? Or some hybrid of these? Specific and concrete answers to these questions generally prove elusive, but in this chapter I try to address these questions in broad terms.

There are a few pieces of firm ground in this quicksand of shifting contexts. First, the phlyax vases, like most South Italian red-figure, were made for local use and not for export markets.[12] They were also relatively cheap and available to a broad cross-section of society.[13] Secondly, apart from a few exceptional and roughly drawn examples, the phlyax genre is peculiar to the West and is not found in Attica or mainland Greece.[14] Within the western context, however, although the vases can be characterized generally as Apulian, Paestan, or Sicilian, the provenances of the vases include a great number of places within these regions, and, moreover, some vases have been attributed to other regions, including Lucania and Campania more broadly.[15] Thirdly, individual vases have been associated with many different painters, and, with the possible exception of Asteas and Python in Paestum, none of these artists seems to have made a specialty of

---

[11] Even recognizing the difficulty of establishing chronologies, which as Alexandre Mitchell reminds us, are "difficult to arrive at and most are conventional". Mitchell (2009) 24.

[12] McPhee and Pemberton (2004) 59: "[. . .] these red-figure fabrics were mainly intended for local use and were rarely exported beyond the immediate area of manufacture. Some South Italian red-figure vases reached southern France and Spain, a few have been found at Spina at the mouth of the Po, and in the Greek colonies on the coast of Albania, and occasional pieces even reached further afield, to North Africa, the Black Sea, and even Alexandria. In 1975 Trendall could write that 'as yet no vase which may with certainty be attributed to a South Italian fabric has actually been found on Greek soil.' Even today, the harvest from mainland Greece is minimal: a small stamnoid and a fragmentary bell-krater in Corfu, plus the pieces from Corinth." Robertson (2004) 195: "It is probable, in my view, that the foundation of red-figure workshops in South Italy was heavily conditioned by the Italian market."

[13] Mitchell (2009) 21.   [14] Cf. Csapo (2010) 23–9 on Attic comic vases.

[15] Although their work has been questioned and debated (e.g. Lippolis (1996) 359–60), I follow here the attributions of Trendall, Cambitoglou et al. in their magisterial collections on red-figure vases of South Italy and Sicily.

the vases, but rather produced a few of them as part of large and varied oeuvres. Although it is widely agreed either that the earliest red-figure vase-painters in the West working in the third quarter of the fifth century were trained in Attic workshops or that Attic vase-painters emigrated to the West, there is no evidence, of which I am aware, that the fourth-century painters who painted the phlyax vases came directly from Athens, although they seem in some cases to be influenced by Attic vase-painting styles.[16] Indeed some of the phlyax vases seem to have been made like other red-figure by several workers in what might perhaps be described as a kind of assembly-line process.[17] As Carpenter notes, both the volute krater and the Apulian column krater are found in Italic tombs, and the former only rarely and the latter never in western Greek tombs. The famous Pronomos vase depicting the cast of a satyr play offstage is one such volute krater and was found in an Italic grave in Ruvo.[18] On the other hand, the calyx-krater, a very popular type for phlyax paintings, is almost always found in Greek tombs, and rarely in Italic. In sum, these vases were widely available, varied, and of varying degrees of grandeur, made and painted in local workshops by, as far as can be ascertained, western Greeks at, for example, Metapontum, and by Italic vase-painters at workshops in Apulia, Lucania, Sicily, Campania, and so on. The dramatic subjects appealed to Italiotes and Italics, Sikeliotes and native Sicilians alike.

Despite the tragedy of clandestine excavations, which has left many vases with no known provenance, and the added complication of fakes,[19] specialists have made great progress in the study of Sicilian vases, and in cataloguing and identifying a close relationship between the workshops of Sicily and Campania. In the case of the phlyax vases, this work suggests that the vibrant tradition of phlyax painting in Paestum was first sparked by Sikeliote vase-painters or vase-painters working in Sicily who moved north to Paestum after the fall of Dionysius I and the resulting chaos in Sicily. The Painter of Louvre K 240 and perhaps also Asteas are now thought to have

---

[16] Carpenter (2009) 28–9; Giudice (2002).

[17] Lippolis (1996) 357: "I sogetti rappresentati su uno stesso vaso possono anche essere, così, il prodotto di una collaborazione di più mani, non solo quando i due lati di un cratere mostrano impegno e livello qualitativi diversi, ma anche nei casi in cui le complesse decorazioni accessorie e il completamento del vaso possono richiedere l'opera di specialisti con capacità operative differenti, dalla sovraddipintura alla campitura dello sfondo."

[18] Carpenter (2009) 32; Green (1991) 53 notes that the column kraters, which seem to have been manufactured primarily for trade with the Italic peoples of Apulia, have no comic scenes on them. Green sees this as evidence that it is unlikely that the Italic peoples were particularly interested in comedy. For an authoritative collection of essays devoted to the Pronomos vase, see Taplin and Wyles (2010).

[19] Cf. Robinson (2004); Carpenter (2009) 32.

begun work in Sicily and to have brought traditions of painting with them to Paestum.[20]

Despite a strikingly wide distribution of provenances, comic vases have not appeared everywhere in the West: no examples have yet been found at Locri on the south-east tip of Italy among its rich deposits of figurines and vases, for example, or at Velia further north on the western side, which boasts a stone theater, or grand Selinus on the south-west coast of Sicily. That is, there appears not to be a necessary connection between Greek settlement and the performance of comic drama. In Sicily itself, many of the findspots of the twenty-eight extant phlyax vases are known and these cluster in the Lentini-Manfria region, with some also nearer to Catania, others from Lipari and from Messina. Despite the useful categorization of the Lentini-Manfria group, many of these vases were found scattered in different places. It is curious that, with a few exceptions, they have been found in sites close to the non-Greek hinterland, rather than near the heart of great Sikeliote cities, where one might expect the greatest amount of theater, particularly if, as is now widely accepted, the images represent Aristophanes and Old and Middle Comedy.

Apart from the earliest vases, which are thought to predate the Paestan tradition, most of the Sicilian vases are dated to the third quarter of the fourth century, more precisely between 340–330. This date corresponds to the period of Timoleon's reforms and the beginning of renewed wealth and stability for the island, and it appears that this dating is unfortunately, but necessarily, somewhat circular.

The Paestan tradition, so closely linked to the Sicilian because of the apparent migration to Paestum of Sicilian potters in the second quarter of the fourth century, comprises a main workshop operated by Asteas and his student Python, and secondary or later workshops. Though some vases have been found in surrounding towns, these workshops remain firmly associated with the city. The city itself, however, was conquered early in the fourth century by Lucanians, who became the ruling class and remained in control, though they may have been ousted for a brief time in the third quarter of the fourth century.[21]

Likewise, influence from Sicilian vase-painters has been identified in the workshops in the region just north of Paestum, Campania, to which some twelve phlyax vases have been attributed. Other red-figure images by Campanian vase-painters show women in Samnite dress and appear to

---

[20] E.g. Hughes (2003).   [21] Wonder (2002).

be inspired by local Italian custom. From Lucania, one comic vase survives, remarkable also as the earliest of the phlyax tradition.[22]

Apulian vases from the Italic area around Taranto and vases from Metaponto seem to evolve from a slightly separate tradition, and no Sicilian forerunners are usually identified. Several of these are dated very early, to the beginning of the fourth century, and it is here that most vases with non-Doric, probably Attic, inscriptions have been found. It is, moreover, from this collection of vases that nearly all the examples (with the notable exception of the Paestan Phrynis and Pyronides vase) of the influence of Aristophanes and Old Comedy are drawn. Yet here, too, the vases are distributed in an unexpected way. Most with known provenances come from non-Greek graves, well inside Daunian, Peucetian, or Messapian regions. As discussed below, Carpenter and Robinson have argued that these Italic peoples had direct contact with Athens and with Athenian vase-painting from an early stage; we need not postulate Doric Tarentum as the middle-man between Attic vase trade and the Italic tribes of Apulia.[23]

Thus, Sicilian, Paestan, Campanian, and Apulian traditions of comic vases developed in proximity to or in regions under the control of native Sicilian and Italic populations. It is, of course, true that most Greek cities in the West were relatively proximate to non-Greek populations, and non-Greeks often mingled with Greeks sometimes enslaved, sometimes employed, sometimes in power, sometimes integrating on a more equal footing through marriage.[24] It is somewhat simplistic to point out a general connection to the non-Greek world, as relationships varied drastically in different regions, but it is nevertheless striking that these comic vases do not appear to have been exclusively made or owned by Greeks, but quite often made and owned by non-Greeks as well.

In sum, the broad context in which these vases have been found seems to be peculiarly western, and distinct from that of Athens: namely, the Italic and native Sicilian market for the vases seems to have played a significant role in the growth of the phlyax vase industry. Far from evoking a picture of isolated Greeks clinging to the culture of distant Athens through esoteric and obscure comic paintings, the evidence points to lively interaction with

---

[22] Berlin F 3043 attr. to the Amykos painter. For discussion of Lucanian comic vase-painting, see Green (2012).

[23] Robinson (2004); Carpenter (2009).

[24] See Leighton (1999) and Antonaccio (2001) on pre-Greek culture and Greek interactions. An elegantly readable, but now out of date, history of Sicily is Finley (1979); see now De Angelis (2016). Pugliese Carratelli's (1996) richly illustrated volume (in which Vagnetti and Garbini's essays can be found) includes a range of essays on many aspects of the western Greeks.

local markets, both Greek and non-Greek, and to a widespread and joint appreciation of this comic tradition.

Moreover, as Csapo has pointed out, even the Greeks in question were not colonists from Athens, nor part of or subject to the Athenian empire. The four main Greek cities where theater seems to have been popular had been settled by Doric colonists from Sparta (Taras) and Corinth (Syracuse), and Achaian colonists with the leadership of Sybaris (Metaponto and Poseidonia). As Csapo notes: "Who would have thought that the evidence for it ["the translation of Athenian drama into Greek classics"] would come not from Athens or Athens' colonies, empire, or neighbors, but from the distant and (in the late fifth-century) mainly hostile state of the Dorian West?"[25] These western cities had not, of course, remained isolated from the literary and performance developments in the larger Greek world, nor from the flourishing theater industry in Athens; and the close literary and dramatic ties between Athens and Syracuse in particular in the fifth century were set out in the first chapters of this book. As Csapo also argues, these cities' love for drama must have been, to some degree, examples of a broad and growing Panhellenic interest in the genre, which by the end of the fourth century was to sweep the Greek world with the wildly popular and accessible New Comedy, more and more uniformly produced by professional acting troupes. There are, however, particular characteristics of the western Greek situation that should not be discounted. Italic people and native Sicilians also delighted in the comic images and were probably in direct contact with Attic traders and perhaps also visited Athens themselves; Doric Greeks put great emphasis on distinguishing their own Doric traditions of theater from those of Athens; and Hellenistic and Roman imitators took care to distinguish between their Attic and Sicilian models. So, although Greek theater writ large must be recognized as an umbrella category, comprising and uniting Athenian and all local traditions of theater, Greek theater can, *at the same time*, be divided into regional traditions and the audience and viewers of comic vases in the West can be understood to have been quite different from their counterparts in other parts of the Mediterranean.[26]

Thus, the viewers of these comic vases seem to have been a mixture of western Greek, Italic, and native Sicilian. The vases often seem to have been

[25] Csapo (2010) 39.

[26] It is too awkward to separate study of more precise audiences (e.g. Samnite versus Tarentine versus Sicilian) from study of the comic paintings themselves. Therefore, I take up the more precise distinction between regional tastes for the vases in the second section in the context of discussion of some vases in particular.

produced in both Greek and non-Greek settlements, and they were prized
and carried into the underworld by all parties.

5.2   Comic Vases: a Review of Scholarly Interpretations of the Comic Phlyax Vases

In addition to the grand stone theaters built in at least fourteen cities in Sicily
(see Map 6.1) and the tragic vases discussed below, relatively inexpensive comic
theatrical pots and terracotta figurines mark the popularity of theater in the
fourth century. Early studies of drama in Sicily separated the evidence of the
theaters and the comic vases: whereas the former seemed to have been built for
large-scale dramatic productions, the latter were thought to depict small-scale,
local farces.[27] Not only did the material of the vases and figurines suggest that
they were inexpensive, but the characters depicted on them seemed to be
drawn from a lowbrow, popular, farcical theater. Therefore, beginning at least
in the late nineteenth century, the comic vase paintings from South Italy and
Sicily were generally thought to represent a local sub-literary native tradition.
Scholars gave the vases the name "phlyax," a word drawn from several ancient
sources, but most explicitly defined in Athenaeus' *Deipnosophistae* as the name
the Italiotes gave their local form of comic theater:[28]

ὡς οὐ τὸ σεῦτλον ταὐτὸν ὂν τῶι τευτλίωι. ἐκαλοῦντο δ᾽οἱ μετιόντες τὴν
τοιαύτην παιδιὰν παρὰ τοῖς Λάκωσι δικηλισταί, ὡς ἄν τις σκευοποιοὺς
εἴπηι καὶ μιμητάς. τοῦ δὲ εἴδους τῶν δικηλιστῶν πολλαὶ κατὰ τόπους εἰσὶ
προσηγορίαι. Σικυώνιοι μὲν γὰρ φαλλοφόρους αὐτοὺς καλοῦσιν, ἄλλοι

---

[27] This separation has since been revised, cf. Hughes (1996) on phlyax or wooden stages in stone
theaters.

[28] In this passage, Athenaeus is citing Sosibius, and Taplin argues that Sosibius might, as
a patriotic historian of Laconia, have been eager to associate South Italian drama with "Spartan
mumming – however primitive and dissimilar – rather than with the celebrated achievements
of effete Athens" (1993, 49). Cf. Pollux, *Onom.* IX.149 (Test. *PCG* I p. 259). Cf. Heydemann
(1886); Dearden (1988) 33; Taplin (1993) 52–4. The etymology of the word has not been
conclusively determined, although scholars have suggested two possible alternatives: see
Todisco (2002) 89; Castaldo and Rocconi (2012) 343–4. One is that it was derived from the verb
phluarein, which is used in Herodotus meaning "to play the fool" (2.131), in Aristophanes
meaning "to talk nonsense" (*Knights* 545), and in Plato of the assaults made on Socrates by
comic playwrights (*Apology* 19c). The other is that it was connected with the verb *phleein*, "teem
with" or "abound in," with either negative associations of excess (see e.g. Aesch. *Ag.* 377) or
positive ones of ripe abundance (Aesch., *Ag.* 1416). The latter alternative might have had
connections with the "swelling" of actors' bodies by padded costumes, or with the epithet of
Dionysus *phleos* founded on an inscription in Priene (φλέος, epith. of Dionysus (*SIG* 1003.1).
Hesychius glosses *phleein* as "babble" which may mean he believed there was an etymological
connection between the verb and phlyax plays.

δ'αὐτοκαβδάλους, οἳ δὲ φλύακας, ὡς Ἰταλοί, σοφιστὰς δὲ οἱ πολλοί·
Athenaeus, *Deipnosophistae*, XIV 621–2[29]

The main literary exponent of the phlyakes comedy seems to have been
Rhinthon, who worked in Tarentum around 300 BCE, though he was
apparently Syracusan by birth. In an epitaph, Nossis of Lokroi, credits
him with plays called tragic phlyakes:

καὶ καπυρὸν γελάσας παραμείβεο καὶ φίλον εἰπὼν
ῥῆμ' ἐπ' ἐμοί. Ῥίνθων εἰμ' ὁ Συρακόσιος,
Μουσάων ὀλίγη τις ἀηδονίς· ἀλλὰ φλυάκων
ἐκ τραγικῶν ἴδιον κισσὸν ἐδρεψάμεθα.

> Nossis epigram 10 Gow-Page, *The Greek Anthology*,
> *PCG* I Rhinthon Test. 1, 2, 3[30]

In later ancient scholarship, Rhinthon is again named as a writer of
phlyakes, both by the *Suda*, where φλυακογραφία, *phlyuagraphia*, is glossed
as ἱλαροτραγωιδία, *hilarotragoidia*, and by Stephanus Byzantius, who
praises Rhinthon for turning tragedy into comedy.[31]

In the late nineteenth century, Heydemann argued that Rhinthon created the kinds of plays represented on the phlyax comedy, and that his
successors continued to write phlyax comedy through the third century.
Heydemann dated the vases to the third century and argued that they
represented Rhinthon's plays and those of his successors.[32] This view was
considerably shaken, however, when Trendall dated the earliest of these
vases to about 400 and the latest to about 320,[33] which meant that the vases
ceased to be produced before Rhinthon began writing. T. B. L. Webster

---

[29] (Test. *PCG* I p. 259): "Those taking part in such revelry were called 'dikelistai' by the Laconians,
as someone might call makers of masks, or mime artists. There are many names, according to
regions, for the sort of thing the 'dikelistai' are. For the Sikionians call them 'phallus-bearers,'
others call them 'buffoons,' and still others 'phlyakes' like the Italians, and many call them
'sophists'."

[30] Speak kindly of me, passerby,
 And, laughing loudly, walk on.
A lesser nightingale am I
 – The Syracusan Rhinthon –
Yet still I plucked an ivy wreath
 From farces lewd and tragic,
Not stock the muses oft bequeath,
 But idiosyncratic.

[31] Cf. *Suda* ρ 170, Cf. Dearden (1988) 33, and note 3. Heydemann (1886); Taplin argues that
Rhinthon was not building on "some sort of buffoonish folk-theatre," but was the originator of
a new genre, (1993, 51–2). Cf. Csapo's analysis of Rhinthon's role (1986, 388), with Trendall
(1991) 169.

[32] Taplin (1993) 52–4. [33] Trendall (1936). Cf. Csapo (1986) 388.

then suggested that the phlyax vases represented Athenian comedy. His thesis was opposed by Pickard-Cambridge in favor of the argument that the phlyax vases could still depict a tradition of local South Italian or Sicilian burlesque that remained essentially sub-literary until about 300 BCE, when Rhinthon elevated the comedies to a literary form;[34] this does not, however, explain why the vases *stopped* being produced in Rhinthon's heyday. Webster's view was widely accepted by other scholars, including Gigante and Trendall,[35] many of whom viewed the western Greek situation as sophisticated, well informed and up to date with developments in Attic drama.[36]

The recognition of the influence of Attic tragedy and comedy did not, however, lead all of these scholars to discount the possible influence of the playwrights of the West. In 1966, Marcello Gigante, for example, developed Heydemann's theory in a slightly different direction and showed how similar some of the themes represented on the vases are to the plays of Epicharmus. Like Rhinthon's *hilarotragoidia*, which depended upon sophisticated knowledge of Greek tragedy, Epicharmus' plays should not be discounted as buffoonish, rudimentary comedy, but as sophisticated dramas that were as famous in antiquity as the now better-known comedy of Athens.[37] In ascribing the comedies on the vases to Epicharmus, Gigante trod a neat path between the inescapable fact that vases depicting these kinds of comic scenes or actors, with only a handful of poor exceptions, were produced in the West for a western market and a growing awareness that the comedies represented on them may not have been as lowbrow as earlier assumed. I summarize some of his astute comparisons between the images on the vases and the extant fragments of Epicharmus below. Building on Gigante's arguments in the same book, I propose further that if the other evidence for theater in the West, including the grand stone theaters and evidence for the performance of tragic theater, is added to the evidence of the comic vases and fragmentary comic playwrights, a picture of an even more developed and sophisticated Sicilian theater emerges.

---

[34] Webster (1948); Pickard-Cambridge (1946).

[35] Trendall (1967b) agreed with Webster, but nevertheless identified Rhinthon as the highest proponent of the kind of drama presented on the vases. Cf. Csapo (1986) 388.

[36] Gigante (1966) 91–3, and concluding on p. 93 that, "nel IV sec. in Magna Grecia il teatro di Aristofane era popolare."

[37] See Chapters 2 and 4 for analysis of Epicharmus' sophistication and that of his plays. Gigante (1966): "[...] Rintone era *poeta doctus* e conosceva i modelli attici, ma naturalmente viveva in quello stesso clima culturale creato dagli artisti grecoitalici nel corso del IV sec. e non ignorava gli *ateliers* dei vasai e dei pittori [...]."

In the 1980s and 1990s, the interpretation of the comic vases was advanced by the appearance of new examples, at least one of which uncontroversially represents imported Athenian comedies, and Old Comedy at that. In 1986 and 1987 respectively, Csapo and Taplin showed that a fourth-century South Italian phlyax vase, the "Würzburg Telephos," depicts a comedy of Aristophanes.[38] Unaware of each other's research, both scholars independently concluded that this Apulian bell-krater represents a scene from Aristophanes' *Thesmophoriazusae*.[39] The close correspondences which Csapo and Taplin noted between the vase and the *Thesmophoriazusae* leave little doubt that this vase is a depiction of the murder of the wineskin "baby," Aristophanes' spoof on the scene in Euripides' *Telephus* when the hero, finding himself in danger at the Argive court, seizes the infant Orestes.

Then, in 1989 , a bell-krater, also Apulian and painted with an unknown comedy, was sold in New York (Figure 5.1).[40] Trendall published it as the "*Choregoi*," after the two puzzling characters both labeled χορηγός which appear on it, and dated the vase to about 380 BCE.[41] In his seminal work, *Comic Angels* (1993), Taplin argued that the two puzzling figures were Athenian "*choregoi*," that is, producers or funders of Attic theater, and he used the vase as the foundation of an argument that the phlyax vases of Southern Italy and Sicily depict Athenian comedies (I discuss the interpretation of this vase in greater detail below).[42]

To the fairly certain identification of an Athenian comedy on the "Würzburg Telephos" and the compelling argument for another on the "*Choregoi*" vase, Csapo and Taplin add the evidence of other vases, some of

---

[38] Bell-krater, Würzburg H 5697: Trendall and Cambitoglou (1978) 65, num. 4a (Schiller Painter); Kossatz-Deissmann (1980); Csapo (1986); Taplin (1987) and (1993).

[39] The argument has been widely accepted. Small (2003) presents a case that vase-paintings are rarely derived from literary texts, but even she agrees that (p. 66) "[. . .] the Würzburg vase is one of the rare examples of a scene that may truly illustrate a text, or, if not a text directly, then a performance of a text."

[40] The "*Choregoi*" was bought in 1989 by Lawrence and Barbara Fleischman (Taplin (1993) 55). The article in which Taplin notes his awareness of a vase with a chorus, writing that he was "now aware of an unpublished vase on the market which provides the first counter-example," was published two years earlier in 1987. However, since he does not mention any other vase which fits this description (cf. Taplin (1993) 75–8), I assume that he heard of the "*Choregoi*" before it was officially on the market. The vase, from clandestine excavations in South Italy, has been repatriated to Italy: Godart and De Caro (2007) 170–1, num. 45.

[41] Rasmussen and Spivey (1991) and more fully in Trendall and Cambitoglou (1991–1992), I, 77–8, num. 6. Cf. Taplin's review of Trendall's analysis, Taplin (1993) 55–6. Trendall and Cambitoglou attributed the vase to the same artist as the "Milan Cake Eaters," whom they called "The *Choregos* Painter."

[42] Taplin (1993). Cf. his analysis of Attic tragedy represented on South Italian pots, Taplin (1998).

Figure 5.1 Apulian bell-krater depicting Aegisthus, two *choregoi*, and Pyrrhias on stage. *Choregos* Painter. Once Malibu, J. Paul Getty Museum 96.AE.29, now Naples, Museo Archeologico Nazionale 248778, ca 380 BCE

which have inscriptions in Attic dialect, like the New York "Goose Play" (Figure 5.11), and others give evidence of links with the Athenian theater scene, such as the Paestan Phrynis and Pyronides vase, which explicitly references two famous Athenian musicians.[43] Still more vases, though they cannot be linked to particular Athenian comedies, seem to reflect the kind of themes prevalent in Aristophanes' Old Comedy. These associations between the vases and Aristophanes mark an important turning point in our understanding of the early dissemination of Athenian drama, for they show that Old Comedy spread far more widely and far earlier than had hitherto been thought.

Like Gigante and Trendall before him, Christopher Dearden, taking into account the persuasive attribution of the "Würzburg Telephos" and other

[43] Würzburg Telephos, ca 380: see above 180. New York Goose Play, ca 400: Taplin (1993) 30–2, 41–2; bell-krater (Phrynis and Pyronides vase), Salerno, Museo Provinciale Pc 1812, from Pontecagnano: Trendall (1987) 65, num. 19 (Asteas), pls. 20c–d.

evidence and admitting that the evidence for western Greek drama is "tantalizingly inconclusive," has argued that the vases more likely represent a "melding together of both local and imported drama."[44] This combination theory is consistent with the literary evidence for a combination of imported plays and regional adaptations or new versions discussed in Chapter 4.

5.3   Phlyakes among Images

As the studies by Mitchell (2009) and Walsh (2009) demonstrate, the phlyax vases belong not only to the controversial and complex world of vases associated with Greek comic performance, but also to a much wider set of funny Greek vases. Mitchell's painstaking examination of thousands of vases allowed him to identify a category of humorous vase-painting, which he defines as those which in themselves make a joke or are funny, by juxtaposing odd elements or parodying other vases or bringing stereotypical decoration into the action of the scene, as distinct from vases representing comic performance. He was able to make statistical studies of the number of humorous vases from different places, concluding, for example, that about 4–5 percent of Attic vases and about 25 percent of Kabeiric vases were humorous, making Attic vases the largest raw number of humorous vases, whereas very few of the tens of thousands of Corinthian or Spartan vases fall into this category.[45] David Walsh, for his part, examines vases that burlesque divinities, and, in addition to a large number of phlyax vases, he

---

[44] Dearden (1990a) 159–61. Cf. Dearden (1988) 35: "Athenian tragedy had been an acquired taste of audiences in Magna Graecia from the fifth century B.C. . . . It would be strange if audiences acquired a taste for sophisticated tragedy and looked to Athens as the center of the theatrical world but for comedy preferred to remain with the rustic and improvised, ignoring contemporary Athenian productions, even though some of their own sons were writing there." Contra, see Csapo (1986) 388.

[45] Mitchell (2009) 28; ibid. 3: "Tens of thousands of Corinthian vases were produced in the 7th and 6th centuries but show very few instances of humour if any. Why was Athens such a special centre for the production of vases? There were a number of circumstances that made this possible: an abundance of suitable clay, a specialized knowledge, built up over centuries, in competition with other cities such as Corinth. The reason why visual humour was particularly an Athenian tradition was because there was space for freedom of expression and unruliness in daily life only within democracy! The Athenians were independently minded people in a society where people could to a certain extent, think for themselves: they produced the first fully democratic society. Laconian (Spartan) vase-painting is a prolific medium, but it does not produce any visual humour. . . . Humour, as in most places, was probably present in Spartans' words, gestures, and thoughts, but the absence of freedom of expression is enough to explain the lack of humour in Laconian visual culture but also in many other city-states."

surveys a wide range of comic burlesque images from various places. These include Corinthian komos vases, Boeotian Kabeiric vases, satyr vases, vases portraying grotesques and pygmies, and the Caeretan Hydriai made for Etruscans and Greeks in settlements not far north of Paestum. The relationship between these vase types and comic performance is fraught with difficulty; even the Kabeiric vases, found in a sanctuary that boasts an early theater, are not always thought to represent dramatic performance. Yet, many of the comic figures depicted sport elements that are prominent on phlyax vases, for example, padded stomach and buttocks (komasts), short stature (pygmies), masks and prominent phalloi.[46] These overlaps in comic exaggeration yield some insight into the antecedents of the phlyax form for, as Walsh writes, "such physical distortions are found over a large part of the Greek world up to two hundred years *before* comedy was produced at Athens. Greek drama, therefore, exhibits the similarities of physicality rather than accounting for them."[47]

These are useful frameworks within which to examine possible antecedents or influences on the western phlyax vases, not least because examples of all of these other kinds of comic vases have also been found in Magna Graecia and Sicily. Despite the widespread similarity of comic representation extending from Etruscan, to Doric, to Attic painting traditions, and despite the relatively few examples of comic figures in performance (as opposed to humorous paintings) in Attic vase-painting, Attic models have recently been singled out as the original example from which phlyax vases derived. From Athens, as Csapo most recently points out, there are a few early vases that exhibit figures similar to those on the phlyax vases.[48] Yet seen against the background of the humorous and burlesque images painstakingly gathered by Mitchell and by Walsh respectively, these Attic forerunners seem less significant than they might otherwise. For, as Mitchell demonstrates, relative to the many Attic vases that make jokes, both lewd and proper, there are incredibly few Attic vases that depict phlyax figures. Attic vase-painters could and did play fast and loose with serious images, more than any other region's vase-painters by Mitchell's calculation, a proclivity he attributes to the

---

[46] For several extended discussions evaluating the associations between komast vases and early comedy, see Csapo and Miller (2007) 41–117.

[47] Walsh (2009) 248.

[48] Csapo (2010) 23–9. On earlier theories about an original Doric farce, cf. Csapo and Miller (2007); Gigante (1966) 91, who cites Körte (1893) 62–3, "nel 1893 il Körte sosteneva che l'elemento comune alla commedia attica e alla farsa fliacica risale alla *Urform* della farsa dorica."

freedom of expression allowed in a democracy.[49] Yet, despite a few early attempts, the fad of painting comic performance did not catch on at Athens. We cannot explain this away as an insistence on serious and respectable images at Athens, if Athens produced the greatest number of humorous images in the Greek world. Instead, we are left with the curious, unexplained conclusion that the Athenians simply did not paint comic *performance*, unlike their South Italian and Sicilian counterparts. Moreover, Walsh demonstrates that the majority of the burlesque images (including the phlyax images) come from regions outside Attica. Early black-figure burlesque images, which evince elements of the later phlyax vase, are found all over the West. As phlyax comedy was, according to Athenaeus, one variation among many similar types of ribald comedy,[50] so the phlyax vases were one among many similar types of comic vases.

Whether or not an evolution can be traced between ritual or performative events portrayed on the black-figure vases in question and theater proper, as it appears on the phlyax vases, is uncertain. As Osborne cautions, there is no straightforward connection between patterned dances on black-figure comic vases and comic performance itself.[51] Nevertheless, the broad spectrum of comic images on vases helps put into perspective both the unremarkable choice of the South Italians and Sicilians to develop their own variant of funny vases, and their remarkable interest in presenting specifically theatrical moments.

5.4 Attic Comedy in the West

Given the ubiquity of comic vases of various types throughout the Mediterranean world and the commonalities among them, it is perhaps not surprising that the western Greeks adopted a variant for itself and that the phlyax image and type became so quickly popular and was so frequently reproduced in South Italy and Sicily. Yet, unlike some of the other types of comic vases, vases in the phlyax category almost always insist on a marked theatricality, even metatheatricality, with stage, or costume, or mask, clearly expressed. This emphasis on the moment of performance distinguishes them, not only from the other comic vases among which they otherwise belong, but also from the Athenian theatrical vases which usually present actors offstage or together with

---

[49] See n. 45.   [50] See the quotation from Athenaeus on p. 175.   [51] Osborne (2008).

Dionysus in celebration or in thanks following a victory.[52] This marked theatricality has elicited an almost unanimous response among scholars to try to identify *which* or *what kind* of play the vases or vase represents.[53] Marcello Gigante and C. W. Dearden both argue that the vases may represent more than one tradition of theater, or a blended tradition made up of both local and imported plays. This conclusion is also the one to which my efforts have brought me, with the added specification that the key unifying feature of the vases is this very emphasis on performance, that is, on the moment of setting a play, farce, or spoof on stage. The substance of the production may range from imported Athenian to local spoof, as I argue below, but in all cases the vases refer to the moment of performance, rather than to a specific text or comic idea itself.

Although my focus is on the Sicilian, and by extension Paestan, vases, I begin here with a discussion of some Apulian vases, since these are the ones which have received most attention in scholarship and since many of these come from a relatively early period. As noted in the review of scholarship on the question in 5.2, it is from among these vases, loosely grouped under the category Apulian, that most clear evidence for the influence of Attic comedy, in particular Aristophanes, has been found.

Workshops at Metapontum, Heraclea-Policoro, in the non-Greek centers of Apulia, and at Tarentum itself seem to have produced many vases, and among these are some painted with phlyax scenes and some with scenes of tragedy. The earliest vases were very much influenced by Athenian models and similar in style to each other, and, moreover, as Carpenter has pointed out, "Attic red-figure vases dated to the fifth century B.C.E. have been found at 40 Italic sites in Apulia as well as at Taranto."[54] Nevertheless, as Trendall writes, "It was not long before the two fabrics developed clearly defined styles of their own."[55] Indeed, by the end of the fifth century, as Robinson notes, Tarentine pottery was available in central, non-Greek Apulia.[56] As early as the sixth century, moreover, local kilns in non-Greek Basilicata began producing terracottas, and increasingly Italic workshops have been identified throughout non-Greek Apulia and

---

[52] See Csapo (2010) 1–37. An important exception is the fragment of the Athenian krater, found in Olbia Pontica and depicting tragic chorusmen and musicians performing, in the Kiev Archaeological Museum of the Institute of Archaeology (AM 1097/5219) discussed in Braund and Hall (2015).

[53] With the exception of Beare (1954), who argues that the vases do not represent performance at all. See Csapo (1986) 388 n. 26 on the debate between Webster and Beare.

[54] Carpenter (2009) 30; Trendall (1991) 217–8. Contra: Green (1991) 50–1.

[55] Trendall (1991) 217–8.   [56] Robinson (1990) 264.

Basilicata.[57] In the fourth century, Adamesteanu argues, the wave of encroaching Greek control into the hinterland began to be reversed and native settlements become increasingly strong and seem to push back against the Greeks. This fourth-century date, perhaps not entirely coincidentally, corresponds to the beginnings of the phlyax vase phenomenon in the area.

The rising dominance of the Italics may have worked hand in hand with cultural connections with Athens. Towards the close of the Peloponnesian War, when the Athenian expedition set out on their disastrous expedition for Sicily, they paused on the way along the coast of Messapia where they received assistance from Metaponto, Thurii, and the local Messapians (Thuc. 7.33.3–4). It was prisoners from this same expedition whom Plutarch immortalized by claiming that they won their freedom from the Syracusans by reciting Euripides (Plut. *Vit. Nic.* 29.2), and, in Thucydides' tale of landing on the coast of Messapia, we might have a glimpse into one meeting between many Athenians, presumably eager to please, and many Italiotes and Italics in the generation before the comic and dramatic vases of Apulia become so prominent in the art-historical record. Not long before, Thurii, a nominally Panhellenic, but essentially Athenian settlement, counting Herodotus among its citizens, had been founded just south of Sybaris. Carpenter has recently pointed out that evidence for the spread of red-figure pottery does not prove that relations improved between the Tarentines and the Italic peoples towards the end of the fifth century and he argues that the Italic peoples might have had direct contact with Athens, rather than Tarentum.[58]

The Doric cities of the Gulf of Taranto, however, were resistant to the encroachment of Athens. Taras, in particular, founded by Sparta, was hostile towards Athens and hostility seems to have extended more broadly between Doric cities and those affiliated with Athens. Taras later had good relations with Dionysius I and Syracuse, whereas Thurii was later attacked by Dionysius I of Syracuse.[59] In his efforts to control Apulia, as well as the markets in the region of present-day Albania that could be reached by sea setting out from the coast of Apulia, Dionysius made friends with native

---

[57] Adamesteanu (1990); Robinson (1990) 252 on the Xenon group of vases: "The vases are most frequently met in tombs of the second half of the 4th century BC. This was a time when an explosion of Tarentine culture seems to have been taking place in native Apulia, to judge from the enormous increase of Italiote red-figure and Gnathia pottery in tombs, and the likelihood that workshops of both fabrics were established in native centres at around the same date."

[58] Carpenter (2009) 28. See discussion of Thurii in chapter 2, p. 44.

[59] De Sensi Sestito (2002) 393. In 389, Dionysius' general Leptines fought with the Lucanians against Thurii.

groups.[60] Likewise, he granted Italiots autonomy as "a tool in assuring his control over the affairs of Magna Graecia."[61] Thus various non-Greeks of this region may have found themselves courted by both the Athenian and the Doric powers in the region. Whether the Athenians and the Syracusans regaled their Italic allies with comic and tragic performances and recitations, we cannot know for sure, but it is likely that there were many opportunities for this kind of cultural exchange. Dionysius I, looking back at the successful theater propaganda techniques used by Hieron I before him might have promoted this kind of exchange. He is credited with the success of the red-figure vase trade elsewhere in the region and for creating the conditions for artisans to travel.[62] As Robinson warns, however, politics often provide illusory and misleading leads for understanding the spread of cultural production.[63]

Political and historical figures, unfortunately, appear more clearly in the fragmentary record than those of literary and dramatic figures. Just as there are no mentions of Aristophanes or any other Athenian comic playwright in the fragmentary literature that survives from Tarentum and the Achaean colonies to the south or in later ancient scholars discussing this region at this time, there is no specific mention of the Sicilian Epicharmus or Sophron early in the fourth century.[64] However, by the beginning of the next century, Rhinthon, who worked in Tarentum, is associated with Syracuse. Moreover, a few generations later, Ennius of Tarentum wrote a long poem on Epicharmus.[65] The Doric tradition, if it had lapsed in fifth- and fourth-century Tarentum, was, it appears, reappropriated by the third century. It may be that, despite the hotbed of comic production in Athens, Tarentines did not exclusively watch Athenian comedy. Indeed, given the

---

[60] Relations between the Italic peoples and Tarentum, however, were often strained and sometimes violent, Carpenter (2009) 113; Hdt. 7.170; Paus. 10.10.6, 10.13.10; Thuc. 6.44, 7.33; Strabo 6.3.4.

[61] Sanders (2002) 478 and *passim.*

[62] Ceka (2002) 77–80, where Ceka suggests (80) that not only vase-painters but other artisans profited from the trade routes opened by Dionysius I; d'Andria (2002) 127–8 notes that the chronology of red-figure vase-painters in Epidamnos corresponds with the presence of Dionysius I in the Adriatic.

[63] Robinson (1990) 264.

[64] The *Life of Aristophanes* does record that Plato sent a copy of Aristophanes to Dionysius I of Sicily to teach him about the government of Athens (*PCG* 3.2, Test. 1. 40). One might interpret this anecdote in a straightforward way to mean that, although the tyrant Dionysius was a successful contestant at the theatrical Lenaia at Athens, he was not familiar with Aristophanes. The note is so ridiculous, though, that it is more likely to be an entertaining story about the cheekiness of Athenians in their dealings with tyrants. On Dionysius I, the theater, and Plato, see the two essays in Bosher (2012a) by Duncan (2012) and Monoson (2012) respectively.

[65] See discussion on pp. 80–2 on Epicharmus.

antagonistic relationship between Tarentum and Metapontum/Thurii, it is tempting to imagine that the two cities might not have always enjoyed the same plays (the former might have been better pleased by plays or skits that would buttress the Doric world, and the latter by Athenian imports). Such speculation is rendered even more problematic, however, by the non-Greek, Italian markets for theatrical vases. As the argument about the referent of the vases has in earlier discussions concentrated on interpretation of the vases themselves, I consider below two important Apulian examples in greater detail.

5.5 Würzburg Telephos

As noted above, Csapo and Taplin have demonstrated that the Würzburg Telephos vase of ca 370 depicts a scene from Aristophanes' *Thesmophoriazusae.*[66] Trendall and Cambitoglou attributed the vase to the Schiller Painter, a follower of the Tarporley Painter.[67] As with other vase-painters classed as followers of the Tarporley Painter and indeed the Tarporley Painter himself, most of the vases attributed to the Schiller Painter are on Dionysiac themes.[68] As Trendall notes, other vase-painters, who also follow Tarporley, sometimes also depict "Oscan warriors, either in battle or in a domestic setting, and scenes from phlyax plays."[69] This group of vase-painters was, it seems, very interested in depicting the theater and the associated Dionysiac world, but also, rather strikingly, Italic traditions and non-Greek people.

It is difficult to be sure whether the images were painted for an Italiote or Italic market in the first instance. Most of the Schiller Painter's vases are without provenance, and are now housed in museums throughout Europe and America. At least three of his vases, however, do have findspots, one from the Etruscan city of Pontecagnano, near Paestum (Pontecagnano 3762, from T 784), one from Crispiano (Taranto 6242) in the hinterland of Taranto, and one from Pisticci (Taranto 6954). Without putting too much emphasis on this very meager evidence, it is curious to note that the only vases with provenance data by this artist come from outside major

---

[66] See above p. 177. Austin and Olson (2004) lxxv–lxxvii point out some discrepancies between the image and the play itself, arguing that "this is something other than a simple straightforward depiction of a South Italian theatrical performance."

[67] Trendall and Cambitoglou (1978) 65.

[68] See Trendall and Cambitoglou (1978) 63. See Carpenter (2009) for a summary of the importance and ubiquity of Dionysus on Apulian red-figure.

[69] Trendall and Cambitoglou (1978) 63.

Greek settlements. As has been extensively examined, Dionysus was well represented in Etruscan iconography and on Greek pottery from Etruscan sites; indeed the dramatic increase in production of Attic Dionysus and *thiasos* vases has been linked to demand from the Etruscan market.[70] The cult of Dionysus (*bakchoi* or *sectatores Liberi Patris*) was already a significant part of life in the early Greek colony of Cumae, and throughout Campania. T. P. Wiseman has shown, moreover, that the mythological world of Dionysus was very much alive among non-Greek cultures of Italy and pre-literary theatrical forms are also well attested in the iconographic material.[71] Whether the Würzburg Telephos itself was owned by a western Greek or by one of his non-Greek neighbors we shall never know, but its connection to the world of Dionysus would perhaps have made it fit well in either place.

Not only the general Dionysiac association of an Attic Old Comedy play, but the subject of Telephos and the depiction of this scene from the myth in particular are likely to have been familiar to audiences in the West. First, the myth of Telephos seems to have been popular and well known in the West. A number of playwrights wrote a play by the name *Telephos*,[72] in particular, Epicharmus' contemporary, the Syracusan comic playwright Deinolochus, and, from several generations later, the Tarentine and Sicilian Rhinthon. Deinolochus' play survives only in a list of titles preserved in a papyrus from Oxyrhynchus, and in two brief notes about vocabulary in Athenaeus and Antiattes.[73] The only evidence for Rhinthon's *Telephos* is Pollux's note that Rhinthon used the word, κράββατον, *krābbaton*, "couch or mattress."[74] The word *krābbatos* appears rarely until later Greek texts, and, if its cognate in Latin, *grabatus*, maintains the same register it is a rough word for a lowly kind of bedding (Ver.

---

[70] Isler-Kerényi (2009) 64; Carpenter (1986) 35.

[71] Wiseman (2000), e.g. 286: "complex iconographic evidence presented here indicates, I think, a common fourth-century culture of mimetic representation extending far beyond the Greek cities of Southern Italy and into Etruria and Latium." See also Robinson (2004) 204–6.

[72] A play by the name *Telephos* was written by Aeschylus, Sophocles, Euripides, Iophon, Agathon, Cleophon, Moschion, Ennius, and Accius (K-A, p. 180).

[73] Cf. K.-A. Deinolochus Test. 3: *POxy.* 2659 fr. 2 col. Ii; Deinolochus fr. 6: Athenaeus III, p. 111 C; Deinolochus fr. 7: Antiattikistes, p. 112, 28. Curiously, Athenaeus' note records a Messapian term for bread, ἄρτος, artos, followed by a note that Deinolochus used the Dorian words πανία, pania, with the stress on the penultimate syllable ("satiety") *and* πάνια, pania, with the stress on the first syllable ("filling, satisfying"), in his *Telephos* as did Blaisos in *Mesotribai* and Rhinthon in the *Amphitryon*, and that the Romans then adopted πᾶνα for bread, presumably implying an etymological link between all these words. I do not think that Athenaeus' juxtaposition of the Messapian word and the words of the West Greek comic poets can suggest a borrowing of Messapian dialect by the poets, but I would be delighted to be proven wrong.

[74] *PCG* Rhinthon fr. 9: Pollux X.35. Gigante (1966) 90–1 suggests that Rhinthon's play includes the same moment as that parodically represented on the Telephos vase.

Mor. 5; Lucilius 251). It is perhaps not completely irrelevant that rough bedding is depicted on some phlyax vases, and the world conjured up by comic phlyax characters is often one of a transient and traveling lifestyle.[75] There is not, however, enough text remaining to make specific connections between the vase and the plays by Deinolochus or Rhinthon, but, at least, as both Csapo and Taplin note, the evidence of Telephos plays by Deinolochus and Rhinthon suggests that the myth, in a comic form, would have been readily accessible to western audiences. This familiarity is further demonstrated by depictions of the myth or perhaps an unidentified tragedy about Telephos on South Italian and Attic vases which are strikingly similar to the image on the Würzburg Telephos.[76]

Secondly, the festival of the Thesmophoria in celebration of Demeter, which is the setting of Aristophanes' play, was not foreign to western Greek settlements. Demeter was enormously important in Sicilian myth, religion, and, by way of the Deinomenids, fifth-century politics.[77] Indeed, the Thesmophoria was the "principal festival of the Syracusans" and celebrated for ten days in the city. White suggests, moreover, that elements of the festival were very similar to those at Athens.[78] Although the cults of Tarentum are difficult to identify with great precision because of meager evidence, there does seem to have been a cult of Demeter and Kore, with remains in the Contrada Pizzone necropolis that have yielded finds very similar to those excavated at Sicilian cult sites.[79] Moreover, Hinz has gathered evidence for Demeter cults or cults closely related in Messapia and Lucania, suggesting that even non-Greeks, living far from Greek centers, are likely to have had excellent reference points from which to understand Aristophanes' play.[80] Thus, western audiences would have been well prepared to appreciate the parody in Aristophanes' play, both of the festival, and of the myth of Telephos.

[75] For example, the following four vases seem to depict bedrolls together with other baggage: Malibu, J. Paul Getty Museum 86.AE.412; Moscow, Pushkin Museum 735 (Green (2012) revised Trendall's identification of a shield as a bedroll); London 1849.6-20.13 (F 151); Bari 2970, from Bitonto. See Gigante (1971) 84–5, n. 19, for some notes on the peculiarities of Rhinthon's dialect, including the word Καλαβρία, Calabria, "the Messapian region." Although the word *krābbaton* is rare, it also occurs in a play by the comic playwright Crito entitled *Messenia*. The few remaining titles of Crito's plays (*Aitolian, Ephesians, Messenia*) and a brief fragment of the *Philopragmon* in which he characterizes a Phoenician as a parasite suggest that Crito delighted in satirizing regional characters. Perhaps the word, which was repudiated as not Attic by Phryn. 44, was in use in the Doric dialect of Messenia as well as the Doric of Rhinthon.

[76] For discussion and examples, see Taplin (2007) 205–10; Taplin (1987) 103.

[77] See Chapter 3 for a full discussion of the connection between Demeter and theater in Syracuse. Cf. Hinz (1998) 55–167.

[78] White (1963) 126. See also Chapter 3.   [79] Lippolis (1982); Hinz (1998) 182–7.

[80] Hinz (1998) 194–202.

Thirdly, as thoroughly examined by Gigante half a century ago, the tradition of Doric *hilarotragoidia* made famous or perhaps invented by Rhinthon seems to be based on a deep and extensive knowledge of Euripides. Since it is unlikely that Rhinthon would have been popular if his audience was unfamiliar with the Euripides parodied, it seems likely that Tarentines and non-Greek people in nearby cities and towns alike would have been well acquainted with Euripides. Thus, the parodies of Euripides in the latter half of *Thesmophoriazusae* would, presumably, have been accessible to many in an audience in this region.

This vase, therefore, seems to represent an Athenian play particularly well suited to local festivals and cult and in tune with local theater. Aristophanes' *Thesmophoriazusae* might have been staged in South Italy, as Aeschylus' *Persians* was staged in Syracuse 100 years before, because it engaged the interests of local audiences, Greek or not, and because it fit into the tradition of theater already in place. Thus, the vase may mark not so much a wave of encroaching Athenian comedy taking the West by surprise, but rather one example of an Athenian comedy that was similar to western Greek comedy, and appealed to western taste.

In sum, I do not mean to argue in the case of the Würzburg Telephos, nor for most of the other vases discussed below, that the association with Aristophanes is mistaken. In several of these cases, Aristophanes does seem to be a very likely referent. Nevertheless, whether Aristophanes or no, we can in all cases see how the comedies represented on the vases would fit particularly well into the traditions of South Italian and Sicilian mime and comedy and into the wider dramatic and cultural context.

5.6   The "*Choregoi*"

Among the vases known for many generations, several have been considered good evidence for the influence of Old Comedy in the West. Among these, the Paestan Phrynis and Pyronides vase was long ago thought by Webster to represent Attic comedy.[81] Likewise, an Apulian calyx-krater, known as the New York Goose vase (Figure 5.11), on which phrases apparently in Attic Greek emanate from the mouths of the three comic actors, is often thought to represent an Attic drama.[82] As Taplin points out,

---

[81]   Webster (1978) 45.

[82]   *PhV* 84 Apulian calyx-krater attributed to Tarporley Painter, New York, Metropolitan Museum of Art 24.97.104, *RVAp* 46, 3. Dearden (2012) 283–4; Taplin (2012) 249; Gigante (1966) 105–6.

it is notable that when the vases from Apulia have inscriptions, these are not in Tarentine or even a Doric dialect, but appear to be in Attic, or at least a dialect compatible with Attic.[83]

Dialect, however, may not settle the problem of which drama the vases depict. There are two reasons for this: first, the tragedy regularly parodied by Rhinthon was that of Euripides and, as Cassio has noted, the fragments of Rhinthon's comedy that seem to be atticized in dialect may in fact be genuine: he might have written in Attic.[84] This argument might be extended to any parody of Attic tragedy: western Greek comic writers might have chosen Attic when they parodied Attic tragedy. Indeed, quite a few Sicilian writers, including poets of New Comedy, adopted Attic in their writing. Philemon of Syracuse and Alexis of Thurii, for example, moved to Athens and seem to have had successful careers composing plays in Attic dialect.[85] As Hordern notes, the mime tradition in the West (Epicharmus, Sophron, Herodas, Theocritus) is somewhat exceptional for its use of regional Doric dialects.[86] On the one hand, given that South Italian and Sicilian writers frequently adopted Attic dialect, it may be possible to put too much emphasis on the Attic dialect on some of the vases; on the other hand, the choice of a non-Doric dialect does suggest that these scenes were not extracted from a comedy or mime written in Doric.

If the dialect is, however, a signal of Attic drama on both of these vases (the Attic Greek and the name labels of Phrynis and Pyronides respectively) then it seems to be an explicit one: modern scholars are not, in these cases, inferring a relationship to a drama presented in Attic from some kind of assumed gesture or quirk of depiction, but rather reading labels which have been added for guidance. In both the case of the New York Goose vase (Figure 5.11) and the Phrynis and Pyronides vase, the vase-painters overtly identify the images with text. In the first case, the two famous Athenian performers are identified by the labels and in the second the play is identified as acted in Attic Greek. It is not certain that we should read these vases, together with the Würzburg Telephos, back onto the other couple of hundred phlyax vases as evidence that the comic phlyax images as a type represent Attic comedy. We might equally infer that the marked and labeled vases are to be understood as Athenian drama or, indeed, spoofs on Athenian drama, as distinct from the others.

---

[83] Taplin (2012) 227–8; see also Taplin (1993) 41–2.   [84] Cassio (2001) 435.

[85] Cf. Taplin (2012) 228, who makes this point to support the opposite argument that western Greek comedy was essentially Attic.

[86] Hordern (2004) 11.

Two comic figures on the "*Choregoi*" vase are labeled "χορηγός", *choregos*, with the Attic eta instead of the alpha one would expect in Doric dialect. Does this point in the direction of an Attic comedy? In what follows I review Oliver Taplin's extensive and ground-breaking interpretation of the vase, and, building on that interpretation, I propose that this image reflects a Sicilian spoof on Athenian theater.

Taplin notes that a "substantial argument" against the hypothesis that the phlyax vases represent Athenian comedy is that the vases show no trace of the chorus that was so prominent both in Old Comedy and on earlier theatrical comic vases, particularly those from Athens.[87] In 1989, however, an Apulian bell-krater painted with an unknown comedy, and, perhaps, a chorus, was sold in New York (Figure 5.1).[88] Trendall published it as the "*Choregoi*" and Taplin used the vase to strengthen the argument that the phlyax vases of Southern Italy and Sicily depict Athenian comedies.[89]

He begins with the label χορηγός, *choregos*, above the figure in the middle and the one on the right. Trendall understands *choregos* as "chorus-leader." However, Taplin objects that the word never appears in comedy (it is only in Alcman and later high lyric contexts, except in an imitation of a Spartan lyric at the end of Aristophanes' *Lysistrata*), and that the chorus does not usually appear on the Athenian *skene* (they are confined to the orchestra).[90] He argues instead that the labels refer to the official duty of that peculiarly Athenian institution for funding, among other things, the theater. The chorus members would be citizens performing the duty of *choregos* and therefore labeled *choregoi*.

The *choregoi* then, represent two halves of a chorus, a white-haired older half and a dark-haired younger half. These halves would be in opposition to each other, an agonistic structure paralleled, for example, in the choruses of old men and old women of Aristophanes' *Lysistrata*. Two competing "choruses" of angels would make the play intensely metatheatrical, and

---

[87] Taplin (1987) 107. Cf. Taplin (1993) 75–8 in which he reviews other possible representations of choruses. Csapo (2010) 74–6 argues that choruses are no longer as interesting in the fourth century in general and their absence on South Italian and Sicilian vases, as distinct from the sixth- and fifth-century Athenian vases, represents a general shift in the wider Greek world away from the chorus and a growing fascination with the actor.

[88] Trendall (1991) 8: "They [the *choregoi*] are presumably the two leaders of the semi-chorus." The "*Choregoi*" was bought in 1989 by Lawrence and Barbara Fleischman (Taplin (1993) 55).

[89] Taplin (1993). Cf. his analysis of Attic tragedy represented on South Italian pots, Taplin (1998, 2007).

[90] On the place of the chorus in the orchestra, cf. for example, Sifakis (1962) 39: "The orchestra is always considered the appropriate place for the chorus." And he dismisses the "other modern view that the chorus, perhaps diminished in number, went on to the high stage [in the Hellenistic period]..."

Taplin adduces a number of examples of other Athenian plays which seem to have a similarly self-referential approach: Kratinos' Διδασκαλίαι, Didaskaliai ("Stage Productions"), Aristophanes' Δράματα, Dramata ("Dramas"), and Phrynichos' Μοῦσαι, Mousai ("Muses") and Τραγωιδοῖ Tragoidoi ("Tragic Actors" or "Tragedians").

He then turns to the tragic and comic figures, labeled Aegisthus and Pyrrhias respectively. After reviewing all other phlyax vases which have figures who may be somewhat parallel to the puzzling Aegisthus figure on the far left of the vase, Taplin concludes that Aesgisthus must be "representative of tragedy." If Aegisthus stands for tragedy, then the slave Pyrrhias stands for comedy (and this symbolic role accounts for his statuesque pose). This kind of competition between the two genres would have been natural in Athens, where comedy and tragedy shared the same festival, and comedy often made fun of tragedy.

In sum, the opposition of tragedy and comedy was familiar at Athens.[91] The liturgy (act of public benefaction) known as the *choregia*, moreover, was instituted at Athens, and not, it seems, anywhere else in the Greek world.[92] Both the use of the term *choregos* and the opposition of tragedy and comedy imply a metatheatrical approach, which was fairly common in Athenian comedy. This can be seen, as Taplin writes, in the addresses to the audience, disguise and dressing-up scenes, and metatheatrical business with the *aulos*-players. Thus, Taplin concludes that "the comedy captured here must surely be Athenian."[93] His argument is persuasive.

Some of the details Taplin mentions, however, might also point away from an Athenian source and towards a more local one. It is the incongruous absence of the word *choregos* in Aristophanes' plays which led him to suggest that the *choregos/i* were two Athenian producers, one of comedy and the other of tragedy, probably themselves representing two whole choruses of *choregoi* in some sort of agonistic structure. Pollux, however, notes that, unlike Aristophanes, the Sicilian Epicharmus did usually use the word *choregos* in his plays.[94] In his play *Odysseus Automolos* and perhaps also in *Harpagai* he seems to have used it to mean *didaskalos*, i.e. director/ writer. If this meaning of the term is applied to the vase labels, instead of two producers having an argument as Taplin suggests, we might imagine that the labels identify two directors, one of comedy and one of tragedy. This could explain the awkward stance of the other two characters, Pyrrhias and Aegisthus. If his "director" is making him rehearse a part, Pyrrhias

---

[91] Taplin (1986). [92] Wilson (2000). [93] Taplin (1993) 63.
[94] Pollux IX.41.42. Cf. Hesychius 631–2.

might comically adopt an exaggerated declamatory pose facing directly forward and gesticulating.[95] Likewise, the puzzled look of the tragic figure might mean that he is trying to understand acting directions which the older *choregos* is giving him.[96]

Taplin's interpretation of the two figures as leaders of a chorus is, as he notes himself, difficult because they are on stage, whereas Athenian comic and tragic choruses were confined to the orchestra. We know very little, however, about the choruses of Epicharmus; it has been proven neither that he used a chorus, nor that he did not.[97] Later Doric mime traditions appear not to have had a chorus. If Epicharmus did, moreover, we have no reason to think that it would have been relegated strictly to the orchestra. There is no evidence for the formalities of chorus placement in early western theaters, or, more particularly, for the plays of Epicharmus; in fact, there is no particular reason to believe that there were any formalities at all. The small size of the orchestra in the first trapezoidal theater at Syracuse suggests to Anti and Polacco that Epicharmus had no chorus.[98] However, since Aeschylus' plays, performed at the same time and probably in the same place, did have a chorus, the small orchestra may indicate not the absence of a chorus, but its placement on the stage.[99] At the very least, it suggests that the formal divisions of stage and orchestra were not so clearly defined in Syracuse, and thus that there may have been more freedom of movement for both actors and chorus. Even if Epicharmus did not regularly make use of a chorus, it is not inconceivable that he would have parodied the Athenian chorus, which would have been strikingly present in the plays of Aeschylus imported with much fanfare by Hieron, since Epicharmus parodied so much else in the daily life and culture of Syracuse. Moreover, if these *choregoi* are parodies, it is reasonable that they should appear on stage; for they would not then be a standard choral backdrop, but an integral part of the plot. If the play is in mockery of Aeschylus, or Attic tragedy, then the Attic form of *choregos*, as it appears on the vase, rather than the Doric *choregos*, is perhaps not so out of place. Indeed, Rhinthon,

---

[95] Cf. Green (2003) 121, who interprets the character labeled Pyrrhias as a parody of an archon choosing between two plays in a *proagon*. The slave's name, Pyrrhias, seems an odd choice for an archon, and the neat parallel of tragedy vs. comedy is undermined if Pyrrhias does not represent comedy in counterpoint to the tragic Aegisthus.

[96] Taplin (1993) 59 notes how difficult it is to interpret the expression on Aegisthus' face.

[97] Cf. Chapter 3 for a review of arguments about the presence of a chorus in Epicharmus.

[98] Polacco and Anti (1981/1990) 166. Cf. below (266) for dissenting views about Polacco and Anti's reconstruction of the early phases of the large theater at Syracuse. On the small size of the *orchestrai* of Sicilian theaters in general, see Chapter 6.

[99] On the number of chorus members in Aeschylus, cf. Fitton Brown (1957).

who writes in Tarentum but several generations after the painting of this vase, may have employed exactly this kind of mixed dialect. The few remaining fragments of Rhinthon's work include Atticisms which, as Cassio notes, may remain from his parody of Attic tragedy. The bizarre conjunction of a tragic hero, a comic slave, and two chorus-members on the same stage is distinctly metatheatrical, as Taplin noted, and suggests that the play may have been some sort of metatheatrical farce and comedy. Perhaps, then, in the hands of Epicharmus, it would be a parody not only of tragedy and comedy, as Taplin suggests, but also of the Attic "chorus" itself, whose members seem to play an equal role on this eclectic stage.

Taplin suggests that the differing hair colors of the two *choregoi* mark two halves of a chorus. If this is so, the phlyax vases may repeatedly show choruses, for there are a large number of them with two similar figures, one with dark and one with white hair.[100] In a few cases, however, these figures are named specifically, which is an impossible treatment of a generic chorus member. One might instead imagine the two figures as recurring comic characters, or comic types, who get up to trouble in various guises in various plays.[101] They might function as a chorus in a limited way, if they turn up repeatedly in different plays; on the other hand, their frequent presence, often alone on stage, suggests that they may play more central roles. On this view, then, the figures are characters on stage in the role of *choregoi* – either directors as Epicharmus seems to have meant, directing an assortment of Athenian dramatic stereotypes, or parodying Athenian *choregoi* and the Athenian system of *choregia* more directly.

Taplin notes the agonistic structure of what he identifies as the two hemichoruses and adduces a number of other examples in Athenian comedy to show how a play such as this would have suited the general mood of Athenian comedy. But the origin of this sort of "agōn" may have been not Athens, but Syracuse. For it seems possible that Epicharmus' development of the "agōn" in the play *Logos kai Logina* was copied by Aristophanes in the contest between the Just and Unjust arguments in *Clouds*.[102] An agonistic exchange between tragedy and comedy would be at least as likely in Epicharmus' plays as in those of Aristophanes.

---

[100] Vases with a light- and dark-haired comic actor, who seem to form a pair, are plentiful, e.g. Trendall (1967b) 18, 34, 37, 45 pl. 2, 58 pl. 3b, 59 pl. 4a, 84. The masks are not necessarily exactly the same from vase to vase, but the pattern of a light-haired and dark-haired duo seems fairly common.

[101] Green (2003) 120–4 traces the changing roles of the character wearing the mask of the character Pyrrhias on the "*Choregoi*" vase, noting that he is called Xanthias on another vase (London F 151), and seems to play various roles on different vases.

[102] Herington (1967) 74.

Without more information about the two *choregoi* represented on the vase, it is impossible to be certain what their role is. However, Epicharmus' work, slight and fragmentary as the remains are, seems to offer a fairly likely source for these two characters. If Epicharmus is the source, the figures may be the *choregoi* – directors whom he discusses in his plays, or they may be a parody of the choruses of Aristophanes or Athenian choruses more generally. They may also, on this already hybrid stage of tragedy and comedy, be some conflation of both.[103]

Secondly, the confrontation of tragedy and comedy, or parody of tragedy in comedy, seems to have appealed to Epicharmus just as it did to Aristophanes, and he made fun of Aeschylus in particular. A scholiast to the *Eumenides*, for example, noted that Epicharmus made particular fun of Aeschylus' use of the word τιμαλφούμενον.[104] Aeschylus, moreover, famously came to Syracuse and put on his *Persians*. Epicharmus wrote a *Persians* of his own, perhaps a parody of Aeschylus' version. Only a few words survive from the play of Epicharmus. One of these, σκωλοβατίζειν, *skolobatizein*, apparently means "to walk on stilts."[105] If the short stumpy stature of comic characters on vases was likewise a feature of characters on stage, and was constrasted on stage, as on the pots, to the tall, elegant figures of tragedy, then "stilt-walking" might have to do with a comic character trying, comically, to redress the imbalance in height. The comedian on this vase, Pyrrhias, seems to have solved the problem by standing on a basket.

Finally, the metatheater implied by the confrontation between tragedy and comedy, and by the presence of the *choregoi* would not be any more peculiar in Epicharmus' plays than it would be in those of Aristophanes. In addition to mocking Aeschylus, and using the word *choregos*, we know that in his play *Logos kai Logina*, he referred to the alterations in the use of the iambic meter made by another playwright, Aristoxenus.[106]

Thus, on this reading, the vase might also represent themes we expect from the plays of Epicharmus, or the tradition of parodying Attic tragedy picked up and perhaps brought to a new level of perfection by Rhinthon. By this comparison all I mean to show is that the themes which can be identified that might associate the vase with Attic theater can also point back to the early theater of Epicharmus in Syracuse or forward to the later

---

[103] See Dearden (1999) 243 for a similar argument that the image is self-referential: Aegisthus is the playwright, Pyrrhias the auctioneer, and the two *choregoi* are competing for the right to fund the performance.

[104] *timalphoumenon*, "honored." See Schol. M on Aeschylus' *Eumenides* 626 (*PCG* I, Epicharmus Test. 221) and the longer discussions above on pp. 18 and 84.

[105] Etymologicum Genuinum, s.v. a 1283 (*PCG* I Epich. Test. 111).   [106] Epicharmus *PCG* I77.

theater of Rhinthon in Tarentum and Syracuse. I think this might help to explain the ready acceptance of Aristophanes in the late fifth and early fourth centuries.

Evaluating the social conditions which must have obtained in South Italy for the successful dissemination of Athenian drama, Taplin remarks that: "even if the relatively surface topicality is cut or altered, the comedies [of Aristophanes] still demand considerable cross-cultural understanding from their audiences. These plays simply would not be accessible to narrow-minded provincials with an undeveloped sense of cultural and political relativity."[107] He suggests that we should consider the wealth and literary prowess of western Greek cities such as Syracuse in order to understand how they were able to appreciate Aristophanes' comedies. I would like to take this argument one step further to suggest that western audiences, including Daunians, Peucetians, Messapians, and Tarentines, were not only generally cultivated, but that, perhaps drawing on the much earlier tradition of Epicharmus, they had grown accustomed to a sophisticated tradition of comic theater, specifically, which prepared them for the urbane wit of Aristophanes.

5.7   Sicily and Paestum

In this section, I turn from the better-studied Apulian vases to look more closely at Sicilian and, by extension, Paestan vases. The earliest red-figure painting in Sicily has been dated to the late fifth century, when, as Trendall points out, it might have suddenly become more difficult to import red-figure vases from hostile Athens. Early fourth-century Sicilian workshops were scattered: they seem to have been located at Syracuse and Himera, and some vases by a single painter have been found at various sites in the south of the island, including Agrigento, Vassallaggi, and Selinunte.[108] Through stylistic analysis, Trendall demonstrated that the Paestan tradition of red-figure vase painting was influenced at its outset by Sicilian vase-painters, including most importantly for the tradition of comic vases, the Dirce Painter. Trendall suggests that followers of the Dirce Painter emigrated to Campania in 370–360, perhaps in order to escape the social and political upheaval following the death of Dionysius I in 367.[109] His death might also

---

[107] Taplin (1993) 96–7.   [108] Trendall (1967a) 30.

[109] More recently, this theory has been called into question, the migration of vase-painters being explained instead by a particularly strong commercial relationship between Sicily and Campania under Dionysius I: see more recently Barresi (2013) 212.

have heralded steep cuts in funding for theatrical production and, by extension, a reduced market for vase paintings of Dionysiac and theatrical subjects. In this same period, the middle of the fourth century, there is a gap in comic painting from Sicily. It is not until the 340s that phlyax paintings again appear in Sicily, and this time Trendall postulates an influence back from Campania on Sicilian artists. These vases, clustering in the decade from 340 to 330, are notable for their particularly clear representation of stages and dramatic scenes, rather than single actors in the company of Dionysus or other Dionysiac figures.[110] Some general characteristics of these vases may point to performance traditions associated with Epicharmus and also with Sophron. More specifically, some idiosyncracies of these vase paintings, notably their representation of women and female *aulos*-players, give clues about the fourth-century theater scene in Campania and Sicily.

Thematically, many of these vases are not incompatible with Epicharmus' comedies. The comic vase identified as the earliest of the Sicilian-Paestan tradition, for example, depicts Zeus leaning heavily on his cane, perhaps weighed down by the thunderbolt he carries in his left hand. He is flanked by a man, perhaps a slave, holding a wine flask and a basket of food, and by a piper wearing the mask of a hetaira.[111] As is the case with most phlyax vases, there is no clear play to which this image refers; it may even reflect an Attic comedy performed in Sicily. Nevertheless, as with the Apulian vases discussed above, the scene here seems to fit the type of play popularized by Epicharmus. Even in the pitifully small remains of Epicharmus, Zeus makes not infrequent appearances: in *Logos kai Logina* (*Argument and Argumentina*), he provides a feast; in *Muses* or *The Marriage of Hebe* he reserves a sturgeon for himself and his wife; and in a third, unidentified, play he performs a sacrifice.[112] In all these festive contexts, moreover, music would be appropriate, as would a slave carrying a wine-flask and offering of food.

The pipe-playing comic male actor masked as a hetaira, a figure who is striking in his own right, is also notable as belonging to a set of Campanian

---

[110] Although the comic vase traditions of Paestum and Sicily may be derivative of Apulian (Green (1991) 50, "it seems reasonably clear that the idea of painting such scenes came to them from Taranto"), the fragmented production sites in the Apulian region, together with the confused evidence for a major center of production in Tarentum, renders the family tree of vases a little less schematically clear.

[111] Madrid 11026: Trendall (1967b) *PhV* 53, num. 82, and Green (2012) 319 identify this mask as female.

[112] *PCG* 76, 1; 88, 2; 198. In *Trojans* he is described as dwelling on snowcapped Gargara and Mt. Ida, but this may simply be a reference to him in a speech rather than imply any appearance on stage (*PCG* 128).

vases all of which depict female pipe-players. Of the thirteen Campanian phlyax vases cited in *PhV* 2 and in *LCS*, three, and likely five, show women playing pipes.[113] Another example of a woman pipe-player appears on a second Sicilian vase, where she seems to be playing in a symposium context closely followed by a phlyax character (Lipari 18431).[114] These Sicilian and Campanian scenes may be compared with one, or arguably two, female pipe-players on extant Apulian phlyax vases.[115] On both Apulian vases, the female pipe-player is not the central figure, and in fact is studiously ignored by the comic characters represented. On the *Obeliaphoroi* ("Skewer-Carriers") vase, where the piper is unambiguously a woman, the comic phlyax figure closer to her looks away from her and back towards his companion phlyax character. She is, moreover, markedly smaller than the comic characters and perhaps meant to be in some perspective relationship or else to be of less importance than the two larger, self-involved comic figures. Likewise, on the Bari Pipers, two male pipers, in comic phlyax dress, dominate the stage and are the object of a third comic man's gaze. The piper who may perhaps be a woman crouches behind a tree out of sight.[116] Taplin has thoroughly discussed the implications for these figures in the context of Athenian drama, suggesting very persuasively that they might indicate the female pipe-players who sometimes accompanied performances both in Athens and among the western Greeks.[117] Of the latter he writes: "The comic vases (the 'phlyakes') reflect the activities of travelling players; and the *aulos*-players who accompanied

[113] Frankfurt α 2562; Rio de Janeiro 1500; Madrid 11026; Cambridge, Fitzwilliam Museum GR 29/1952 (I include in this list Cambridge, Fitzwilliam Museum GR 29/1952 which is given a place in *PhV* because of the comic mask hanging in the background); two further vases (Princeton 50–64 and Melbourne, National Gallery of Victoria D14/1973 (Figure 5.2)) probably also show female pipe-players, cf. Taplin (1993) 72; Taplin (1991) 33.

[114] Campanian calyx-krater, Lipari, Museo Archeologico Regionale Luigi Bernabò Brea 18431, from Lipari, t. 2515: Bernabò Brea, Cavalier, and Spigo 1994, 91 (workshop of the NYN Painter) 94, fig. 66.

[115] Certain female pipe-players on Apulian vase with *obeliaphoroi*: either in Leningrad 2074 [W. 1122] or in St. Petersburg Hermitage Museum, inv. 2074 [W. 1122]. Possible female pipe-player on Apulian vase: Bari, coll. of Contessa Malaguzzi-Valeri, no. 52. Several Apulian vases depict male phlyax characters playing the pipe (Syracuse (NY) University), *PhV* 118; Ruvo, Jatta coll. 1528, from Ruvo, *PhV* 137; Bari, coll. of Contessa Malaguzzi-Valeri, no. 52 (which has two male pipe-players and one of ambiguous gender), and at least one Paestan vase shows a male piper. Cf Taplin (1993) 70–1 and (1991) for discussions of Athenian vases, most of which depict male *auletes*. He also takes up South Italian and Sicilian vases, and the problem of references and metatheatrical references to *aulos*-players in Attic comedy.

[116] See Taplin (1993) 70–1 and (1991).

[117] On the particular significance of the *aulos* among the western Greeks, see Bellia (2014).

these troupes were sometimes women – and perhaps towards the later fourth-century they were usually women."[118]

Given the relationship identified by Trendall and Cambitoglou between Campanian and Sicilian vases (see above), the cluster of Sicilian and Campanian female auletrides might be considered together as a type, somewhat distinct from the Apulian tradition and perhaps the Athenian tradition, which is discussed by Taplin.[119] Unlike the female pipers on Apulian vases, who are not dominant characters in the scenes represented, the women on Campanian and Sicilian vases regularly upstage the other characters. Even though on the Madrid vase, Zeus has his back turned to the piper and seems to be moving towards the other male character, the piper is eye-catching and arguably dominates the scene because of the disjunction of female courtesan mask and very obvious male costume in every other respect. On the other Sicilian vase, the auletris travels at a lower level from the banqueters at the symposium, but she is closely followed by the comic actor and appears to be the focus of his attention. Among Campanian vases, the female pipers are similarly dominant. On the Melbourne vase (Figure 5.2), for example, both comic characters stare at the female piper, and one seems to be addressing her;[120] on the Rio vase (Figure 5.3), she takes center place between the fish-eater and another comic character who seems to be waving his arms at her;[121] on the Frankfurt vase, the phlyax character stares back at her over his shoulder.[122]

In sum, the relatively frequent appearance of female pipe-players on Campanian vases is reinforced by their dominant position in the scene. This pictorial evidence is not enough to suggest that the *aulos*-players were considered to be actors, but it does suggest that the vase-painters, at least, found female pipers to be important figures in comic performance contexts. This may, in turn, suggest that the performance traditions that developed or were adapted in Campania and perhaps in Sicily gave a more prominent position to the *aulos*-player (and female ones at that). This privileging of a musician, a non-actor, points us in the direction of shows and performances that were not strictly or formally full versions of plays, but rather more varied medleys in which the *aulos*-player at times

---

[118] Taplin (1991) 43.   [119] Taplin (1991); Taplin (1993) 70–1 and appendix II.

[120] Campanian bell-krater, Melbourne, National Gallery of Art D 14/1973: Trendall (1973) 222, num. 337b (Libation Painter).

[121] Campanian bell-krater, Rio de Janeiro, Museu Nacional 1500: Trendall (1967b) *PhV* 42–3, num. 56 (near to the Painter of New York GR 1000).

[122] Campanian bell-krater, Frankfurt, Museum für Vor- und Frühgeschichte α 2562: Trendall (1967b) *PhV* 31, num. 26 (Libation Painter).

Figure 5.2 Campanian bell-krater depicting a wreathed man bending forward towards a female flute player. Libation Painter. Melbourne, National Gallery of Victoria, Felton Bequest 1973 (D 14–1973). Third quarter of the fourth century BCE

Figure 5.3 Rio Fish Eater, Campanian bell-krater. Rio de Janeiro, Museu Nacional, 1500, 375–350 BCE

took a central position. The well-known Lipari acrobat vase (Lipari 18431, Figure 5.4) further suggests that sometimes these little acts could be performed in conjunction with a symposium.

In the same vein, a series of Sicilian and Paestan vases show apparently unmasked women together with comic phlyax actors: they are either the focus of the phlyax characters' attention, or, in fact, the women stand squarely on

Figure 5.4 Dionysus and two comic figures watching acrobat. Painter of Louvre K 240. Lipari, Museo Archeologico Regionale Luigi Bernabò Brea 927, 350–340 BCE

a stage.[123] These may be compared to a set of vases for which masks have been assumed for the female characters on stage, but the paint of the masks has rubbed off sufficiently that it is not possible to be certain that they did wear masks. Most remarkable among these are two Sicilian vases, one now in Messina and another in Paris.[124] On the first (Figure 5.5), a young man, a slave dressed as a woman, and an old man stare at a woman (whose face has rubbed off) who is dressed modestly, with no signs of padding or other theatrical dress. On the second (Figure 5.6), two women, both modestly dressed, also with no sign of comic padding, stand on a stage, flanking two men in discussion; in this case as well, the paint has largely rubbed off the women's faces. Were these modestly dressed young women wearing masks?

Hughes compared the frequency of masked female figures on Apulian and Paestan vase painting and made the interesting observation that masked female characters were never represented on stage in the Paestan tradition, but 15 percent of the characters on Apulian vases wore female masks. Further, he noted that in the Paestan tradition, although there were no characters depicted in female mask, there were a significant number of disembodied female masks shown hanging on the vases, all of which

123 E.g. Glasgow 1903.70f, from Lipari. Hughes (2003) 295 suggests that the many women on the Sicilian Manfria vases anticipate the conventions of New Comedy.

124 Sicilian calyx-krater, Messina Soprintendenza 11039, from Messina, via S. Marta, t. 33: U. Spigo in Bacci and Spigo (2002) 32; Sicilian calyx-krater, Paris Louvre CA 7249.

Figure 5.5 Sicilian calyx-krater. Young woman, young man, slave (?) dressed as a woman, old man on stage. Manfria Painter. Messina, Soprintendenza 11039. Third quarter of the fourth century BCE

Figure 5.6 Sicilian calyx-krater. Two young women, a young man, and an old man on stage. Paris Louvre CA 7249, Lentini-Manfria Group. Third quarter of the fourth century BCE

Figure 5.7 Bell-krater, Apulian (Greek), Puglia. Object 1849,0620.13 © The Trustees of the British Museum

represented young women. In the Apulian tradition, by contrast, of the 15 percent of characters sporting female masks, half were masks of old women.[125] Although there are no masked women on extant Paestan vases, these (and Sicilian) vases do however depict women with closed mouths and no apparent mask. Many of the female figures, including most of the window damsels found only on Paestan vases, are not obviously wearing masks or look at all grotesque. By contract, the two women in the background to an Apulian scene of Cheiron being pushed up the stairs do wear masks (see Figure 5.7).[126] Who are the unmasked women on Paestan and

---

[125] Hughes (2003) 290–1.

[126] Apulian bell-krater, London, British Museum F 151: Trendall and Cambitoglou 1978, 100, num. 252 (Eumenides Group).

perhaps also on Sicilian vases and can we associate them at all with the unmasked female pipers who are often presented together with comic phlyax figures?

Aulos accompaniment seems, as it was in the plays of Aristophanes, to be an expected part of the dramas of Epicharmus.[127] In the *Sphinx*, one of the two extant fragments gives an order by an unidentified character, "Let someone pipe me a tune of Chitone [apparently an epithet of Artemis in Sicily as well as in Attica, Miletus, Segesta, and elsewhere in the Greek world]!" and Athenaeus (XIV p. 629 E) notes that among the Syracusans there was a distinctive dance and *aulos*-performance in honor of Artemis Chitonea.[128] Music-loving women are warmly praised by Epicharmus. A main fragment remaining from the play, *Megaris,* for example, probably referring to a *hetaira* as Kerkhof speculates,[129] is a single line that describes a woman as celebrated in hymns, delighting in all music, and loving the lyre:

εὔυμνος καὶ μουσικὰν ἔχουσα πᾶσαν, φιλόλυρος.

Epicharmus, *PCG* 80, Hephaestion 1, 8

The other main fragment from the play is a volley of insults about someone's appearance, comparing the person to fish.[130]

On the "Rio Fish Eater" (Figure 5.3),[131] one of the Campanian vases, these two themes of music and fish converge: a woman plays a double *aulos* and accompanies a man who seems to be engaged in flamboyantly eating a fish. Epicharmus' liking for very long lists of obscure fish, presumably as comic examples of excess, is perhaps exaggerated because one of our main sources for his fragments is Athenaeus. Nevertheless, thanks to Athenaeus, we have forty-five lines of fish names preserved from a single play, *The Marriage of Hebe*, and six more from *The Muses*, and scattered references from other plays. Fish-eaters seem to have been stock characters in his

---

[127] See further Wilson (2002).

[128] On other evidence for the female "chiton-dance" for Artemis, who was customarily portrayed in a short chiton, see further Lawler (1943) 67–8.

[129] Kerkhof (2001) 130.

[130]

> τὰς πλευρὰς οἱόνπερ βατίς,
> τὰν δ'ὀπισθίαν ἔχεις, Θεάγενες, οἱόνπερ βάτος,
> τὰν δὲ κεφαλὰν ὀστέων οἱόνπερ ἔλαφος οὐ βατίς,
> τὰν δὲ λαπάραν σκορπίος παῖς ἐπιθαλάττιος τεοῦ.

> Your sides look as flat as a skate's, Theagenes, your tail looks a ray-fish, your bony head like a stag not a ray, and your flanks like a baby sea-scorpion.
>
> Epicharmus *PCG* I 79, quoted by Athenaeus VII.286

[131] See Smith (1962).

plays. On this vase, the figure on the right is dropping a fish into his mouth with a dramatic gesture. Of course, there is not enough to connect the scene pictured here with a particular moment in Epicharmus, but it is clear that the fish joke, which seems to have appealed so much to the comic poet, also seems to figure prominently on the vase. Whether this vase represents a play by Epicharmus, another local playwright, or an Athenian comic writer, the themes that the vase-painter drew from the play are similar to the combination of themes we can trace in the *Megaris* by Epicharmus.

Women, moreover, figured prominently in the mime tradition made famous by Sophron at the end of the fifth century in Syracuse. It seems possible that both female and male actors in this tradition did not wear masks. Although it is not possible to draw a tight connection between any single picture and the very fragmentary remains of Doric mime, the framework of female performers, perhaps without masks, may be a useful one in which to understand the Campanian and Sicilian vases. On the one hand, this view is extremely old-fashioned, but, on the other, the new advances in linking a few Apulian vases to Attic comedy may not be enough to warrant abandoning a century's worth of study on the connection between Doric mime and the vases. The appearance of unmasked, or likely unmasked, women on the Sicilian and Campanian comic vases as a link to the Doric mime tradition, has not, as far as I know, been noted before. It is perhaps instructive that the women on vases from Apulia are almost exclusively masked with comic masks and with bodies filled out with some comic padding: these artifices have led some to infer that the women are all meant to be old, but it may just be that they are masked and costumed, and therefore ugly, rather than old.

Alan Hughes noted the difference between the women on Apulian (generally masked and costumed) and Paestan and Sicilian (in windows, or unmasked) vases, suggesting that Sicilian vases may be depicting New Comedy and that Paestan vases may, in fact, have been painted from the artist's memory rather than in some relation to theatrical performance in Paestum.[132] Apart from the absence of masked women, the heart of his argument lies in the fact that many of the Paestan vases seem to show actors in the company of Dionysus or otherwise offstage. There are three points which, I think, suggest that an absence of performance is not the most likely explanation. First, as Csapo has now shown, the Athenians painted many

---

[132] Hughes (2003).

vases with actors, offstage, together with Dionysus, at the height of their own theatrical industry in the fifth century.[133] It may be, in fact, that the Paestan vases that show actors together with Dionysus offstage are more closely linked to the Athenian tradition, and, perhaps, are also a roundabout piece of evidence that, like the Athenians, the Paestans enjoyed theater. Secondly, what Hughes describes as an absence of female characters (despite the abundance of female characters in Attic comedy) is, I think, really an absence of clearly *masked* female characters: there are certainly many unmasked women, including unmasked women in windows. If the hypothesis of a mixed set of performers and performance traditions appearing on the vases is accepted, then these unmasked women may represent a mime tradition, another musical performance tradition, or simply a variation in the conventions of performance in Paestum. Finally, and related to the second point, Xenophon's *Symposium* 9 describes a performance at the end of an Athenian symposium, given by a male and a female slave belonging to a Syracusan traveling entertainer, who even uses Doric forms in his speech; they enact the playful lovemaking of Dionysus and Ariadne in her bridal chamber. The performance is accompanied by pipe music. It seems unlikely that these performers wore grotesque masks or padded costumes, or, indeed, were associated in any way with the comic stage. Rather, these mime artists (a beautiful Dionysus and charming Ariadne) danced beautifully and skillfully and are explicitly said to be distinguished for their great good looks and the tender erotic naturalness of their physical movements.[134] If, in the West, such mime traditions were regarded as part of a larger category of performances together with comedy, and perhaps tragedy, then here is another reason for the appearance of unmasked women on local vases.

5.8 Tragic Vases

A large number of vases showing myth and very likely to be related to tragedy have been found in the West. Their relationship to Attic tragedy

---

[133] Csapo (2010) 1–37.

[134] The emphasis on the erotic appeal, beauty, and silence of the actors, balletically representing a scene from elevated myth, intriguingly suggests that, rather than crude or grotesque mime, an early prototype of the medium of pantomime, usually thought to have been invented in the Greek East in the first century BCE, was already known in Sicily in Xenophon's time. See further Hall and Wyles (2008).

has been a subject of interest for many years. Taplin has recently examined a range of tragic vases, comparing them in detail to known plays and fragments of Aeschylus, Sophocles, and Euripides.[135] Although some of the vases he discusses are Attic, most are from South Italy and Sicily.[136] Taplin makes a compelling argument that most of the 109 vases he examined reflect a play by one of the three great Attic tragedians, or else a play closely related to theirs.[137] This study confirms the conclusions drawn by, for example, Marcello Gigante that Greek tragedy and Euripides, in particular, must have been well known in the West. Gigante's painstaking study of Rhinthon's fragments and the fragments of other western Greek authors revealed that they, and presumably their audiences, must have had a great familiarity with Attic tragedy. Patricia Easterling added to this evidence through her study of references in Euripides which, she argues, were included in order to appeal to audiences outside Athens, including audiences from Syracuse, Thurii, and Macedonia.[138] William Allan built on her work to argue from vase-paintings that Euripides' *Children of Heracles* was performed at the end of the fifth century in South Italy, and likewise Chris Dearden has done much to work out the complex dramatic scene of South Italy and Sicily.[139] The evidence of the tragic vases recently set out by Taplin further confirms that, after Aeschylus' productions and his residency and death in Sicily in the mid-fifth century, the western Greeks, and perhaps the native populations of South Italy and Sicily (Sikels, Sikanians, Daunians, and Lucanians, etc.) continued to delight in Greek tragedy.[140]

Non-Greeks (Sikels, Sikanians, Daunians, etc.) become important players in this debate because many of the vases have been found at non-Greek sites, and others at Greek sites under the control of non-Greeks (for example Paestum). Many Apulian vases have been associated with non-Greek burials and have engendered a debate about whether non-Greeks would have had access to performance of tragedy and whether they would

---

[135] Taplin (2007).

[136] Taplin (2007) vi, " . . . except for the five painted in Athens, they (the pots) were all painted in the Greek West, the great majority in Apulia. . . " For example, in his discussion of twenty-one vases associated with the plays of Aeschylus, only two are Attic, three are Lucanian, and the rest are Apulian; of Sophocles, two are Sicilian, one is Lucanian, and the remaining five are Apulian; of Euripides, three are Attic, one Sicilian, six Lucanian, four Paestan, one Campanian, and the remaining twelve are Apulian.

[137] Taplin (2007) 3–4. But for a different perspective, emphasizing the autonomy of vase-painters and the importance of epic poetry, alongside with drama, as a source of inspiration, see Giuliani (2009).

[138] Easterling (1994). For a study of Attic tragedians' poetic treatment of the Greek West, see Burelli (1979).

[139] Allan (2001) and Dearden (1990a) and (1991).   [140] Taplin (2007).

have appreciated it if they did.[141] As discussed above in the context of comic vases, new archaeological and art historical work has strengthened the evidence found in the ancient historians that the Italics had had direct contact with Athens from the end of the archaic period. It may be that some traveling or local players staged tragedy along with comedy in the wealthy centers of non-Greek Apulia.[142] More generally, the vases are associated with a wide array of places: their provenances or attributions include Sicily, Paestum, Lucania, Campania, as well as Apulia. Thus, it appears that tragedy was widely known and appreciated, and perhaps watched, in many places in the western Greek world, although perhaps above all in Apulia with its close ties to Athens.

Unlike the comic phlyax vases, on which actors and stage are usually clearly signaled, most tragic vases are difficult to distinguish from vases that represent myth directly.[143] Some scholars doubt whether the vases reflect actual performance and others doubt whether the images were associated with plays at all: the former suggest other methods for explaining how the myths on the vases were explained to the owners of the vases;[144] the latter argue that the images should be examined in themselves and do not need text to be interpreted.[145] Although there is, of course, great value in studying vases on their own and for their own sake, it can also be profitable to consider them within a theatrical context. From a socio-historical perspective, as opposed, for example, to an art-historical or an etymological study, the links between vases, texts, and performances give crucial evidence about the world of the original creators and users of the vases. As Taplin puts it, "it is impoverishing to treat their [philology and art] interests as separate worlds that run parallel to one another, rather than treating them as coexisting worlds in constant interaction."[146] Nevertheless, in the case of Sicily, where we have a relatively thin record of play performances and we possess only tiny fragments of tragedies that were written on the island, by for example, Dionysius I, it may also be profitable to consider the vases together, apart from Attic play texts, as evidence of specifically Sicilian theatrical events which may have only a tenuous relationship to well-known Attic tragedies.

---

[141] Todisco (2012) 251–71; Taplin (2012) 226–50.   [142] Taplin (2012) 226–50.
[143] See Taplin (2007) and (1993) 21–9.   [144] E.g. Todisco (2012).
[145] E.g. Small (2003). These arguments for separating the paintings from performances and even from the plays have recently been refuted by Taplin (2007) 3 and by Csapo (2010) 1–2.
[146] Taplin (2007) 3.

5.9   Characters on Stage: a Link between Tragic and Comic Sicilian Vases

The Sicilian tragic vases share a characteristic that distinguishes them from the tragedy-related vases of other western regions: they are explicit in signaling performance. Taplin, discussing the name-vase of the Sicilian Dirce Painter[147] dated to ca 380, writes: "This closeness of vase-painting to performance may have been particularly cultivated in Sicily."[148] He suggests that the configuration of figures in the painting "strongly suggests that in a production in Sicily the *ekkyklema* was used for the human scene (in which Lykos is revealed), and the *mēchanē*, the flying machine, for the epiphany of Hermes."[149] Even more striking, three other Sicilian vases from the third quarter of the fourth century (Syracuse 66557 (Figure 5.9); Caltanissetta 1301bis (Figure 5.8);[150] Contessa Entellina, E856[151]) all show stages, whereas no tragic vases so far discovered elsewhere do. By the age of Timoleon, therefore, there was some interest in seeing performance itself represented on the vases. This corresponds with a series of Sicilian comic vases dated to the same period on which the stage is also clearly drawn.[152]

The most strikingly performative of the Sicilian tragic vases is the just-mentioned calyx-krater by the Capodarso Painter (Gibil Gabib Group) in Caltanissetta depicting an unknown play (Figure 5.8). Four figures stand on a stage with three visible supports. From left to right, the figures are a young woman, a young man, another young woman and an elderly *paidagogos* or messenger figure. The young woman on the left is turning away from the young man who is looking and gesturing towards her, but kneeling so that the rest of his body faces another woman on his left (the right of the vase). This woman on the right of the vase is turned away from him, holding her hands up towards her face and facing the diminutive, elderly *paidagogos* or messenger figure, who, in turn, faces her with his hands gesturing as if he is explaining something. Noting the unusual number of figures on the stage – there are four,

---

[147] Early Sicilian calyx-krater: Berlin F 3296, from Palazzolo: (1983) 99, num. 49 (Dirce Painter).
[148] Taplin (2007) 189.   [149] Taplin (2007) 189.
[150] Sicilian calyx-krater, Caltanissetta Museo Archeologico 1301bis, from Capodarso: Trendall (1967a) 601, num. 98 (Gibil Gabib Group), pl. 235.2–3.
[151] Sicilian fragmentary skyphos (?), Contessa Entellina E856, from Rocca d'Entella: De Cesare (2003) 257–8 (Gibil Gabib Group), pl. 48.2. Green (forthcoming *PhV*) identifies this fragment as belonging to a comic vase.
[152] E.g. Agrigento, from Monte Raffe: Trendall (1967a) 596, num. 76; Lentini, from Lentini (Figure 5.10): see below 151–2; Syracuse, Museo Archeologico Regionale Paolo Orsi, from Grammichele; Gela 643, from Manfria; Milan, Museo Teatrale alla Scala 12, from Centuripe: Trendall (1967a) 595, num. 68, pl. 231.1; Paris, Louvre CA 7249 (Figure 5.6): see above 213, n. 125; and there are some additional examples which may represent a stage, though it is not certain.

Figure 5.8 Sicilian calyx-krater. Two young women, a young man, and an old man. Capodarso Painter. Caltanissetta, Museo Archeologico Regionale 1301 bis, ca 330 BCE

but Attic tragedy only allows for three speaking characters – Taplin suggests that the painter might have actually painted two scenes in a single image, conflating, in this way, the practice of depicting tragedy in a synoptic form as a sort of summary of the whole story with the practice of depicting a single scene from comedy.[153] This interpretation is appealing, but two objections can be raised to it. First, in this painting, the young man is drawn so that he is facing and gesturing towards one woman while he looks back at and gestures at the other. It seems to me that this position and these gestures strongly unite all three characters in the single scene. Indeed, the striking feature of this scene is that the young man appears to be caught between two women, both of whom are turning away from him. A key aspect of the play represented must, I think, be this dilemma or unhappy triangle. Secondly, as Taplin notes, the other tragic Sicilian vase fragment that is large enough to give a sense of the full scene, conventionally (but very problematically) assumed to represent a scene from the *Oedipus Tyrannus,* also has four main characters on it plus two clearly significant children (curiously, it also has two women and two men) (see Figure 5.9).

Moreover, though many of the Sicilian comic vases are too fragmentary to reveal how many characters are represented, two comic Sicilian vases also

[153] Taplin (2007) 261–2.

Figure 5.9 Sicilian calyx-krater. Scene from *Oedipus Tyrannus*? Gibil Gabib Group. Syracuse, Museo Archeologico Regionale Paolo Orsi 66557, from Syracuse, ca 330 BCE

Figure 5.10 Sicilian calyx-krater. Heracles and young woman. Manfria Painter. Lentini, Museo Archeologico Regionale, from Lentini, ca 340–330 BCE

show four figures on a stage (Lentini, from Lentini; Paris Louvre CA 7249) (see Figures 5.6 and 5.10). It is curious, though perhaps only accidental, that on all of these vases there are also two men and two women. Although both of the tragic scenes may be explained away, in the first case by supposing that two scenes are presented and in the second case by excluding the fourth woman as an attendant of the main woman, perhaps Jocasta, it seems to me that we should also consider the possibility that these are plays with four speaking characters.[154] They are, perhaps, adaptations of Attic tragedy, rather than Attic tragedy proper or perhaps even new plays on mythical themes.

More curious still, another Sicilian vase, representing a comedy, was recently unearthed in Messina (Figure 5.5) which depicts four characters in, essentially, the same relationship one to another as they are on Caltanissetta 1301 bis (Figure 5.8): on the far left of the stage, a modestly dressed woman appears facing towards (rather than away as on the tragic vase) a young man. The young man is standing, but, like the young man on the tragic vase, his body is positioned towards the woman to his left, although, also like the tragic vase, he is himself looking back at the woman to his right. To his left, a slave dressed up as a woman, raises his/her hands like the second woman on the tragic vase, but, unlike his/her tragic counterpart, s/he faces the young man and other young woman, rather than the old man or *paidagogos*. The old man or *paidagogos*, for his part, seems to be observing, whereas on the tragic vase, he seemed to be explaining. Apart from the confused gender of the central woman (though Bernabò Brea, for example, suggests that this character is simply an ugly old woman, rather than a slave)[155] the main change between the two vases is that on the tragic vase, both women are facing away from the young man, whereas on the comic vase, both are facing towards him. Thus, on the tragic vase, the gender relations take on one relationship: the young man pleads with the two young women and they turn away femininely. On the comic vase, the roles are reversed: the young man is taken aback and surprised by the women, and so, perhaps, in the subordinate role. Could the comic vase represent a parody or comic skit spoofing the play represented on the tragic vase?

At least, we do have here a similar placement of actors on both a tragic and a comic stage from roughly the same period and found in places that are not too far apart. If the similarity between the vases can be entertained as more than mere accident, these two vases interpreted together yield information about some of the associations made on Sicilian phlyax vases. For example, if the *paidagogos* figure on the tragic vase is parallel to the old man figure on the comic vase, it may be that the comic old man figure on several other comic vases also bears some relationship to the tragic

---

[154] Taplin (2007) 92. The connection of this vase-painting with the *Oedipus Tyrannus* has now widely been called into question since the children are not boys but girls: see Hall (2016).

[155] Bernabò Brea (2001) 58.

paidagogos, or messenger. That is, the comic vases may spoof not just a play, but a type of character. As often noted, the old *paidagogos*/messenger figure appears frequently on tragic vases, and is, indeed, often the best indicator that the vase represents a drama.[156] The relative frequency of the appearance of an old man with cane on the comic vases may, perhaps, reflect the appeal of this character or even a spoof of messengers informing everyone of the latest catastrophe.

It might be worth noting that the young man on the comic vase is modestly dressed, with no phallus in sight, just as the Aegisthos character on the "*Choregoi*" vase, clearly pulled from tragedy, is also dressed for tragedy and has no obvious comic costume. Indeed, tragic, or at least, not obviously comic, figures on comic vases have posed an interpretative problem for some time, not only on Sicilian vases, but also on Apulian. If the comic vases are parody, or spoof of tragedy, the interpretation of some of these problematic vases might be furthered, as well. Not only does the Aegisthos figure appear on stage with three comic characters on the "*Choregoi*" vase, but also the young man labeled "tragoidos" has seemed out of place on the New York Goose vase (Figure 5.11).[157] If four was a common number of main characters on the western Greek stage, and if we can accept that tragic figures wander on or are spoofed on comic vases, then it may be that the naked "tragoidos" figure is simply the fourth character in the play. It may also be the case that the label may apply not to the diminutive figure out of whose stomach it seems to be protruding, but rather to the young man in naked costume directly below. In this case, the young onlooker is a second naked figure (presumably also a tragic one) who should be understood as somehow associated with the central naked young man. The central naked young man speaks unintelligibly,[158] gestures arrogantly and, as tragic characters are probably wont to do in parody, gives the poor old comic characters a hard time (Figure 5.11).

Relying very much on the work of experts, such as Taplin, Todisco, and Giuliani, I have tried to glimpse some features of Sicilian fourth-century tragic painting and to examine some relationships between the tragic and comic vases that survive from the island. Given the difficulties of

---

[156] See e.g. Green (1999).

[157] New York 1924.97.104. See, e.g., Dearden (2012) 284, n. 52; Marshall (2001) 64–6.

[158] The words emanating from the young man's mouth seem to be gobbledygook – at least, they have not yet been satisfactorily deciphered. Tragic playwrights are often accused of incomprehensible jargon (most famously perhaps Aeschylus in Aristophanes' *Frogs*, especially line 962), but Epicharmus also mocks Aeschylus' vocabulary (see Chapter 2). So, this string of unintelligible syllables may, perhaps, be the visual representation of tragic characters' high-flown, incomprehensible speech.

Figure 5.11 New York Goose vase, Apulian calyx-krater. Tarporley Painter. New York, The Metropolitan Museum of Art 1924.97.104, ca 400–390 BCE

identifying tragic performances in the West, however, and the even more complicated problems of tracing their influence on comedies, my efforts in this direction have been very preliminary and most of this aspect of the complex history of theater in the West preserves its secrets. In this respect, as in many others, my picture of theater in Sicily is incomplete and conjectural; I offer it simply as part of a first tentative reconstruction of the development of western Greek theater.

5.10 The Combination Theory: Doric and Attic Comic Traditions Merge in the West

In the 1980s, at a time when the theory that the phlyax vases were related to Attic comedy was only beginning to be accepted, Eric Csapo suggested that the argument that they represent both Attic and Doric traditions was a weak compromise. He argued for a strong and, as far as could be ascertained, exclusive connection between the vases and Attic comedy: "Since Webster, scholars have hedged their bets, acknowledging Attic 'influence' but resuscitating the theory that the vases illustrate an independent Doric farce."[159] He extended his analysis of the Würzburg krater to suggest that Athenian comedy may have been the model for all phlyax vases. He writes:

> To date, the Würzburg crater is the strongest confirmation of Webster's argument that the Italian paintings might depict Attic comedy and Old Comedy at that. . . . True, the Würzburg vase cannot be used to characterize the 'phlyax' group as a whole. It is but a single instance in which Webster's thesis holds good. At least there are reasons . . . why Attic comedy seems a likely subject for these illustrations. For an independent contemporary theatre in South Italy there is not a shred of evidence.[160]

Over the course of the following two decades, however, his original and controversial arguments linking the vases to Attic comedy have come to be widely accepted.[161] Together with Oliver Taplin, who has likewise made a strong case for the link, Csapo has changed the scholarly view of theater in South Italy and Sicily. As a result of their work, we now have a new understanding not only of the performance traditions in the West, but also of the early spread and popularity of Attic comedy and tragedy. Most recently, however, Csapo has linked his study of the vases with his work on Greek theater in Attica and has offered a large-scale history of the development of Greek drama, and its evolution in Roman theater. In this more synthetic work, he proposes that Sicilian drama, particularly that of Epicharmus in the early fifth century, might well have contributed to the development of Greek drama in general. That is, he has proposed a melding of the Doric and Attic traditions at a fundamental level. He concludes that by the fourth century (and it is, of course, at the beginning of the fourth century that the phlyax vases first appear) Greek drama was no longer linked so closely with Athens, or for that matter, with Syracuse,

---

[159] Csapo (1986) 388.   [160] Csapo (1986) 390.

[161] E.g. Slater (2005) *BMCR* review of Taplin (2003): "I had intended to start this review by stating that it was no longer 'controversial', as Taplin says [p.3], to argue that Old Comedy was performed outside Athens. That seemed to me to have been reasonably certain since the publication of the Würzburg comic 'Telephus' in 1980, with the independent commentaries of Taplin, 'Phallology' *PCPhS* 33 (1987) 92ff. and Csapo, *Phoenix* 40 (1986) 379ff. I have since discovered that there are still some who believe in an independent South Italian comic tradition. Even so, I should still maintain that the case made here for the influence of Attic Comedy on Southern Italy is so strong, that it is now up to its opponents to refute it."

but had come to be recognized as a Greek tradition, which the Panhellenic world could claim as their own. This melting-pot theory may, perhaps, support the argument I have laid out here that some of the comic and tragic vases from the West are influenced by Sicilian traditions and norms.[162]

Other scholars have long supported the view that the comic vases represent both traditions. Dearden, for example, taking into account Csapo's persuasive attribution of the "Würzburg Telephos" and admitting that the evidence was "tantalizingly inconclusive," still considers the possibility of a "melding together of both local and imported drama."[163] The evidence does seem to point in both directions at once, to the Attic and Doric worlds, to mainland Greece, and to Syracuse and Sicily. To Dearden's argument may be added the possibility that theater in the West was not only sophisticated and literary, but was, in large part, funded and supported by the western tyrants. Their Panhellenic view of the world led them not only to support local artists and theater projects, but also to import Athenian plays. Unlike the sub-literary, grassroots western tradition, which, though very likely to have existed, has not left much mark in the historical record, as Csapo noted, this theory of a sophisticated local theater produced in conjunction with Athenian plays, and supported by the tyrants, can be supported with some historical, literary, and archaeological evidence. It is possible that the sudden profusion of phlyax vases in the fourth century is due to the sudden advent of Athenian drama, but the theatrical sophistication we must assume of the western audiences encourages one to look for a dramatic antecedent closer by. That is, the western Greeks of South Italy and Sicily came to appreciate topical Athenian comedy, because they were already accustomed to it through their own theatrical tradition.

In the four previous chapters, I have tried to show how the Sicilians and South Italians developed their own theatrical tradition. Less than 100 years before, Epicharmus, along with his contemporaries Deinolochus and Phormis, produced many outrageous comedies. In the intervening years,

---

[162] Csapo (2010). Although I am completely persuaded by most of his book, I believe that there continued to be strong Sicilian theatrical traditions which were distinguished in antiquity from those of Athens, see Bosher (2013a) and (2011).

[163] Dearden (1990a) 159–61. Cf. Dearden (1988) 35: "Athenian tragedy had been an acquired taste of audiences in Magna Graecia from the fifth century B.C. [. . .] It would be strange if audiences acquired a taste for sophisticated tragedy and looked to Athens as the center of the theatrical world but for comedy preferred to remain with the rustic and improvised, ignoring contemporary Athenian productions, even though some of their own sons were writing there."

a related tradition was carried on by Sophron, whose work may have fed directly into that of Xenophanes, a writer of mime working under Dionysius I, in the Syracusan court.[164] In this chapter, I have suggested that the phlyax vases seem to reflect the themes of Epicharmus' plays, as much as they do those of Aristophanes. Although we know much less about tragic performance in Sicily, the few vases that remain, particularly if considered together with similar comic vases, show original features which may point towards particular Sicilian developments in the genre of tragedy and tragic-comedy, or, more straightforwardly, in the staging of tragedy or tragic-comedy.

Scholars insisting on a mainly Athenian influence on the phlyax vases point out that there was no comedy native to the West after Deinolochus and before Rhinthon.[165] This position is tenable, indeed bullet-proof, if the definition of comedy employed is a strict one, using the Athenian example as an inflexible model. To be sure, if comedy is generically distinct from mime, has a chorus, preferably a parabasis, lyric interludes, and is performed as part of a festival, preferably one which can be imagined to be modeled on the Athenian Dionysia, then there certainly was no comedy native to the West then, or perhaps ever, if we take it as a possibility that Epicharmus had no chorus and was perhaps not performed in the context of a festival. If, with C. W. Dearden and T. P. Wiseman, however, we consider the generic boundaries in the West to have been more flexible, and group together, as surely Sosibius, by way of Athenaeus, suggests we do, comic performances, whether or not they followed the Athenian norm, then the theatrical world of South Italy and Sicily revives considerably.

In this chapter, I have argued that the comic vases are in the tradition of the plays of Epicharmus, first performed in early fifth-century Syracuse, just as much as they are reflections of Aristophanes; likewise, the Sicilian tragic vases give intimations of original developments in genre or performance. In the next chapter, I will take up the evidence for local architectural and social influences on the development of theaters in the West, and argue for their role as places of political assembly. In these two chapters, then, I aim to show how the later, better-known, and imposing developments of the fourth century, especially the vases and theater buildings, fit into not

---

[164] For further discussion of Sophron, see Chapter 7, Conclusion.

[165] Csapo (1986) 389; probably Olson (2007); Taplin (1993) 51, n. 6: "Epicharmos had successors, especially Deinolochus, but, so far as we know, there was no longer significant independent Syracusan comedy by the end of the fifth century."

only the history of Athenian theatrical expansion but also the more local tradition of Sicilian theater itself.[166]

---

[166] In both cases, a much more detailed archaeological analysis of the material will eventually be required. Both Taplin and Green have suggested that the next big step in the study of phlyax vases is to distinguish their provenances more precisely, which may require clay analysis of the vases, revisions of the attributions already made, and consideration of the social and historical circumstances of each city or area that produced vases. Likewise, the architectural elements of Sicilian theater buildings, which seem to imitate that of Syracuse, need to be more extensively compared, which would require long study at the sites of the theaters themselves (Cf. Dearden (1990a) 232). In future research, I hope to take up some of these questions more thoroughly.

6 | Drama in Public

Stone Theaters in the West

By the Hellenistic period, monumental stone theaters were being built throughout the Greek world in such great number that Pausanias later suggested that a polis without a theater (and from his context it is likely that he means a stone-built theater rather than a place in or near a sanctuary where wooden seats could be erected) was hardly worthy.[1] Western Greek cities took part in this urban development, in some cases as early as the fourth century. Archaeological remains of eighteen stone theaters have been identified in Sicily and South Italy and at least ten others are suggested by literary sources (Map 6.1).[2]

The widespread popularity of theater in the Hellenistic period, marked by the new monumental theaters, has often been linked to the theater's abandonment of political themes and social engagement in favor of pure entertainment. Brigitte Le Guen, for example, summarizes this scholarly view of the degeneration of theater into entertainment: "Les siècles suivants [i.e., the Hellenistic Period], quant à eux, correspondaient à une époque de déclin inexorable où le théâtre ne survivait plus qu'à titre de divertissement compensatoire offert à des citoyens désabusés et profondément dépolitisés."[3] J. R. Green agrees: "The 'political' role of tragedy has largely gone. [...] The retreat from the problems of the political world in the face of

---

[1] Pausanias X 4.1: "It is twenty stades from Chaeroneia to Panapoeus, a Phocian city, if one can call it a city where they have no government offices, no gymnasium, no theater, no market-place, no water channelled to a fountain, but live in rude shelters like mountain cabins, right on a ravine." Cf. Rossetto and Pisani Sartorio (1994). See more recently Hesberg (2009).

[2] Some of these literary sources suggest that theaters had been built already in the fifth century and I take up what we can glean about these fifth-century theaters in the second section of Chapter 2.

[3] Le Guen (1997) VII (Le Guen's article is a bibliographical study of recent works which counter this long-held idea.). For many persuasive arguments in support of a re-evaluation of Hellenistic tragedy as a flourishing and dynamic art form, see also Le Guen (2007), including a neat explanation of Aristotle's opposition of the classical actors who declaim "politically" and the Hellenistic actors who declaim "rhetorically" (110–11), extremely useful appendices gathering all known works of Hellenistic tragedians (120–9), and a translation into French of all surviving fragments (129–34); LeGuen (1995).

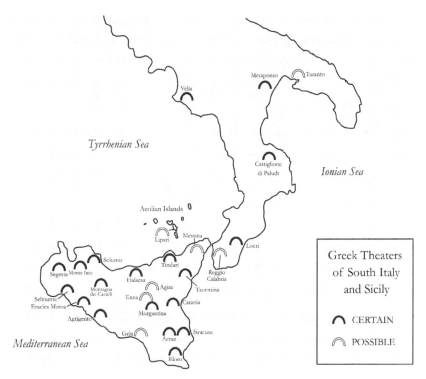

Map 6.1 Greek Theaters of South Italy and Sicily.

economic pressures and other crises of confidence in the traditional system is already reflected in the later plays of Aristophanes."[4]

Although these interpretations reflect the decrease in specific political references in many plays of the period, they do not take account of the political relevance of theater on a larger scale. Like the fragments of Epicharmus, which, on closer inspection, seem to be more engaged in the politics of Syracuse under Gelon and Hieron than is usually thought, monumental theater building in the West can also be understood as a product of the Sicilian tyrants' propaganda tactics. Many theaters housed political assemblies as well as theatrical productions, and, in so doing, they bridged the theatrical and political worlds not only in a practical way, but also symbolically. In this chapter, I argue that Sicilian theaters in themselves were symbolic of the melding of tyrannical and aristocratic wealth, which funded them, with the popular assemblies, which met in them.

---

[4] Green (1994) 50, 62.

In the five sections of this chapter, I aim to demonstrate that theaters must have been built explicitly for public assembly and that the main actors responsible for building them were not councils or city governments, but wealthy individuals and, often, tyrants. In the first section, I examine the development and function of the Greek theater in several places in the Mediterranean and argue that the theater served as an *ekklesiasterion* in most places. In Sicily, in particular, the architecture of the theater building diverges from the canonical form of the theater of Dionysus at Athens in ways that are particularly suited to assemblies, as I argue in the second section. In the third section, I suggest that although Timoleon has often been credited with creating the conditions necessary for new building projects, including theaters, the evidence for his intervention is slight and more agency should be attributed to the Dionysioi who preceded him and to the new tyrants, Agathocles and Hieron II, who followed. In the last section, I argue that theater buildings, whether serving as a democratic veneer, a show of wealth, culture and power, for public performances and festivals, for assemblies, or some combination of all of the above, seem to be most strikingly associated with tyrants and with violent popular backlashes against them. Late classical and Hellenistic theatrical performances and the buildings that house them, all showy and expensive forms of public display, not only accord well with the theatrical aspirations of Dionysius I and other fourth-century tyrants, but also echo the propaganda techniques of Gelon and Hieron explored in the first chapters of this book. Nevertheless, the tinderbox combination of massive public gatherings and tyrannical rule inevitably, perhaps, explodes at many points and later ancient historians record bloody encounters between autocrats and crowds in those very same theaters.

6.1   Assemblies and the Theater

Since the function and symbolism of theaters developed over the course of several centuries in the Greek world, their function in South Italy and Sicily can be better understood in the context of several large-scale historical developments. One of these is the structural origin of the standard semi-circular orchestra and *koilon*.

Although the Greek theater was long thought to have developed from religious spaces designed for circular dance patterns, there is now evidence to suggest that the early forms of the building may have been rectilinear.[5] Not only are many of the earliest known theaters in Attica rectilinear in form, most famously Thorikos, but the influential studies of the late nineteenth and early twentieth centuries that presented the earliest orchestra at Athens itself as circular have now been shown to be without strong archaeological support and to have been influenced by the shape of later Hellenistic theaters, particularly Epidaurus.[6] Indeed, as Elizabeth Gebhard has argued, there is good evidence to assume that the primary element of the Greek theater was not an orchestra of any shape, but rather the *koilon* or *theatron*. As she argues, it is likely that the orchestra adapted itself to the hollow shape of the *koilon* rather than the other way around.[7] Shifting the architectural focus from the orchestra to the *koilon* prompts a reconsideration of the original impetus for building theaters: although the *koilon* may sometimes have been used to gather participants for specific religious or festival activities, its more basic function was simply to provide a structure for people to assemble.[8]

That stone theaters doubled as political meeting places and can therefore be symbolic of civic assemblies, as well as of drama, seems to be both intuitively obvious and supported by literary sources.[9] This notion was, however, challenged in 1994 by Hansen and Fischer-Hansen in their extremely useful analysis of monumental political buildings. In 1994, at

---

[5] For detailed discussion of the archaeology, see Goette (2005); Moretti (1999–2000); Gebhard (1974); Anti (1947); Frederiksen et al. (2015). Evidence for the rectilinear orchestra is drawn primarily from excavations of early theaters outside of Athens. Polacco and Anti (1981/1990), for example, began with study of the theater at Syracuse; Gebhard (1974) surveyed a number of early Greek theaters in Greece, including the Theater of Dionysus; and Nielsen (2002) concentrated on "cult theaters," beginning with early Near Eastern and Egyptian examples and tracing her model into late antiquity. Nielsen notes in particular that the most typically "Greek" addition was the seating arrangement of the *theatron*, since, further East, cult dramas tended to be performed before (and with) a standing audience. For a review of the literature, see Bosher (2006) 147–60, summarized in Bosher (2008–2009) 3–7.

[6] See now Papastamati-Von Moock (2015) for a new reconstruction of the earliest theater at Athens of the late sixth century BCE with a rectilinear *koilon* and orchestra. Early rectilinear theaters have been found at several other places, including Ikaria, Trachones, Chaeronea, Argos, Rhamnous, and, most relevant here, Syracuse. Cf. Goette (2005) for a discussion of Thorikos, Ikaria, Rhamnous, Trachones, Chaeroneia, Isthmia, Tegea, Phlious, Argos, Peiraieus, Oropos, and Cyrene. Cf. Bosher (2008–2009) for an argument that the term orchestra came to be applied to the circular dancing place only in the fourth century, when those rounded dancing places first appeared. See Bosher (2006) 147–60 for a summary and discussion of the problematic literature on the Athenian orchestra, particularly the influential interpretations of Dörpfeld (1896) and Fiechter (1914), which assumed an original circular orchestra predated the building of the theater.

[7] Gebhard (1974); literary evidence supports this archaeological finding – see Bosher (2008–2009).

[8] On cult theaters, see Nielsen (2001); Sokolicek (2015).

[9] E.g. Isler (1981)162–3; Marconi (2012) 185–7.

the beginning of a five-year "Polis Project," Mogens Herman Hansen and Tobias Fischer-Hansen set out to determine which buildings in a Greek polis could be described as "monumental political buildings."[10] They rejected most political buildings as not monumental: *prytaneia* (central government offices) *dikasteria* (lawcourts), *bouleuteria* (council houses, though the Hellenistic *bouleuteria* are included), and *stoai* (public colonnades). Although they categorize theaters as monumental, they reject them as apolitical. Indeed, for the early periods (archaic and classical) the only building type they accept as both monumental and political is the *ekklesiasterion*. Hansen and Fischer-Hansen's contention that the theater is not a political building is founded on a distinction they make between the *ekklesiasterion*, a secular and political building, and the theater, a religious and theatrical building; they argue that the former is primarily a political building, and the latter is not.[11] The criteria Hansen and Fischer-Hansen use to exclude theaters from the category of political buildings may be summarized as follows: (1) Greek theaters are not secular but part of a sanctuary; (2) we should expect to find a stone *bema* (speaking platform) and benches, instead of a *skene*, in a building which is primarily intended for political meetings; (3) theaters are much bigger than needed to house the largest political assembly, the *ekklesia*.

(1) First, even those buildings in the West which have been generally recognized as *ekklesiasteria* (the assembly areas at Agrigento, Morgantina, and Metaponto) seem, like theaters, to have been part of or close to a sanctuary.[12] Conversely, many Sicilian theaters are not only built next to a small *bouleuterion*, but are also located near the central market space and political heart of the polis.[13] It is, therefore, difficult to make a distinction between the two categories based on their physical proximity to religious or cult sanctuaries. (2) Secondly, although the presence of a *bema* might confirm the political character of a building, its absence does not prove the opposite, since most political buildings do not, in fact, have one.[14] (3) Finally, although it is true that the enormous size of many theaters suggests that their function as festival halls for huge crowds was important, this does not necessarily mean that the assembly would have felt that they were in a building that was not intended for their meetings. The proof of this lies, I think, in Hansen and

---

[10] Hansen and Fischer-Hansen's focus (1994) is on archaic and classical architecture, but their list of relevant buildings includes examples from later periods and their judgment of the theater building as a non-political edifice is not limited to these earlier periods.

[11] For an extended discussion of Hansen and Fischer-Hansen's point of view and an examination of *ekklesiasteria* throughout the Greek world, see Bosher (2006) 160–73.

[12] See Chapter 3.   [13] Marconi (2012) 187–9.

[14] With some notable exceptions, for example the Pnyx. Cf. also the agora at Assos, and the theatral area at Olbia and at Gortyn. Cf. Bosher (2006) 164, table 6.4.

Fischer-Hansen's own definition of a monumental building: that it be bigger and grander *than its intended function.* The example they cite is the *bouleuterion* at Miletus which has seats for 1,500 people, though the *boule* meeting in it probably had fewer than 500 members.[15] In Athens, for example, the theater of Dionysus may have accommodated about 14,000, and the *ekklesia* included about 6,000.[16] The proportion of seats to citizens in other theaters is sometimes much greater than this,[17] but it is not possible to determine whether the excess space made the building seem inappropriate or monumental. In my view, Hansen and Fischer-Hansen's criteria cannot maintain a clear distinction between building types, for, although they isolate a small group of *ekklesiasteria* that may not have functioned as theaters, they do not distinguish most theaters from *ekklesiasteria*. In other words, although not all *ekklesiasteria* may have served as theaters, all theaters could have served and probably did serve as *ekklesiasteria*.

Not only did many theaters serve as assembly halls, as well as theaters,[18] but at least one, the Panionion at Mycale in Asia Minor, was built explicitly for a political assembly of the league of Ionian cities.[19] In form, the Panionion seems to be modeled on the typical shape of a theater. The diameter of the orchestra is 19 m and that of the orchestra and *koilon* together is 31.80 m. The *koilon* of limestone consists of ten rows of seats divided into three cunei by two rows of steps.[20] At the base of the *koilon* is a slightly raised platform that supports the *prohedria* and this form of the *prohedria* is almost identical to the arrangement at the theater at Priene. Moreover, in the center of the orchestra is a flat slab of rock that may have supported an altar

---

[15] "including the forecourt, the bouleuterion at Miletus covered 2,100 m² and the auditorium itself could accommodate 1,200 – 1,500 persons, but most councils had less than 500 members ..." Hansen and Fischer-Hansen (1994).

[16] For arguments about the capacity of the theater at Athens, and suggestions ranging from 3,700 to 17,000, see, e.g., Csapo and Miller (2007) 97, Goette (2007) 120, Roselli (2011) 72–5. Summarized in Bosher (2013c).

[17] The theater at Delphi could fit 5,000 but the *ekklesia* was attended by about 450. Hansen and Fischer-Hansen (1994) 53.

[18] Bosher (2006) 163–70, and tables 6.4 and 6.5.

[19] On this league and the planning and building of the Panionion, see Bean (1979), Kleiner et al. (1967), and MacDonald (1943). Though the league was nominally religious, gathering at an altar to celebrate Poseidon, it seems also, from its inception, to have been a political organization: "Und zweitens fällt auf, dass an diesem 'Heiligtum aller Ionier' nur die zwölf Städte und nicht auch die anderen Ionier teilhaben durften, wie bei Herodot ausdrücklich hinzugefügt ist. Der besondere politische Charakter des Bundes geht noch aus dieser Ausschliesslichkeit hervor. Aber natürlich versammelte man sich an einem Altar." Kleiner et al. (1967) 13.

[20] Isler (1994) 446.

similar to the one found in the theater at Priene,[21] and, as Hansen and Fischer-Hansen note, in the *ekklesiasterion* at Poseidonia.[22] In front of the orchestra is a trapezoidal foundation without traces of any other structure on it. It may have supported a *bema*, as Hansen and Fischer-Hansen suggest,[23] but the archaeological record leaves this question open: it may equally well have supported a wooden *skene* for dramatic performances. Perhaps the well-known political function of the league and the equally well-known festival celebrated at the sanctuary, which may have included dramatic performances, were both served by this trapezoidal foundation: either a *bema* or a *skene* could be erected to suit the needs of the moment. The unit of measurement that was used for the Panionion (0.295 m.) seems to have been the one introduced in Priene by Pytheos.[24] Indeed, the structure of the Panionion is so similar to that of the theater at Priene that it is often dated in relation to the latter.[25]

The blending of categories in this building is difficult to disentangle: Kleiner stresses that it remains imperative that we question the relative dates of the theater and of the *bouleuterion*.[26] In function, the Panionion is most regularly described as the meeting place of the Panionian league. Representatives from each of the twelve member states came to a collective council meeting that was called the *boule* of the Ionians. Thus, as Hansen and Fischer-Hansen point out, "constitutionally speaking, the building is a *bouleuterion*, but of a confederation, not of a *polis*. The size and type of the meeting place however, more properly characterize it as an *ekklesiasterion* . . ."[27] In sum, the only building in Asia Minor which might be called an *ekklesiasterion* resembled a typical Greek theater, and especially the nearby theater of Priene. Nevertheless, its political importance both as the seat of the Ionian *boule* and as a monument to the league are certain. This is, without doubt, a monumental political building.

Historical sources allow us to identify the political function of the Panionion, despite its apparently theatrical architecture; there is no comparable historical evidence for the Sicilian theaters. In nearby South Italy, however, the curious case of Metapontum suggests that a similar overlap of theater and assembly place obtained in the West. In this Achaean city south of Tarentum, a large circular assembly area, called an *ekklesiasterion* by its excavators, was built as early as the mid-sixth century. In the fourth

---

[21] However, the altar at Priene may have been erected much later. De Bernardi Ferrero dates it to 190 BCE (1966–1974), III, 18.

[22] Hansen and Fischer-Hansen (1994) 69.   [23] Hansen and Fischer-Hansen (1994) 69.

[24] Carter (1983) 28.   [25] Kleiner et al. (1967) *passim*.   [26] Kleiner et al. (1967) 13.

[27] Hansen and Fischer-Hansen (1994) 69.

century, a theater seems to have replaced the *ekklesiasterion* in exactly the same place. Although we cannot be certain of it, it is likely that the new theater retained some of the functions of the old *ekklesiasterion*, including that of providing a place for public gathering.[28]

The theater at Metaponto, like so many in Sicily, was situated immediately next to the agora and the central political spaces of the city. On a recent count, in fact, six of the Sicilian theaters were adjacent to smaller council chambers, or *bouleuteria*.[29] Since the smaller council chambers may have provided a venue for small meetings, it seems possible that they were built near larger theaters because these in turn provided a place for large assemblies.

This archaeological evidence for the use of theaters for assemblies is supported by literary and epigraphical sources. Inscriptions about and literary references to assemblies in theaters are found all over the Greek world.[30] MacDonald has assembled a list of fifty-seven decrees from Athens, the earliest dating from 327/6 BCE and the latest from 40–42 CE, which refer to assemblies in the theater. He suggests that there are so many because, whenever the *ekklesia* was not to be held in the usual place (i.e. the *ekklesiasterion*, which, in the case of Athens, is the Pnyx), it was necessary to note the change.[31] Inscriptions announcing *ekklesiai* held in various other places (for example, the Peiraeus) support this interpretation. Kolb, however, argues that, far from being an exceptional alternative to the regular meeting place, theaters were primarily constructed *for political assembly*: "die griechischen Theatergebäude waren wohl sogar von vornherein in erster Linie für die Volksversammlung gedacht."[32] In this context, it is interesting to note that the Athenian assembly was transferred from the Pnyx to the theater of Dionysus sometime after 332 and before the end of the third century BCE, after it had undergone the Lycurgan renovations.[33]

[28] Cf. Carter (1990) 405: "No single discovery has been more provocative than that of the circular building found under the 4th-century BC theatre. It dates in its earliest phase to the mid-6th century BC and has been provisionally identified as an *ekklesiasterion* for the assembled citizens. The excavators estimate its capacity at 8,000." Mertens and de Siena (1982); Mertens (2006) 161–3, 334–7; Lippolis, Livadiotti, and Rocco (2007) 789.

[29] Marconi (2012) 187.

[30] Kolb has assembled a comprehensive list of inscriptions and literary references (Kolb 1981, 88, n. 9). Hansen and Fischer-Hansen disagree with a number of his citations (1994, 48 n. 103), but not enough to alter the general picture of theaters being used for assemblies.

[31] MacDonald (1943) 57–8, n. 74.   [32] Kolb (1981) 90. See especially n. 14.

[33] "... after the completion [of the Lycurgan renovations] the Theater must have been much the best equipped meeting place in Athens for any large group." MacDonald (1943) 58. Cf. Pollux VIII.133, and Athenaeus, *Deipnosophistae* V, 212 e–f, 213, d. For the return to the Pnyx later, cf. Lucian, *Jupiter Trageodus*, 11.

There are, moreover, explicit references to assemblies held in the theaters of Catania (Front. *Str.* 3.2.6), Skotoussa (Paus. 6.5.2), Thebes (Plut., *Mor.*, 799 E–F), Syracuse (Plut., *Tim.*, 34.6), Enna (Livy 24.39.4–5), Engyion (Plut., *Marc.* 2 0.3), Rhodes (Polybius, 15.23.2), Tralles (Vitruvius 7.5.5), Epidaurus (*IG* IV2 1 84.23–4), Ephesus (Paul I. *Ephesians*, 28.19–20), and Taras (Val. Max. 2.2.5).[34] Although these sources themselves are relatively late, several of them refer to assemblies held much earlier, at the end of the fifth century (e.g. Frontin. *Str.* 3.2.6) or the fourth century (e.g. Paus. 6.5.2); others mention that it is the habit of the Greeks to hold assemblies in the theater (e.g. Val. Max. 2.2.5); and still others seem to assume that the reader hardly needs to be told that the assembly was in the theater (e.g. Livy 24.39.4–5).

The word *ekklesiasterion*, on the other hand, is "known only from a few literary notices and inscriptions."[35] Large meeting places seem to have acquired their own private names, e.g. Pnyx or Thersilion, and are not called by a generic name which identifies them by type, as theaters invariably are. Thus, the rarity of references to meetings in an *ekklesiasterion* might mean not, as MacDonald and Hansen and Fischer-Hansen suggest, that the meetings were so frequently held in an *ekklesiasterion* that there was no need to announce them, but that there was no strict notion of an *ekklesiasterion* as such.[36] If theaters, on the other hand, were *commonly* used for the *ekklesiai*, then perhaps this meeting place would be assumed without explicit reference to the theater building, especially in cities where there was no obvious alternative venue (i.e. most cities).[37] MacDonald's argument from silence, adopted by Hansen and Fischer-Hansen, that no mention of a meeting place probably meant that the most common place was used,[38] for which there would be no need to specify location, could equally well apply to theaters when these had become the standard place for assemblies. The *ekklesia* would meet wherever was most suitable, and the most suitable structure would be, in most places, the theater. Vitruvius, for example, notes that the citizens of Tralles called their theater an *ekklesiasterion* (Vitruvius 7.5.5). Indeed, the Romans thought that the Greeks typically used the theater for meetings of the assembly:

> Graecorum autem totae res publicae sedentis contionis temeritate administrantur. ... Cum in theatro imperiti homines rerum omnium rudes

---

[34] Cf. Hansen and Fischer-Hansen (1994) 49–50.

[35] MacDonald (1943) 62 referring to Olbia, Delos, Tralles.

[36] This interpretation is supported *by the lack of* a standard structure for an *ekklesiasterion*.

[37] For a chart of cities with both an *ekklesiasterion* and a theater, see Bosher (2006) 165, table 6.5.

[38] MacDonald (1943) 57–8, n. 74.

ignarique consederant, tum bella inutilia suscipiebant, tum seditiosos homines rei publicae praeficiebant, tum optime meritos ciuis e ciuitate eiciebant. Cicero, *Pro Flacco* 16.[39]

The fundamental overlaps between theater and *ekklesiasterion* suggest that separation of secular, political meeting places from religious, theatrical places is a modern distinction rather than an ancient one. Not only in Athens, but throughout the Greek world, theaters seem to have been recognized as places for political assembly. Building a theater, therefore, is not only evidence of interest in providing entertainment, but also of all that a public meeting house entails.

6.2   Theater Design and the Influence of Athens

Even if ancient Greek theaters do seem to have been political buildings, both practically and symbolically, modern scholars often associate them with Athens and the popularity of Attic drama, sometimes overlooking local political purposes and affiliations. As in the case of the plays, Athens is often understood to be both the conceptual and architectural model for other theaters. Paul Cartledge summarized this widely held view in the first chapter of *The Cambridge Companion to Greek Tragedy*:[40]

> The experience of Greek Sicily and South Italy, however, was just the most vivid illustration of a universal Greek theatrical phenomenon, whereby following the Athenian model a purpose-built stone theatre came to be as much a fixture in Hellenic civic architecture as the *agora*.[41]

To what extent did Athenian theater and the theater of Dionysus serve as a model for Sicilian theaters? In this chapter, I approach the question from two angles: first, in this second section, I take up some arguments for the distinctive architecture of Sicilian theater buildings; secondly, in sections three and four, I consider some local political and social reasons for building theaters in Sicily.

---

[39] "All public affairs of the Greeks are run by the recklessness of a seated public assembly. . . . When men, ignorant, unversed and inexperienced in all things sit down together in the theater, then they take up useless wars, then they put factious men in charge of the government, then they throw those most worthy of the citizenry out of the state." Cf. Hansen and Fischer-Hansen (1994) 51.

[40] On the idea of a Greek drama, incorporating Athenian and other regional theater already by the classical and Hellenistic periods, see Csapo (2010), ch. 2.

[41] Cartledge (1997) 5.

Although Athenian theater must have exerted a strong influence in the West, western theater-building was not dominated as completely and definitively by the theater of Dionysus as overviews of the period sometimes suggest.[42] Approaching the archaeological evidence from the Sicilian perspective reveals architectural and historical idiosyncracies in the Sicilian material that distinguish it from its better-known counterpart in Athens. Several scholars have tabulated and examined the differences between western Greek and mainland Greek theaters.[43] Indeed, so many of these have been identified that Moretti suggests that performing in a Sicilian theater and in a mainland Greek theater would have been fundamentally different experiences for an actor.[44]

In this section, I outline a few differences that reveal that Sicilian theaters were particularly well suited for assemblies as well as theatrical events. A reduced orchestra with limited entryways, combined with strong evidence of temporary wooden stages, suggests that the theaters may not have been designed with the choral dancing space or perhaps even with the performance area itself as the determining or the most important element. When stone *skenai* were built, moreover, their permanent and ornate sculptural decoration, in contrast to the changeable and painted decoration on their mainland Greek counterparts, suggests that the *skene* building was specially designed to mark the status and wealth of the sponsor or city rather than to provide a flexible performance area.

As Moretti has pointed out, a significant difference in the structure of Sicilian theaters is that their orchestra was smaller than that of theaters on the Greek mainland.[45] The relatively small Sicilian orchestra may have influenced the later Roman orchestra, whose size is generally explained as a result of the diminution and absence of the chorus in the Roman theater.[46] Did the Sicilians give less space to the orchestra than their counterparts in

---

[42] Although Dörpfeld (1896) does not appear to have distinguished western Greek theater building from that of the mainland, Bethe (1896) and later Fiechter (1914) did recognize features of the western buildings that differed from those of the mainland. Courtois (1989) 11–14 and Moretti (1993) provide concise literature reviews of the study of western Greek theaters. Isler (2000) 217 notes the basic design influence of Athens on Iaitas, Segesta, Solunto, and Tyndaris: "Comune a tutti i monumenti menzionati è una pianta a parasceni, tipo di pianta che risale senza dubbio al primo teatro in pietra del mondo greco, quello di Dioniso ad Atene."

[43] For catalogues and general discussions, see Courtois (1989) and Mitens (1988). See also Moretti (1993) for a summary and discussion.

[44] Moretti (1993) 95–6.

[45] Ibid. 96–7. The shape of the orchestra of the theater at Heracleia Minoa is anomalous in the Mediterranean world (97).

[46] Ibid. 97. On the influence of Sicilian theaters on Roman theaters more generally, see, e.g., Isler (1994); Courtois (1989); Mitens (1988).

mainland Greece because staples of their theater, the comic drama of Epicharmus in the early fifth century and later the mimes of Sophron, Xenarchus, and others did not include a chorus?[47] The art-historical and literary evidence of the popularity of Greek tragedy in Sicily well into the fourth century suggests that Attic tragedy, perhaps with a chorus, was performed in the West well into the Hellenistic period, and Sicilian theaters do, of course, have space for choral dance.[48] Images of tragedy on Sicilian and South Italian vases, however, tend not to privilege the chorus, as opposed to Attic representations, where the chorus is dominant.[49] It is possible, nevertheless, that these western Greek theaters adapted to their local theatrical needs by concentrating less on the large dancing space. Apart from theatrical requirements, a smaller orchestra is well suited to the use of the theater for general assembly: there is no need for an excessively large orchestra for individual speakers or indeed for any relatively static group assembled in front of the seating area.

In addition to a small size, the orchestra of some Sicilian theaters is further distinguished by limited or peculiarly constructed *parodoi*.[50] At Iaitas, for example, Isler remarks on the curious design of the *parodoi* that follow the sides of the *skene* building and then turn inwards toward the center.[51] On the western side, the theater was built up against the slope of the hill that continued forward beyond the front limit of the *koilon*; originally, a small, sloping, retaining wall to the west of and roughly parallel to the side of the *skene* building held the bank of earth in place.[52] In later remodeling of the theater, moreover, a built wall, perpendicular to the *analemma*, continued to limit the western *parodos*. Thus, the bank of earth with the early retaining wall and then later the more developed wall forced the *parodos* to run perpendicular to the *analemma* from the earliest phases of the building.[53] Isler points out that the third stage of the building at

---

[47] On the chorus, or lack of one, in Epicharmus' plays, see Chapter 2.

[48] On the reception of Attic tragedy on South Italian and Sicilian vases, see Taplin (2007).

[49] See further, Chapter 5. An exception is the Pronomos vase (on which see Taplin and Wyles (2010)), most likely found in Ruvo, though it is of Attic manufacture.

[50] For this link between the small orchestra and the closed-off *parodoi* in western theaters, see Moretti (1993) 97.

[51] Isler (2000) 205–6.

[52] Isler (2003) 277, "[. . .] in origine un muretto obliquo tratteneva il terreno ad ouest dell'edificio scenico."

[53] These *parodoi* were corridors, delimited by walls, and, as Courtois (1989) 63 notes, precursors of the *parodoi* of the Roman theater. Courtois (1989) 65 records that this is the only Greek theater she knows to have this type of *parodos*, and suggests that the impetus was a desire to unite the cavea with the scene building. In about 200 BCE or shortly thereafter, Isler concludes

Segesta shares this peculiarly closed orchestra and correspondingly reduced, walled, and probably covered *parodoi*.[54] At Tyndaris, Moretti notes that the *analemmata* were at a tangent to the stage building, which was itself unusually far forward. As a result, he suggests, there would not have been room for formal *parodoi* at this theater, though there do seem to have been other entry points to the orchestra.[55] The uneven remains of the *parodoi* at Syracuse suggested to Polacco and Anti that Sicilian builders developed their own entrance corridors independently, rather than imitating a ready-made Athenian model.[56] Bernabò Brea argues that the *parodoi* at Syracuse were not part of the first stage of the theater, "non risalgono al primo impianto del teatro, e sono stati invece praticati solo in un secondo momento e successivamente ancora approfonditi, allargati e trasformati a piu riprese." [57] Because the theater at Syracuse was excavated deep out of the rock, Bernabò Brea argues that the earliest entry points to the orchestra must have been from directly behind the orchestra: there would have been no lateral entryways for the chorus as we imagine most standardly at the theater of Dionysus, for example. In the case of both Iaitas and Syracuse, topographical constraints seem to have limited the *parodoi*.

Nevertheless, it is perhaps telling that neither of their sites were chosen with a view to accommodating clear open spaces for *parodoi*; nor, once the sites were chosen, was much effort expended to clear a wide path to allow for the construction of *parodoi* on the model of those at Athens. At some other Sicilian theaters, the area of the orchestra and *skene* building has fallen away and it is impossible to determine what the *parodoi* were once like. At Heloros, for example, a canal now flows where the orchestra once was, and the orchestra of the rectilinear theater at Syracuse, likewise, is completely destroyed. Like the small size of the orchestra, the reduced and more limited entryways to extant Sicilian *orchestrai* may reflect the lesser

---

that the stage was built forward into the orchestra; this may have further restricted the *parodoi*. Isler (2000) 207–13, and figs. 7, 8, and 11. On the dating of the theater, see Isler (2003) 290: the first phase of the theater dates to the last quarter of the fourth century; the second phase to around 200 BCE; and the third phase was begun in the course of the first century BCE and suspended in the Augustan period.

[54] Isler (1981) 158.

[55] Moretti (1993) 74. Although much of the evidence at Tyndaris is compromised because of later Roman renovations, Moretti argues that it is still possible to identify these features of the Greek building.

[56] Polacco and Anti (1981/1990) 162, 166.

[57] Bernabò Brea (1967) 99, who notes that the *parodoi* were much mutilated in the imperial period, which obscures the evidence.

importance of the chorus. These irregular *parodoi* also suggest, as Polacco and Anti point out, that Sicilian theaters were not built exactly following the model of the Theater of Dionysus in this respect, but adapted to suit their own circumstances.

Art-historical evidence from the West, likewise, puts emphasis on actors and the stage, rather than on the chorus and the orchestral dancing area. A remarkable number of South Italian and Sicilian red-figure vases depict actors performing on raised wooden platforms; conversely, Attic vases most usually represent choruses or chorus members, without evidence of a stage.[58] Recent arguments about the Athenian subject matter of the comedies depicted on the South Italian and Sicilian vases notwithstanding, the overwhelming majority of depictions of wooden stages come from the Greek West. Regardless of the subject matter of the plays, this evidence gives us valuable information about western performance spaces. Many scholars reasonably incorporate the evidence of the fourth-century phlyax vases, and the more complex evidence from tragic vases, as depictions of temporary wooden stages erected in western Greek theaters.[59] Removable wooden stage buildings, often preceding but sometime coinciding with the high permanent *skene* of the later Hellenistic period, point to a fundamentally adaptable aspect of the Sicilian theater building.[60] Although a wooden stage and *skene* building could be erected in the theater for performances or a season of plays, they were not made in permanent stone like the *koilon*. The bright, colorful stage of performance could be dismantled and the theater would be ready for other functions, including, most likely, assembly meetings and other large-scale gatherings of the population. As Hughes has demonstrated, the wooden stage buildings are not at all incompatible with the grand stone theaters, but these strictly theatrical elements, the stages, could be removed when the theater was required for other purposes.

When permanent stage buildings were built in Sicily later in the Hellenistic period, many of them differed from their mainland Greek counterparts in their sculptural as opposed to painted decoration. Isler specifies that Greek theaters often had painted *pinakes* on the front of the *proskenion*, but that Sicilian theaters with *paraskenia* were decorated instead with real architectural orders, and he notes the similarities between this theatrical

---

[58] See Csapo (2010) 1–37.

[59] Courtois (1989) 21–7, 65; Isler (1981) 138, 152. However, Hughes (1996) has argued convincingly that similar temporary wooden stages were used in stone theaters throughout the Greek world. For discussion of the Perseus Dance vase and similar wooden stages in Athens, see Csapo (2010) 25–7.

[60] At Iaitas, however, the first phase of the stage-building seems to be contemporary with the first phase of the cavea (Isler (2003) 280).

sculptural decoration and much earlier temple decoration, particularly at Agrigento. The Atalantes type of supporting structure, first attested on a theater at Iaitas and then in the third century at Segesta and Syracuse, are very similar to the Atalantes of the temple of Zeus at Agrigento.[61] Thus, the sculpture of local temples may have served as a model for the sculpture on monumental theaters.[62] Marconi notes that resources that had once been devoted to temple building in the archaic and classical periods, were, in many Hellenistic cities, used for building theaters.[63] In this way, monumental theaters came to take the place of temples in city architecture of the fourth century and later. This shift reveals profound changes in the social and religious structure of cities, but it also suggests that the building of theaters was a public act of greater significance than the straightforward provision of space for theatrical performance.

In Sicily, the reduced dimensions of the orchestra, the limited *parodoi*, the evidence for temporary wooden stages, and the grandeur of the *skene* building on the model of earlier temples may suggest that the production of plays was not the only or even the dominant function of the theater building. If an important function for theaters throughout the Greek world was to provide place for assembly, as argued in the first section of this chapter, it appears that Sicilian theaters were, both in their original plans and in later additions, particularly well suited to this function. Not only was the earliest, the most imposing, and the most enduring aspect of Sicilian theaters the *koilon*, monumental stone seating for large groups of people, but the orchestra and performance area seems to have been easily adaptable to the needs of political assemblies. Thus, providing assembly space may not have been only a by-product or secondary function of Sicilian theaters; their primary function may have been to serve as a grand meeting place for public and civic functions.

The evidence is sufficiently complicated that scholars still argue about the extent of the influence of the Theater of Dionysus at Athens on Sicilian theaters.[64] To these archaeological debates, a curious footnote may be added: at least one Sicilian city with particularly close ties to Athens does not appear

---

[61] Isler (1981) 158–9; Isler-Kerenyi (1976) 38, tav. 20. Cf. Courtois (1989) 64 for an argument that Sicilian theaters boasted richer and more varied decorations. For discussion of the major divide between *skene* buildings with *paraskenia* and those with a *proskenion*, see Isler (1981) 148–51.

[62] Isler points to a close regional heir of such architectural decoration in the theaters of the Roman Republic (Isler (1981) 158).

[63] Marconi (2012) 175–6.

[64] Isler (1981) 162 concludes that the main influence was Athens, whereas Moretti (1993) 97 writes that a more satisfying conclusion would consist of supposing "que l'édifice occidental résulte d'une évolution interne régie par des exigences scéniques proprement occidentales d'un edifice classique qui, s'il fut importé de Grèce au Ve s., devait être à l'origine une simple skènè percée d'une ou de trois portes en façade." (98) "Le théâtre hellénistique d'Italie

to have built a theater. Camarina, west of Syracuse, was a strong ally of Athens through the fifth century and appears to have had particularly close trade links with her (a third of the Attic vases in the large museum at Syracuse come from Camarina).[65] Despite this exchange of goods, loyalties, and, presumably, ideas, the city is noticeably devoid of a theater. Likewise, at the Athenian colony of Thurii, a city south of Taras on the Ionian coast, where we might also have expected a theater modeled on that of Athens,[66] no evidence of a stone theater has been found.[67] Our admittedly incomplete evidence reveals the grandest theaters in cities that were often hostile to Athens, most famously, the Doric city of Syracuse. Allan notes that conflict encouraged cultural interaction between cities;[68] a still simpler explanation may be that western Greek cities built theaters for a range of internal, civic reasons rather than because of direct Athenian influence.

6.3 Timoleon

Despite the persistent tradition that Sicilian theaters were modeled on the theater of Dionysus at Athens, the main period of monumental theater building in Sicily is often associated with a Corinthian, Timoleon. The period of renewed prosperity and democracy that Timoleon brought to the island is often thought to have encouraged the building of theaters. Although Timoleon and his reforms must have provided the circumstances necessary for many cities to rebuild and develop grand public buildings, Sicilian theater, as I have tried to demonstrate in this volume, was only tenuously and circuitously connected to democracy. I propose, moreover, that Timoleon's support for theaters is only weakly supported by the sources, and that it is more likely that the impetus and funding for theater building came from wealthy and powerful individuals, often tyrants. Support for monumental theater-building may have begun with the aspiring playwright, Dionysius I, and was certainly continued by later tyrants and monarchs, from Agathocles to Hieron II.

---

méridionale et de Sicile diffère par sa morphologie de son contemporain de Grèce et répond à des exigencies scéniques différentes."

[65] Di Vita (2002) 144; Talbert (1974) 158.

[66] Although see the earlier discussion of Thurii, above p. 44.

[67] The same disjunction is true for vase-paintings, as Robinson (2004) 196 notes: "As Lippolis and others have pointed out, the migration of Attic vase-painters in the second half of the 5th century BC corresponds very poorly with the political alliances of Athens, and with her official colonization; Thurii and Herakleia would have been more 'logical' sites for migration than Metaponto and Taranto or, for that matter, Corinth." Cf. Lippolis (1996) 380.

[68] Allan (2001) 79, n. 68.

The case for Timoleon's role in supporting theater-building in Sicily rests on two basic assumptions: first, that general prosperity and public wealth is an important pre-condition for the building of theaters, and, secondly, that, to some degree, theaters are inherently democratic.[69] It is generally agreed that Timoleon brought prosperity to an island devastated by the megalomania of Dionysius I and successive tyrants, and also that one of his main aims was to restore democracy to the cities of Sicily.[70] Where we have evidence, however, it appears that the general prosperity of a city was not nearly as important in the building of theaters as the patronage of a few, or even a single, wealthy and powerful individuals. This private support for theaters has been confirmed in several places. Inscriptions attesting to support and probably building by Hieron II at Syracuse and Taormina are well known.[71] At Morgantina, as well, an individual "Archelas, son of Eukleidas" is inscribed as the dedicator and so perhaps the sponsor of the theater.[72] Likewise, at Iaitas a fragmentary inscription gives the name "Antallos," whom Isler proposes as the dedicator of the monument.[73] Isler writes that "it is noteworthy that such a public building, of impressive dimensions, was dedicated not by the citizenry, but by a single individual."[74] As far as I have been able to ascertain, there are no corresponding examples of dedications by a city or large public group at other Sicilian theaters, nor are there records of a city's expense in paying for a theater. The repeated acknowledgment of wealthy sponsors begins to make sense, however, if we recognize that the general economic prerequisite for theater-building in Sicily may not have been city wealth and general prosperity, but rather the wealth of key individuals.

As I have tried to demonstrate in this book, moreover, the links between democracy and theater become complex and very difficult to define in the West; much of the best evidence for theater from Sicily (literary fragments, vase-painting, figurines) can be dated to periods of tyrannical control. The model of fifth-century Athenian theater, intimately associated with Athenian democracy and with general prosperity, does not seem to fit very well in

---

[69] Isler (1986) 162: "Il teatro doveva essere invece il simbolo dell'autonomia politica, anche se solo d'apparenza, data da Timoleonte alle città della zona sotto l'influsso di Siracusa."

[70] E.g. Di Vita (2002) 140, "un vero ricostruttore, nel morale e sul terreno, della *polis* in Sicilia: Timoleonte." Cf. Talbert (1974). Contra: Finley (1979) 97: "For all this activity Timoleon had no legitimate Sicilian authority. Were it not for the myth which has been created about him, he would be called a tyrant. And rightly so [. . .]"; Galvagno (2002) 416.

[71] Cerchiai, L. et al. (2002) 167; Bernabò Brea (1967) 102. These inscriptions indicate a date between 238 and 215 BCE.

[72] E. Sjöqvist (1962) 134; R. Stillwell (1964–1965) 586.   [73] Isler (2003) 276.

[74] Isler (2003) 276: "È comunque degna di nota la circonstanza che un tale edificio pubblico, di dimensioni notevoli, venisse dedicato non dalla cittadinanza, ma da un singolo individuo." Isler (2000) 201.

western cities. Isler's cautious remark that Sicilian theaters must have been symbols of political autonomy, *even if only in appearance*, recognizes the enormous complexities of the situation.[75] Indeed, as Galvagno eloquently put it: "La caduta di Dionisio II, con il suo conseguente allontanamento, lasciava la Sicilia senza timoniere. Un ritorno, dopo così lungo tempo, ad un ordinamento democratico, che pure aveva permesso a Siracusa di resistere all'offensiva ateniese, si rivelò impossibile. Sarà compito del moderato Timoleonte, una figura carismatica ma, per certi aspetti, monocratica, riportare l'isola alla sua antica prosperità."[76] It is not entirely clear how distinctly democratic Timoleon's rule was. Moreover, as I have argued in previous chapters, it seems quite likely that Sicilian tyrants, likewise, often maintained a veneer of democracy. They had at least as much invested in developing symbols of prosperity and democracy as Timoleon, particularly in circumstances where there was, in fact, little general wealth and still less democracy.

In sum, where we have epigraphical evidence about the building of a theater, it points to wealthy individuals rather than to the city or assembly. Even if Timoleon's devotion to democracy were not in question, there is no clearly established connection between the theater and democracy in the West.

If we set aside, for the moment, the assumption that city wealth and democratic government are necessary to create the conditions for theater-building, the remaining evidence for Timoleon's role in catalyzing the building of monumental theaters is fairly thin. It is notoriously difficult to date the theaters with any precision, but, where they can be dated, few coincide with Timoleon's rule. As Isler summarizes, Iaitas, Syracuse, Heraclea Minoa, Morgantina, Solunto, Tyndaris, Segesta, and Monte di Cavalli, and maybe also Helorus, and Akrai can be dated to between the second half of the fourth and the first half of the third century.[77] This is a long 100 years during which Sicily was mostly ruled by powerful individuals rather than by democracies.[78] Moreover, whether or not Timoleon himself is labeled a tyrant or a democrat, the period of his power (344–ca 336) was very brief, even if the democratic phase that immediately followed his abdication is included in the accounting.

---

[75] Isler (1986) 162.   [76] Galvagno (2002) 416.

[77] Isler (1986) 162. There is a huge range of scholarly opinion about the dating of most Sicilian theaters; for a summary review of this range, see Moretti (1993); Courtois (1989); and Mitens (1988).

[78] Syracusan rulers often exerted control over much of the rest of the island: Dionysius I (405–367); Dionysius II (367–344); "third democracy," when an oligarchy-friendly council of 600 was in power (344–317); Agathocles (ca 317–289), though he only assumed title of King in 304; "fourth democracy" (289–278); Pyrrhus (278–276); Hieron II (275/4–215), though he only assumed title of King in 269.

Following an interim of small oligarchies when the democracies fell apart, in 317, Agathocles gained control over most of Sicily as tyrant of Syracuse.

Of the fifteen or sixteen or Sicilian theaters known from excavation or literary reports, only one has been independently and fairly securely dated to the period of Timoleon's work in Sicily.[79] This is the newly excavated theater at Montagna di Cavalli, ancient Hippana.[80] Yet, as Stefano Vassallo notes, this theater (and five others) were well within the Punic Eparchy and under Punic control until the middle of the third century. Although Greek influence and commercial and cultural exchange may explain Hippana's urban plan and its grand theater, it is difficult to see how Timoleon himself, or the democratic reforms that he enacted in the brief eight years of his rule, could have had much bearing on the building of this theater. Diodorus Siculus mentions a second theater in his native Agyrium, which he describes as the second most beautiful theater on the island. Although the city itself was founded at the beginning of the fourth century under the tyrant Agyris (Diod. Sic. 14.95), Timoleon seems to have overthrown a later tyrant and introduced many more citizens in 339 (Diod. Sic 16, 82). Diodorus lists the theater in a catalogue of buildings that he attributes to the new wealth brought by Timoleon. Curiously, however, in a section that immediately precedes his note about Agyrium's theater, he ascribes all the other buildings that came from the new wealth introduced by Timoleon specifically to various tyrants (the "Hall of the Sixty Couches" and the "towers along the shore of the harbor" at Syracuse were built by Agathocles; the Olympeium and the altar near the theater at Syracuse were built by Hieron II).[81] He does not, likewise, place the building of the theater at Agyrium at a certain date: it, like all the other monuments he mentions, might have actually been built under a tyrant. Diodorus' report about the theater at Agyrium cannot, moreover, be tested against the archaeological remains, because these have not yet been securely located, much less excavated.[82]

---

[79] See Marconi (2012) for recent estimates of the dates of the theaters. In his survey of archaeological evidence for Timoleon's building program, Talbert could only point to one theater, Heraclea Minoa, as tentatively dated to the period of Timoleon, but the theater is now usually ascribed to a later date, Talbert (1974) 146–53.

[80] Vassallo (2012) and (2019).

[81] Diod. Sic. 16.83.2–3. It is curious that Diodorus mentions Hieron's building of the great altar near the theater, but not his building of the theater itself. Cf. Finley (1979) 101.

[82] Favaloro (1922) 34–9 identifies the location of the theater based on a thirteenth-century religious document which seems to make reference to remains of a theater (proscenium and kerkides (*in chirchia*)), the topography of the hill, and fragments of seats. His findings are also summarized in Pace (1938), vol. II, 321. His appealing and encouraging hypothesis has not, however, been confirmed by archaeological excavation.

Most other extant remains of theaters in Sicily are dated to the last quarter of the fourth century or later, and some more specifically to the period of Agathocles or Hieron II; on archaeological or epigraphical dating, therefore, most theaters belong to a moment after Timoleon had not only resigned power, but his democratic reforms (if such they really were) had been upset by factional fighting and then by a new era of tyrannical rule.[83] At Morgantina, for example, the fill under various parts of the theater points to the mid-third-century BCE.[84] Iaitas was dated by Isler to the last decades of the fourth.[85] Akrai is often dated as late as the second century.[86] In the case of Syracuse, some scholars date the theater by the inscriptions to Hieron II and his wife carved on the stone steps, and others prefer to push the date of the theater earlier to reach towards the period of the great flowering of Sicilian theater in the fifth century.[87] In any case, there is no evidence to assign this theater to the period of Timoleon. In sum, few monumental theaters seem to have been built during the period of Timoleon's reform.

Like Diodorus Siculus, however, most scholars do not argue that Timoleon funded or encouraged the building of specific theaters, but rather that the prosperity and democratic reforms he brought to the island were the basis for their later construction. Although a similar argument about general urban renewal in Sicilian cities is widely accepted and confirmed by archaeological excavation, in the case of theaters, specifically, the evidence is complicated. A brief survey of some of the cities he is credited with reviving most dramatically seems to contradict this argument. In several large cities destroyed under Dionysius I (or earlier) and revived only under Timoleon, including Gela, Megara Hyblaea, and Camarina, there is, as yet, no evidence of a theater. This is particularly notable because some of these cities grew to be important and wealthy: they are the kinds of cities in which one would expect to find a monumental theater. At Agrigento, an *ekklesiasterion* has been excavated and dated to the third century, but this is one of the rare assembly buildings that seems unlikely to have doubled as a theater (Figure 3.1). As its excavator, De Miro, points out, the building, with hardly any rake and wings extending towards a circle far more than in

---

[83] For a recent summary of estimates of dates, see Marconi (2012), table 1.

[84] On recent excavations and finds, see Bonanno (2009), particularly 72; Sposito (2011); Bell (2012) 114 (with dating of the theater to the mid-third century). On the dedication to Dionysus, see Sjöqvist (1962) 138; Sposito (2003) 332.

[85] Isler (1981) 132.   [86] Moretti (1993) 78–9.

[87] Marconi (2012) 179–80 for discussion and an argument for the later date; cf. Polacco and Anti (1981/1990) and Voza (2008) for the earlier date.

most Greek theaters, is not suitable for theatrical performance.[88] Although such difficulties could no doubt be overcome in performance, the form of the *ekklesiasterion* does not conform in significant ways to the typical monumental theater structure. Di Vita points out that the *ekklesiasterion* seating 3,000 is a symbol of the democracy brought by Timoleon.[89] In other words, although it served the purpose of providing an assembly space, which was also a main function of theaters, its architecture does not align with the grand, theatrical monumentality of theaters in other Sicilian cities. These earlier observations have been confirmed by the recent discovery of a monumental stone theater in Agrigento, currently dated to the early third century BCE and the time of Agathocles, not Timoleon. This theater was possibly built on top of a fifth-century BCE wooden predecessor.[90]

It is not only the problematic chronology of the theaters and the lack of them in key cities that upsets the traditional link between Timoleon and theater-building. The second major premise that associates him with theaters is that the theaters, like the reforms he brought to the island, were fundamentally democratic buildings. Indeed, the function of a grand stone theater seems, as discussed in section 6.1, to have been in large part to provide a place for public assembly. Curiously, however, despite the democratic aura that surrounds both the history of Greek plays, and also the concept of public assembly, it is not clear that the grand stone theaters were, in fact, exclusively or even primarily used by *democratic* assemblies. At Athens, for example, movement of the assembly from the Pnyx to the theater at Athens occurred at some undefined moment after 332 and before the end of the third century.[91] For most of this period, despite a few democratic revivals, Athens was not a democracy but was ruled by a succession of autocratic rulers.[92] It is likely, therefore, though it cannot be proven, that the Athenian assembly began to meet regularly in the theater once they no longer, in fact, wielded significant democratic power.

What might be an accidental meeting of monocratic or oligarchic politics and the meeting of the assembly in the theater in Athens appears as part of a pattern in Sicily. As early as the fifth century, Gelon and Hieron I used theater as a propaganda tool, as I argue earlier in this book. In the democratic period

---

[88] De Miro (1967) 165–6. See p. 57, n. 21.   [89] di Vita (2002) 143.   [90] Caliò (2019).

[91] MacDonald (1943) 58. Cf. Pollux VIII.133, and Athenaeus, *Deipnosophistae* V, 212 e–f, 213, d. For the return to the Pnyx later, cf. Lucian, *Jupiter Tragoedus*, 11.

[92] After the Lamian War of 323–2, democracy was only revived for very brief periods at Athens.

that followed (a democracy that brought Sicily enough stability and order that they were able, among other things, to fight off the Athenian invasion of 415–13) relatively little evidence for public theater remains, since the fragments of Sophron may not belong to a public performance genre at all.[93] At the time of Dionysius I, however, interest in theater was manifestly rekindled as can be seen not only in his own efforts at writing tragedy, but also in the sudden proliferation of comic vases, once "phlyax," throughout the western Greek world.[94] His investments in theater seem to have been imitated and expanded by later tyrants, perhaps most obviously Hieron II, who left his name and that of his wife inscribed on seats in the great theater of Syracuse, but also by lesser tyrants such as, for example, Mamercus of Catania, who, like Dionysius, appears to have written dramas.[95] In Sicily, the main support for theater appears to be neither influence of Athens nor democratic conditions, but, rather, a certain kind of ruler or wealthy elite interested in and able to fund theater and theaters. This is not to imply that Athens and the symbols of democracy played no part in the development of Sicilian theater, far from it; but rather that the West and western tyrants borrowed the elements they wanted (e.g. symbolism of democracy, culture, links to wider Hellenic world, good plays) and left out those they did not want (e.g. actual democracy). Indeed, in this respect, as in so many others identified by Bieber, Courtois, and Mitens,[96] Sicily may have led the way for Roman theater. In the Roman world, the great period of theater-building took place not during the Republic but rather under the Empire. As Sear writes:

> It was Augustus who fully realized the potential of the theatre as a propaganda tool. Pompey had shown that the theatre was not simply an entertainment venue. It was also a place where the Roman people met in large numbers, a building hallowed by long tradition, a dignified setting in which the Roman people were assembled in their proper places according to their station. It is no coincidence that the laws of *discrimina ordinum* were more strictly enforced in the theatre than in any other building of public spectacle. Furthermore, the theatre had a focus lacking in the amphitheatre. The audience gazed down on the wealthy and powerful seated around the rim of the orchestra, the presiding magistrates in their boxes close to the stage, the stage decked out with fine hangings and scenery, the majestic tiers of marble columns rising behind, the inscriptions with their message of imperial power, and the images of rulers past and present.[97]

---

[93] Cf. Kutzko (2012) 373–4; Hordern (2004) 8.   [94] See Chapter 5.

[95] Todisco (2002) 65; Talbert (1974) 97.

[96] Bieber (1961); Courtois (1989); Mitens (1989). Cf. Sear (2006) 50.   [97] Sear (2006) 12.

6.4   Dionysius and the Spark of Theater
in the Fourth Century

We do not have any archaeological evidence that Dionysius built theaters, as we do for Augustus long after him. We do have records, however, that in the first half of the fourth century, Dionysius I's devotion to theater was infamous both because of the cool reception of his plays in Athens (despite his victory at the Lenaea in 367) and because of his apparently unselfconscious criticism of tyranny in them ("Tyranny is the mother of injustice," fr. 4). Although criticizing tyranny as a tyrant seems a gross example of unselfconsciousness, it may, in fact, be one small part of a larger deployment of theater to provide a veneer of democratic assembly and popular support which would serve his own propagandistic ends. Dionysius seems, for example, to have called an assembly to have himself voted into power.[98] If Chrysostom can be trusted, he memorialized his engagement with theater in a statue he had built of himself as Dionysus, god of theater.[99]

Did Dionysius I have a hand in building the great theater of Syracuse? As has often been pointed out, because the theater is carved out of the living rock it is extremely difficult to date, and the first secure evidence is provided by the inscriptions carved into seats honoring Hieron II and his wife. Some scholars argue that the wealth of literary evidence of an active theatrical tradition as early as the fifth century in Syracuse support an early date for the theater.[100] Polacco and Anti, and more recently Voza, for example, have argued that the large theater at Syracuse may date to the fifth century and may therefore have existed in some form before Dionysius I came to power in 405.[101] The arguments for dating as early as the fifth century, however, have been criticized from several quarters, since there is no secure archaeological data and proponents of this date must rely heavily on literary sources.[102] As discussed earlier in this book, there does not seem to be a correlation between strong theatrical traditions and monumental

---

[98]   Mafodda (2002) 446.

[99]   Hyg. *Poet. astr.* II, 30 e 41, and Dio Chrys. *Or.* 37.21. It has been argued that the features were those of Apollo rather than Dionysus. See Sanders (1991). Cf. Caltabiano (2002) 44–5, who notes that although many statues of tyrants had been built by the time of Timoleon, this was the only one that represented a tyrant as a god.

[100]   Contra: Marconi (2012) 178–80.

[101]   Voza (2008); Polacco and Anti (1981/1990); in an early publication, Isler (1973) 14 also admitted a fifth-century theater at Syracuse, citing Neppi Modona (1961) 16 ff., figs. 11–15.

[102]   For a discussion of and disagreement with Polacco and Anti's theories, see e.g. Sear (2006) 49 and Moretti (1993). Bernabò Brea (1967) 97–8 responds to Anti's earlier publications of similar conclusions.

theaters, and so the evidence for early performances may not indicate an early date for the theater itself.

Other kinds of comparative evidence may, however, help define a date when the theater came into use. First, although literary and historical records of the performance of plays in Sicily are not good evidence to date specific monumental theaters, literary references, not to drama and performance in general, but to the theater building itself may give stronger support. Plutarch assumes that the theaters at Syracuse and at Messina had been built by the end of Dionysius' reign and the brief years of transition to Timoleon's heyday. Mamercus of Catania and Hippo of Messina are tried and killed in theaters, respectively.[103] Late evidence is suspect, but, to the extent that Plutarch can be trusted, his sensational stories point in the direction of a relatively early date for a theater of some kind in Syracuse and Messina.

Secondly, the larger urban plan and the dating of other monumental buildings at Syracuse may correspond with the building of the theater. As Voza points out, Dionysius I set in motion a great building program at Syracuse, and the theater fits into the new urban landscape that developed at this point.[104] The great amount of stone quarried from the area of the theater would have been very useful in the larger city building project. In an important article of 1967, Bernabò Brea argued that Anti's views about sequences of development in the theater could not be correct because of the coherent design and enormous labor that must have gone into creating it. He estimates that no less than 15,000 cubic meters of stone must have been quarried in order to create the theater.[105] Perhaps a further hypothesis can be drawn from Bernabò Brea's estimate of the enormous amount of stone removed: the stone itself might have been an object. Dionysius is famous for overseeing the rapid building of a long wall around the city of Syracuse. Archaeologists have determined that much of this stone came from small quarries near the wall, but the large quarry at the site of the theater may have served this or another building purpose as well.[106] Moreover, Bernabò Brea notes that the small rectangular cuts in the walls above the *koilon* of the theater should, from comparative data, be dated to the fourth century; this would accord well with a Dionysian quarry on the site of the theater. He points out that there must have been specific reasons to establish the theater here: perhaps its sacred character or the natural shape of the hillside. To these possibilities, we might add that the site might have been chosen not despite the enormous quarrying it would require, but because of it.

---

[103] Plut. *Tim.* 33.3–4.   [104] Voza (2008).   [105] Bernabò Brea (1967) 100.
[106] Mertens (2002) 244–52.

To these pieces of circumstantial evidence, another curious fact can be added. If few theaters were built in cities rehabilitated by Timoleon, as noted above, the opposite seems to have been true for cities that prospered, or at least survived, under Dionysius I. Not only is there a theater at Syracuse, but many other cities that continued under or fell under the sway of Syracuse in the period of Dionysius' conquest of the island also eventually built monumental theaters. The dates of the extant theaters themselves do not correspond to Dionysius' rule, but we can nevertheless see a pattern in these cities that eventually built, or rebuilt, theaters of monumental proportions: they were all prosperous or, at least, in existence, under Dionysius I.

Table 6.1 *Theaters of eastern Sicily and their relation to Syracuse*[107]

City	Foundation Date	Relation to Syracuse	Date of Theater
Akrai	664/663	Founded as military outpost by Syracuse	Hieron II (ca 269–215)[108]
Catania	ca 729 by colonists from Naxos (Chalcidians)	Victim of political expansion by Syracuse at the beginning of the 5th ca BCE; 476 Hieron deported population; 461 population returned; 415/413 joined Athenian side of war; 403 conquered by Syracuse and population sold as slaves; reconquered in 338 and ruler crucified in the theater	Few traces; probably built by 338 BCE
Helorus	8th ca? Syracusan occupation in 6th ca?	Founded as military outpost by Syracuse	4th ca BCE
Morgantina	Orthogonal city plan built mid-5th ca	Controlled by Kamarina from the Congress of Gela in 424, and by Syracuse from 396 until the end of the Punic War[109]	Early to mid-3rd ca BCE

[107] For a recent table of dates for all archaeologically documented Sicilian theaters, see Marconi (2012) 189, table 1.

[108] Bernabò Brea (1956) 39, though he notes that Bulle (1928) dates the theater to 150 BCE.

[109] For the Syracusan control, see Malcolm Bell. Preliminary report XII, III, *AJA*, 92, 1988, 324; *AJA* 71, 1967, 246–7; *Kokalos* 30–1, 1984–1985.

Table 6.1 (*cont.*)

City	Foundation Date	Relation to Syracuse	Date of Theater
Tauromenium	396	Founded by Dionysius I of Syracuse and remained in orbit of Syracuse until Roman conquest	Built in Hellenistic era, little remains of ancient theater, but one of the blocks which does has the name of Hieron II's wife, Philistis, on it[110]
Tyndaris	396	Founded by Dionysius I of Syracuse and remained in orbit of Syracuse until Roman conquest	Late 4th ca BCE

Most of these stone theaters are thought to have been built towards the end of the fourth or in the third centuries BCE. It is unclear whether the earlier foundations of less permanent wooden theaters were eradicated by the building of the stone theaters. Even stone theaters on the same sites may have completely disappeared.[111]

Two cities were built as military outposts by Syracuse: Helorus, where evidence of some Greek occupation can be traced to the eighth century but the main city was built in the sixth,[112] and Akrai, which seems to have been built about 70 years after the foundation of Syracuse itself. As military outposts, both cities were equipped with large walls and extensive fortifications, and both, eventually, with theater buildings.

The case of Helorus is particularly striking because there is so little evidence of public buildings at the site. The history of this small town remains in large part a mystery, apart from the battle of 493. The city was connected to the mother city of Syracuse by the Via Helorina,[113] and the settlement barely took up 10 hectares (or 104,000 m² by Orsi's calculation) and is surrounded by a wall of 1,420 meters.[114] The region is now fairly fertile and the modern town of Avola, a few kilometers inland from

---

[110] Cerchiai, L. et al. (2002) 167.   [111] Bernabò Brea (1967) 97.

[112] Orsi (1966) 216 writes that the small city of Helorus can certainly be dated to the sixth century, and perhaps even to the seventh. M. T. Curro who edited Orsi's excavation report for the 1961 printing agrees with the seventh-century date.

[113] A Greek road which seems to have been used at least as early as the fifth century. Cerchiai et al. (2002) 218.

[114] Orsi (1899) 215. Cf. Akrai, the city wall of which surrounds an area of about 35 hectares (Cerchiai et al. (2002) 220; the island of Ortygia alone covers about 40 hectares (ibid. 205)).

Helorus, is supported by almond and olive farming. In 1899, when Paolo Orsi first excavated the site, he noted the richness of the landscape.[115] It was not, however, for its agricultural richness alone that the location was chosen, but for its military usefulness. Helorus was meant to serve as a buffer for Syracuse against the native Sikels, living a little inland, and later against the Carthaginians. The city, as its three excavators, Orsi (1899 and 1927), Militello (1958–9), and Piscione (1961), have all noted is noticeably devoid of public buildings.[116] Perhaps its military function explains the bareness of the site. Thus it seems unlikely that major buildings have disappeared because they were recycled into something else.

Despite the scarcity of other public buildings on the site, the theater at Helorus is fairly substantial (Map 6.1). It is located just outside the western city wall on the slope of the hill, which leads into a canal. As Militello notes, the flow of water here cannot have existed in antiquity, since it would have completely covered the orchestra of the theater. As it is, the water has destroyed all trace of the orchestra and *skene*, as the two archaeological investigations of Orsi and then Militello have successively proven. It is unclear how many spectators the theater could have held, as the *koilon*, as at Akrai, seems to have been built only partly resting against the hill. The wings, which would probably have extended to either side, have disappeared. Nevertheless, a rough estimate of the audience capacity is 1,250.[117]

6.5   Whose Theater?

Understanding how the wave of theater buildings fits into the larger history of Sicilian theater is difficult not only because of the complicated and fragmentary archaeological evidence, but also because ancient historical sources have what may, I hope, now seem a natural bias: they rarely describe theatrical performances in Sicilian theaters. Instead, they are interested in assemblies. This is consonant with the argument in this chapter that theaters

---

[115] "Bella e prospera regione agricola questa zona costiera fra il Cassibile ed il Tellaro e oggi una delle meglio coltivate della Sicilia . . . La coltura a mandorleti in quel di Avola e più a mezzo di immensi boschi di ulivi, con la loro tinta fredda e grigiastra, danno una intonazione di una certa malinconia ad un paesaggio, se non fosse sempre ravvivato da un fulgido sole e dal terso azzurro specchio dello Jonio, la cui onda ora lambisce placidamente, ora morde rabbiosamente la costa montana ed uniforme, priva di seni e di promontori." (Orsi (1899) 206.)

[116] Orsi (1899) 232: "In tutta l'area urbana non ho mai vista una sola briciola di marmo, e nemmeno del bel calcare candido e compatto, d'ordinario adibito per la costruzione di edifici pubblici."

[117] Orsi (1899) 235, accepted by Todisco (2002) 171–2.

and particularly Sicilian theaters were primarily built as places of public assembly and only secondarily, or symbolically, as places for performance. Plutarch, for example, presents executions and political assemblies in the theaters beginning at least as early as the fourth century.[118] He records an assembly that seems to have met in the theater at Syracuse shortly after the departure of Dionysius II.[119] Likewise, in his *Life of Timoleon*, he describes assemblies in the theaters of two Sicilian cities. First, Hippo, tyrant of Messina, routed in Timoleon's swift takeover, was executed in the theater at Messina before an assembled crowd that included schoolchildren.[120] Shortly thereafter Mamercus, tyrant of Catana, was tried at the theater of Syracuse, where he attempted to dash his brains out against the stone seats.[121] Finally, Plutarch records that the Syracusans continued to assemble regularly in the theater, even after Timoleon gave up power.[122] Plutarch, at least, seems to have thought or assumed that there was a major theater in the cities of Syracuse and Messina by the middle of the fourth century. If he is right, we must assume that these theaters had been built, at the latest, under the tyrants who lost to Timoleon, since it is inconceivable that a monumental stone theater would have been built so rapidly in the first topsy-turvy days of Timoleon's takeover.[123]

Other historians of Sicily record later assemblies and violent events in Sicilian theaters under the Roman occupation. The citizens of Enna, for example, were slaughtered by Romans as they held an assembly in their theater.[124] In the second half of the second century, slaves who had revolted in Enna brought their master into the theater for trial.[125]

These references share a striking feature: they describe the theaters full of assemblies of the entire citizen body and sometimes even of a wider assembly of most of the population of the city. This repeated focus on the assembly and the role of the theaters as meeting places may, I have argued, be a key to understanding the practical and symbolic function of these monumental theaters. The primary purpose of the theaters may have been not to house the performance of plays, but large assemblies.

Taken as a whole, these anecdotes yield two other pieces of information about the function of the Sicilian theaters. First, theaters seem to have been

---

[118] Cf. Marconi (2012) 185 for an argument that Frontinus' mention of Alcibiades making a speech in a theater at Agrigento (Frontin. *Str.* 3.2.6) is too unreliable to be used as evidence of theaters in the fifth century.

[119] Plut. *Dion* 38. The story tells only of an ox that ran wild into the theater, and then through the rest of the town, adding that the Syracusans ignored all of it and elected their generals.

[120] Plut. *Tim.* 34.3.   [121] Plut. *Tim.* 34.4.   [122] Plut. *Tim.* 38.2–3.

[123] These references are collected and discussed in Marconi (2012).

[124] Livy 24.39.1–5; Frontin. *Str.* 4.7.22; Polyaen. 8.21.   [125] Diod. Sic. 34.2.14.

appropriated or perhaps even built for political purposes from the very beginning. Secondly, the stories all reveal a tension between the force of the populace, sometimes in the form of the assembly, and the forces of government. The anecdotes from the Timoleontic period describe savage reprisals on autocratic leaders taken by the assembled crowd in the theater; still later, the gatherings of Greeks in the theater in the Roman period either end in mass slaughter or in rebellion. In the long memory of late ancient sources, the Sicilian theater figures as a locus of struggle and tension between the people and a series of autocratic rulers.

7 | Conclusion

Gelon and especially Hieron I supported and encouraged an active literary circle, including the playwrights Epicharmus, Deinolochus, Phormis, and, more briefly, Aeschylus. Literary and historical evidence suggests that their plays were performed on a grand scale. When the Deinomenids fell, a democratic government came to power and there is little evidence of large-scale public theatrical events for more than half a century.[1] This period of turbulent democracy was brought to an end by Dionysius I (405–367), who not only ruled Syracuse, but extended his control over most of Sicily and up the mainland as far as the gulf of Taras and beyond.[2] His rule coincides with the sudden proliferation of comic theatrical vases which continued to be produced through the tyranny of his son, Dionysius II (367–344), and into the democratic order of Timoleon (344–338), petering out before the reign of Agathocles (317–289).[3] As the vases became less frequent at the end of the fourth century, however, massive theater buildings seem to have been built in a number of cities, both on the mainland and in Sicily. In the Greek sphere of Sicily, these theaters were often built in cities that had enjoyed some prosperity under Dionysus I. In the following century, especially under the rule of Hieron II, more theaters were erected in stone or renovated to more grand proportions. Can these periods of intense theatrical activity (the phlyax vases under Dionysius I in the first half of the fourth century and the proliferation of grand stone theater buildings in the third century under Hieron II) be understood together with Epicharmus' work under the Deinomenid tyrants at the

---

[1] On late fifth-century Apulian and some Sicilian vases that may represent tragic performance, see Dearden (1999) and Taplin (2007). The first Sicilian vases explicitly representing tragedy on stage date to the second half of the fourth century.

[2] Bonacasa et al. (2002). Finley (1968) 78: "the Dionysian empire at its peak included, counting subjects, clients, colonies and such 'allies' as Locri, the whole of Sicily (except for the extreme western sector from the mouth of the Halycus to Solus east of Palermo), the toe of Italy to the Gulf of Taranto, enclaves farther north at Ancona and the Po mouth and also across the Adriatic in the region of Split."

[3] Trendall (1967a).

189

beginning of the fifth century as part of a local and continuous history of theater in Sicily and in the West? Or are they only small outbursts, caused by a series of Athenian imports, which do not reflect local politics or society, except as a reflection of Athenian drama? I think the former is possible. I have tried to show this in the preceding chapters, and in the following conclusion I sketch out the trajectory of Sicilian theater from Epicharmus to Dionysius I, that is through the fifth century, in an effort to demonstrate how theater developed in Sicily.

7.1 The Gap

The introduction of Athenian comedies in the early fourth century, recorded on some of the phlyax vases, seems to echo the events of the early fifth century. Gelon and Hieron's propagandistic use of theater to further their causes seems to have been continued by the later tyrants Dionysius and then Hieron II. The importation of Athenian comedies in the fourth century, just like the importation of Aeschylus' tragedies in the fifth century, helped pull Syracuse and other western cities into the cultural world of Athens, but it also helped support the image (or mirage) of democratic and popular involvement in the local politics of Syracuse. The stage had been set for this introduction of Athenian theater, moreover, by Epicharmus, and perhaps other local playwrights and their patrons.

The great difficulty in associating Epicharmus with the fourth-century vases is that there is a gap of some 50 or 60 years between the end of his productive life, it seems, and the beginning of the production of the vases. Luckily, several figures are mentioned in the ancient sources to help bridge this gap. First, two Syracusans whose working lives seem to have overlapped with Epicharmus, Deinolochus and Phormis, appear to have written comedies.[4] A reference to Phormis developing the backdrop for stage action suggests that the plays were staged and performed in public.[5] Deinolochus is cited as both rival and son of Epicharmus.[6] We cannot be certain of the actual relationship, but these claims do, nevertheless, suggest that he was, at the very least, working at much the same time, and probably

---

[4] Deinolochus: *PCG* Din. Test. 1 (*Suda* δ 338); *PCG* Din. Test. 2 (Aelian, NA IV 51). We have twelve titles of his plays, nine of them recorded in a papyrus list, *PCG* Din. Test. 3 (*POxy.* 2659, fr. 1 col. Ii 12 et fr. 2 col. Ii 1). Phormis: *PCG* Phor. Test. 1 (*Suda* φ 609); *PCG* Phor. Test. 2 (Arist. *Poet.* 5, p. 1449, b 5; *PCG* Phor. Test. 3 (Paus. V 27, 1 sq). We have six titles of Phormis' plays.

[5] *PCG* Phor. Test. 1 (*Suda* φ 609).   [6] *PCG* Din. Test. 2 (Aelian, NA IV 51).

some time after Epicharmus, and that there was a small contingent of comic writers in fifth-century Syracuse; Epicharmus was not the only one.

More important, we have not only references, but also fragments, from Sophron, the mime-writer of the second half of the fifth century. The dating of his work is made difficult by a note in the *Suda* which makes him a contemporary of both Xerxes and Euripides.[7] This impossible conflation of two periods (the early and late fifth century), Kaibel and Norwood suggest, may have arisen because the two writers were confused with each other: Epicharmus (who would have been a contemporary of Xerxes) and Sophron, later in the fifth century, a contemporary of Euripides.[8] In Sophron's work, reflections of Epicharmus can be seen, not only in the Doric dialect both writers use, despite the frequent adoption of Attic or Ionic dialects by other prose writers of Sophron's day, but also in many of the themes he takes up,[9] and also in specific references and jokes. In his edition of Sophron, Hordern suggests that Epicharmus' non-mythological dramas may have exerted important and direct influences on Sophron's work.[10]

Sophron's *Women Watching the Isthmia,* in particular, may echo Epicharmus' *Thearoi,* though Aeschylus' satyr play, *Theoroi* or *Isthmiastai,* may also figure in the background to both. Both comedians also take up marriage as a central theme, the *Marriage of Hebe* and the *Muses* of Epicharmus, and Sophron's *Busied about the Bride.* From these two wedding plays of Epicharmus, thanks to Athenaeus, we have 61 lines of fish names preserved as well as scattered references from other plays. In Sophron as well fish are frequently listed, and one play, *The Tunafishers,* seems to take them up as its central subject. Sophron's *The Fisherman against the Countryman,* from which there have only survived obscure references to fish, recorded in Athenaeus, may be in the same vein as Epicharmus' *Land and Sea,* which, likewise, has survived only in references to obscure fish.

More specifically, a proverb quoted in Sophron, "healthier than a gourd,"[11] is also cited in Athenaeus as used by Epicharmus. Moreover, a commentator recorded on papyrus from Oxyrhynchus notes that Sophron quoted the same line of Homer as did Epicharmus in his *Odysseus the Deserter.* This

---

[7] *PCG* Soph. Test. 1 (*Suda* c 893).

[8] Botzon (1856) 3 suggested that the correct reading made reference to Artaxerxes rather than Xerxes, which would indeed be chronologically compatible with the reference to Euripides.

[9] On the theme of magic and supersition, see Manchado (2013).

[10] Hordern (2004). Cf. Bosher (2013a).

[11] *PCG* Soph. 33 (*Et. Magn.* P. 774, 41); Ath. *Deipnosophistae* VII.29.

line: "Lest some other [god awake the Trojans]"[12] may have become proverbial, but the commentator's effort to note the parallel in both works may
suggest that it was a more direct reference as Hordern suggests. Odysseus is
a favorite subject of Epicharmus, appearing in the title of two plays, and also
figures in one of the eleven extant titles of Deinolochus' corpus. Mythological
themes are not common in extant fragments of Sophron, but there are nods
to mythological characters (Odysseus, Ajax, the Trojans). Finally, Sophron's
mention of "Myrilla"[13] – another name for Democopus, the architect of the
theater at Syracuse in the early fifth century – may be a reference to theater in
the time of Epicharmus.

The tradition of mime-writing did not stop with Sophron, but continued in the fourth century with Xenarchus. Xenarchus, a mime-writer
under Dionysius I, is reported as Sophron's son.[14] This is probably
untrue, but at least it suggests a connection between the work of these
two mime-writers. Though little survives of Xenarchus' work, he is
reported to have written mimes, or some comedy under Dionysius I;
the *Suda* compares him to Sotades, noting that Xenarchus, too, wrote
farces or "phlyakes."

The scanty records of early theater do, in this way, offer some evidence
for a continuous comic tradition in the West to bridge the gap between
Epicharmus and the phlyax vases. As Kutzko points out, moreover, it is
very likely that the formal, literary mimes of Sophron shared some features
with popular mime of his day, which does not survive in text form.[15] Since
our evidence, however, comes from the few fragments of the literary mimes
of Sophron, we are faced with a problem of genre and of public reception. If
Sophron's mimes were only performed at small symposiastic parties of the
elite – which, despite a few suggestions to the contrary,[16] is the prevailing
view – is this likely to have perpetuated a popular comic tradition of
theater? Is the work of Sophron enough to explain the sudden widespread
production of comic vases in the next century?

When the surviving texts are considered on their own, they do not
appear substantial enough, or perhaps even similar enough one to another,
to provide evidence of a continuous tradition. If, however, we look at the
evidence from two fresh angles (first, without the restrictions of strict Attic

---

[12] *PCG* Soph. 140 (*POxy.* 2429).   [13] *PCG* Soph. 123 (Eust. *Od.* P. 1457, 19).

[14] *PCG* Xen. Test. 2 (Phot. P. 485, 21).   [15] Kutzko (2012).

[16] Solinus, *De mirabilibus mundi* 5.13 (on Sicily), claims that it was on this island that comedy and
"staged verbal abuse" originated: "Hic primum inuenta comœdia. Hinc et cauillatio mimica in
scena stetit."; R. L. Hunter (1993) 31–44, on Herondas, also suggests that the mimes were
performed publicly.

genre divisions between formal Comedy and Mime,[17] and, secondly, taking account of the wider political situation in Sicily), it may be possible to trace the links through the fragments of evidence left to us.

There is evidence of popular theater in the early fifth and again in the early fourth centuries. At the beginning of the fifth century, the tyrant Hieron welcomed a production of Aeschylus' *Aetnean Women* and most likely also his *Persians*. At the same court, Epicharmus, Deinolochus, and Phormis seem to have produced many comedies. The theme and content of these tragedies and comedies can be seen to support the tyrant's regime (Chapter 4). Provision of large-scale productions for the assembled Syracusans may also have bolstered the tyrant's image, making him appear both current with Attic dramatic developments and also supportive of the democratic implications of popular assembly and, by extension, mass gathering for theatrical performance. Moreover, on the island of Lipari, some early comic figurines have been found, which Bernabò Brea and Cavalier suggest belong to the same period and perhaps represent the tradition of Epicharmus' theater. Likewise, following the dating proposed by Trendall, the phlyax vases began to be produced at the beginning of the fourth century during the reign of Dionysius I of Syracuse. In this period, Dionysius I made even greater efforts to engage with the Attic theater world than his forebears Gelon and Hieron: he himself wrote tragedies and submitted them to Attic competitions.

I suggest that the conditions were similar in both periods. Both tyrants seem to have supported an active literary scene at their courts: Hieron famously surrounded himself with Bacchylides, Pindar, Aeschylus, as well as Epicharmus, Phormis, and Deinolochus; likewise, Dionysius I not only surrounded himself with poets, but also, infamously, tried his own hand at writing plays. Even more telling, both tyrants seem to have used tragedy to advance their own political ends: Hieron hired Aeschylus to write a play celebrating his establishment of a "new" city, Aetna; Dionysius, infamous in antiquity for the harshness of his rule, seems to have filled his plays, not only with adages about justice and good government, but even more ironically with a criticism of tyranny itself. Both tyrants seem to have used tragedy to whitewash their own dictatorial practices.

Not only tragedy, but, in both cases, comedy seems to have been turned to propagandistic use by the tyrants. Xenarchus (writing mimes in the tradition of Sophron) is reported to have been commissioned by

---

[17] We have a good model for ignoring generic differences in Aristotle, who saw connections between all kinds of literary and performative traditions and their influence on each other in the opening to his *Poetics* (1447–9).

Dionysius to mock the Rhegians;[18] likewise, in his play the *Islands*, Epicharmus described Hieron protecting the Locrians from a harsh dictator, Anaxilas of Rhegium. This episode is recorded in a scholiast to Pindar's *Pythian* 2 near lines about the harshness of Phalaris, who is unfavorably compared with Hieron.[19] It seems likely that the reference was made to Hieron here because the play also attempted to show Hieron's good character in contrast to that of wicked tyrants.

Dionysius' use of theater seems then to be similar to, if not perhaps even modeled on, that of the two Syracusan tyrants who preceded him, Gelon and Hieron. If this is the case, the question of the literary or performative character of Sophron's work is not really the deciding factor. If Sophron was simply composing his mimes for the literati during the turbulent and democratic upheavals of the latter half of the fifth century, this is sufficient for the tradition of comic theater, local theater, to have continued where it mattered, among the powerful, who, when their day came, turned it to their own political purposes, propaganda, as well as using it for the entertainment of the general population.

Here we turn to another puzzle about the phlyax vases: why so suddenly, so widespread, and so similar? As Dearden argues, these similarities among the pictures on the phlyax vases, found all over the West, suggest that they represent some kind of standardized theater. He concludes that this homogeneity "makes it difficult to maintain the concept of impromptu drama," and outlines the correspondences among some vases in a range of fabrics.[20] If we posit Dionysius as a supporter of theater, like his forebears Hieron and Gelon, we have a possible solution to this sudden widespread advent of depictions of popular theater. That is, if Dionysius was actively supporting theater, and public performance, as Hieron had done, then it seems reasonable that similar performances would have within a few years begun to be performed in the various parts of South Italy and Sicily under his control. And perhaps cities outside his control may still have felt the influence of a sudden encouragement of the arts. If we look to the next grand tyrant of Syracuse, Hieron II, the same technique seems to be in evidence, for it is under his rule that many of the great theaters of Sicily were built, some with his name or that of his wife etched on a commemorative stone. As Polacco has argued, most of these theaters, especially in Sicily, show the influence of the theater at Syracuse in various

---

[18] *PCG* Xen. Test. 2 (Phot. P. 485,21).   [19] *PCG* 96 (Schol. Pind. *Pyth.* 1, 99 a II p. 18, 21 Dr.).
[20] Dearden (1988) 34–5.

elements of design, and only exceptionally the influence of the Theater of Dionysus at Athens.[21]

That Epicharmus was still very much in the foreground in these later periods is apparent not only in his influence on Sophron, and also the similarity in themes between his plays and the phlyax vases themselves, but also in the work of the tyrant Dionysius' son, who is reported to have made an edition of Epicharmus' letters.[22] Likewise, under Hieron II, a bronze statue featuring an epigram of Theocritus (well known as an imitator of Sophron), perhaps erected in the theater of Syracuse, commemorated the brilliance of Epicharmus and his tremendous effect on the city of Syracuse as a poet and luminary.[23]

If we imagine the tyrants as the prime movers of large-scale theatrical productions, not only later with Hellenistic buildings of grand theaters, but also in their support of earlier writers like Epicharmus, then we no longer need to base our argument that there was a western, Doric tradition on the problematic assumption that a subliterary native tradition fed into the phlyax vases. The tyrants' ties with the larger Greek world, moreover, give ample opportunity for the importing of Athenian plays, as, for example, Aeschylus in the early part of the fifth century, and perhaps Aristophanes in the beginning of the fourth.

Although the great expansion of Athenian theater westward in the fifth century and later did have an impact on the theatrical scene, there is evidence to suggest that it was less likely that it was the catalyst for theater in the West, than that Athenian theater was absorbed into an active theatrical tradition which the Syracusan tyrants Gelon, and especially Hieron, had developed in the early fifth century and which Dionysius I continued into the fourth century. Although even in the fifth century the Athenian plays of Aeschylus were presented in Sicily, they were imported to serve the particular aims of the tyrant Hieron, and, likewise, Dionysius I may have supported both local and imported plays for reasons of propaganda.

[21] See Chapter 6.   [22] *PCG* Test. 33 (*Suda* d 1179).
[23] *PCG* Test. 18 (Theoc. *Epigr.* 18. (*AP* IX 600). Cf. Handley (2003) for discussion of this epigram.

Bibliography

Abbreviations

LCS   Trendall, A. D. (1967a) *The Red-Figured Vases of Lucania, Campania and Sicily. Oxford.*

PhV   Trendall, A. D. (1967b) *Phlyax Vases. BICS Suppl.* 19. London.

PCG   Kassel, R. and C. Austin (2001) *Poetae Comici Graeci.* Berlin/New York.

Adamesteanu, D. (1962) "L'Ellenizzazione della Sicilia ed il momento di Ducezio." *Kokalos* 8: 167–98.

   (1990) "Greeks and Natives in Basilicata," in J.-P. Descœudres (ed). *Greek Colonists and Native Populations.* Canberra. 143–50.

Ahrens, H. L. (1843) *De Graecae Linguae Dialectis.* Göttingen.

Allan, W. (2001) "Euripides in Megale Hellas." *Greece and Rome* 48.1: 67–86.

Anderson, C. A. (1995) *Athena's Epithets: Their Structural Significance in the Plays of Aristophanes.* Stuttgart.

d'Andria, F. (2002) "L'Adriatico: i rapporti tra le due sponde," in Bonacasa et al.: 117–37.

Anti, C. (1947) *Teatri greci arcaici da Minosse a Pericle.* Padua.

Anti, C. and L. Polacco (1969) *Nuove ricerche sui teatri greci arcaici.* Padua.

Antonaccio, C. M. (2001) "Ethnicity and Colonization," in I. Malkin (ed.) *Ancient Perceptions of Greek Ethnicity.* Cambridge, MA. 113–57.

Arias, P. E. (1934) *Il teatro greco fuori di Atene.* Florence.

Arnott, P. (1962) *Greek Scenic Conventions in the Fifth Century BC.* Oxford.

Ashby, C. (1988) "The Case for the Rectangular/Trapezoidal Orchestra." *Theater Research International* 13: 1–20.

   (1999) *Classical Greek Theatre: New Views of an Old Subject.* Iowa City, IA.

Austin, C. and D. Olson (eds.) (2004) *Aristophanes' Thesmophoriazusae.* Oxford.

Bacci, G. M. and U. Spigo (2002) *Prosopon-persona: testimonianze del teatro antico in Sicilia.* Palermo.

Bakola, E. (2010) *Cratinus and the Art of Comedy.* Oxford.

Barigazzi, A. (1955) "Epicarmo e la figura di Ulisse *hesychos.*" *Rheinisches Museum für Philologie* 98: 121–35.

Barresi, S. (2013) "Sicilian Red-figure Vase Painting," in C. L. Lyons, M. Bennett, and C. Marconi (eds.) *Sicily: Art and Invention between Greece and Rome.* Malibu. 210–19.

196

Basourakos, J. (1998) "Exploring the Moral Sphere through Dramatic Art: the Role of Contemporary Canadian Plays in Moral Pedagogy." *Canadian Journal of Education* 3: 265–80.

Battezzato, L. (2008) "Pythagorean Comedies from Epicharmus to Alexis," *Aevum Antiquum* NS 8: 139–64.

Bean, G. E. (1979) *Aegean Turkey*. London.

Beare, W. (1954) "The Costume of the Actors in Aristophanic Comedy." *CQ* NS 4: 64–75.

Becker, T. (2003) *Griechische Stufenanlagen: Untersuchungen zur Architektur, Entwicklungsgeschichte, Funktion und Repräsentation*. Münster.

Bell, M. (1981) *Morgantina Studies I: the Terracottas*. Princeton, NJ.

(1984–1985) "Recenti scavi nell'Agora di Morgantina." *Kokalos* 30–1: 501–20.

(1988) "Excavations at Morgantina 1980–1985. Preliminary Report XII." III, *AJA* 92: 313–42.

(2012) "Spazio e istituzioni nell'agora greca di Morgantina," in C. Ampolo (ed.) *Agora greca e agorai di Sicilia*. Pisa. 111–18.

Bellia, A. (ed.) (2014) *Musica, culti e riti nell'occidente greco*. Pisa.

Berezin, M. (1994) "Cultural Form and Political Meaning: State-Subsidized Theater, Ideology and the Language of Style in Fascist Italy." *The American Journal of Sociology* 99.5: 1237–86.

Berger, S. (1992) *Revolution and Society in Greek Sicily and Southern Italy. (Historia Einzelschriften* 71). Stuttgart.

Berk, L. (1964) *Epicharmus*. Groningen.

Bernabò Brea, L. (1956) *Akrai*. Catania.

(1967) "Studi sul teatro greco di Siracusa." *Palladio* 17: 97–132.

(1998) *Le maschere ellenistiche della tragedia greca*. Naples.

Bernabò Brea, L. and M. Cavalier (1991) *Meligunis Lipàra*. Rome.

(1997) *La ceramica figurata della Sicilia e della Magna Grecia nella Lipàra del IV sec. a.C.* Milan.

(2001) *Maschere e personaggi del teatro greco nelle terracotte Liparesi*. Rome

(2002) *Terracotte teatrali e buffonesche della Sicilia orientale e centrale*. Palermo.

Bernabò Brea, L., M. Cavalier, and U. Spigo (1994) *Lipari: Museo Archeologico Eoliano*. Palermo.

Bethe, E. (1896) *Prolegomena zu Geschichte des Theaters im Alterthum*. Leipzig.

Bieber, M. (1954) "The Entrances and Exits of Actors and Chorus in Greek Plays." *AJA* 58: 280–301.

(1961) *The History of the Greek and Roman Theater*. Princeton, NJ.

Biers. W. (1970) "Excavations at Phlius 1970." *Hesperia* 40: 436–7, 439–47.

(1973) "The Theater at Phlius: Excavations 1972." *Hesperia* 42: 111–20.

(1975) "The Theater at Phlius: Excavations 1973." *Hesperia* 45: 51–68.

Biers, W. and T. D. Boyd (1982) "Ikarion in Attica: the Theatral Area." *Hesperia* 51: 12–14.

Boedeker, D. and K. A. Raaflaub (eds.) (2001) *Democracy, Empire and the Arts in Fifth-Century Athens*. Cambridge, MA.

Bonacasa, N., L. Braccesi, and E. De Miro (eds.) (2002) *La Sicilia dei due Dionisi*. Rome.

Bonanno, C. (2008) "Gli oscilla discoidali," in C. Bonanno (ed.) *Apollonia: indagini archeologiche sul Monte di San Fratello, Messina, 2003–2005*. Rome. 57–61.

(2009) "Gli scavi nell'area del teatro di Morgantina (2004–2005) e i lavori per la riapertura del Museo di Aidone," in G. Guzzetta (ed.) *Morgantina, a cinquant'anni dall'inizio delle ricerche sistematiche: Atti dell'Incontro di Studi. Aidone, 10 dicembre 2005*. Caltanisetta. 69–85.

Bonanno, M. G. (1972) *Studi su Cratete comico*. Padua.

Bondi, S. F. (1999) "Carthage, Italy, and the 'Vth Century Problem,'" in G. Pisano (ed.) *Phoenicians and Carthaginians in the Western Mediterranean*. Rome. 39–48.

Bookidis, N. and R. Stroud (1997) *The Sanctuary of Demeter and Kore: Topography and Architecture (Corinth, Greece)*. Princeton, NJ.

Bosher, K. (2006). *Theater on the Periphery: a Social and Political History of Theater in Early Sicily*. PhD Dissertation.

(2008–2009) "To Dance in the Orchestra: a Circular Argument," *Illinois Classical Studies*, 33–4: 1–24.

(2011) "Review of Csapo, *Actors and Icons of the Ancient Theater*." *Classical Philology* 106.4: 361–5.

(ed.) (2012a) *Theater outside Athens: Drama in Greek Sicily and South Italy*. Cambridge.

(2012b) "Hieron's Aeschylus," in Bosher (2012a): 97–111.

(2013a) "Problems in Non-Athenian Drama: Some Questions about South Italy and Sicily." *Ramus* 42.1–2 = R. Rader and J. Collins (eds.) *The Enigmatic Context: Approaches to Greek Drama*: 89–103.

(2013b) "Infinite Variety: Drama in Ancient Sicily," in C. L. Lyons, M. Bennett, and C. Marconi (eds.) *Sicily: Art and Invention between Greece and Rome*. Malibu. 110–21.

(2013c) "Ancient Greek Theaters," in H. Roisman (ed.) *Encyclopedia of Greek Tragedy*. Chichester.

(2014) "Epicharmus and Early Sicilian Comedy," in M. Revermann (ed.) *The Cambridge Companion to Greek Comedy*. Cambridge. 79–94.

Botzon, L. (1856) *De Sophrone et Xenarcho mimographis*, progr. Lyck 1856 (non vidi).

Bowra, C. M. (1963) "Two Lines of Eumelus." *CQ* NS 13: 145–53.

Braccesi, L. (1979) *I tragici greci e l'occidente*. Bologna.

Branciforti, M. G. (2010) "Da Katáne a Catina," in M. G. Branciforti and V. La Rosa (eds.) *Tra lava e mare: Contributi all'archaiologhia di Catania*. Catania. 135–258.

Braund, D. and E. Hall (2014a) "Gender and Performance on a Fifth-century Red-figure Fragmentary Athenian Vase from Olbia." *JHS* 134: 1–11.

(2014b) "Greek Theatre in the Fourth-century Black Sea," in Csapo et al.: 371–92.

Braund, D., E. Hall, and R. Wyles (eds.) (2019) *Theatre and Performance Culture in the Ancient Black Sea World.* Cambridge.

Bravo, B. (1991) "Citoyens et libres non-citoyens dans les cités coloniales a l'époque archaïque: Le cas de Syracuse," in R. Lonis (ed.) *L'Etranger dans le monde grec. II.* Nancy. 43–85.

Breitholtz, L. (1960). *Die dorische Farce im griechischen Mutterland vor dem 5. Jahrhundert: Hypothese oder Realität?* Stockholm.

Brelich, A. (1964–1965) "La religione greca in Sicilia." *Kokalos* 10/11: 35–63.

Bremer, J. M. (1991) "Poets and Their Patrons," in A. Harder and H. Hofmann (eds.) *Fragmenta Dramatica.* Göttingen. 39–60.

Broadbent, R. J. (1901) *A History of Pantomime.* London.

Broneer, O. (1944) "The Tent of Xerxes and the Greek Theater." *California Publications in Classical Archaeology* 1: 305–11.

Buck, C. D. (1955) *The Greek Dialects: Grammar, Selected Inscriptions, Glossary.* Chicago.

Buckler, C. (1986) "The Myth of the Movable Skene." *AJA* 90: 431–6.

Bulle, H. (1928) *Untersuchungen an griechischen Theatern.* Munich.

Burelli, L. (1979) "Euripide e l'Occidente: Melanippe Prigioniera" in L. Braccesi (ed.) *I Tragici Greci e l'Occidente.* Bologna. 129–67.

Burkert, W. (1972; Eng. trans. 1983) *Homo Necans: The Anthropology of Ancient Greek Sacrificial Ritual and Myth.* Berkeley.

(1977/1985 Eng. trans. 1985) *Greek Religion: Archaic and Classical.* Oxford.

(1979) "Kynaithos, Polycrates and the Homeric Hymn to Apollo," in G. W. Bowersock, W. Burkert, and M. C. J. Putnam (eds.) *Arktouros: Hellenic Studies Presented to B. M. W. Knox.* Berlin. 52–62.

(1987) "The Making of Homer in the 6th Century BC: Rhapsodes versus Stesichorus," in M. True et al. (eds.) *Papers on the Amasis Painter and His World.* Malibu. 51–62.

(2001) *Savage Energies: Lessons of Myth and Ritual in Ancient Greece.* Chicago.

Burn, A. R. (1962; reprinted 1984) *Persia and the Greeks: The Defence of the West c. 546–478 B.C.* London.

Butcher, S. H. (1907; reprinted 1932) *Aristotle's Theory of Poetry and Fine Art.* London.

Caliò, L. (2019) "Il teatro di Agrigento e lo sviluppo della città monumentale," in V. Caminneci, M. C. Parello, and M. S. Rizzo (eds.) *Theaomai: Teatro e società in età ellenistica. Atti delle XI giornate gregoriane* (Agrigento, 2-3 Dicembre 2017), 201–28. Sesto Fiorentino.

Caltabiano, M. (2002) "La monetazione di Dionisio fra economia e propaganda," in Bonacasa et al.: 33–45.

Caminneci, V., M. C. Parello, and M. S. Rizzo (eds.) (2019) *Theaomai: Teatro e società in età ellenistica. Atti delle XI giornate gregoriane (Agrigento, 2–3 Dicembre 2017)*. Sesto Fiorentino.

Camp, J. (2001) *The Archaeology of Athens*. New Haven, CT.

Canac, F. (1967) *Acoustique des théâtres antiques*. Paris.

Carpenter, T. H. (1986) *Dionysian Imagery in Ancient Greek Art*. Oxford.

(2009) "Prolegomenon to the Study of Apulian Red-Figure Pottery." *AJA* 113.1: 27–38.

Carpenter, T. H., K. M. Lynch, and E. G. D. Robinson (eds.) (2014) *The Italic Peoples of Ancient Apulia: New Evidence from Pottery for Workshops, Markets and Customs*. Cambridge.

Carrière, J. C. (1979) *Le carnaval et la politique*. Paris.

Carter, D. M. (2004), "Was Attic Tragedy Democratic?" *Polis* 21: 1–24.

Carter, J. C. (1983) *The Sculpture of Athena Polias at Priene*. London.

(1990) "Metapontum: Land, Wealth, and Population," in J. P. Descoeudres (ed.) *Greek Colonists and Native Populations*. Oxford. 405–41.

Cartledge, P. (1997) "Deep Plays: Theatre as Process in Greek Civic Life," in Easterling (1997b): 3–35.

Casevitz, M. (1991) "Le vocabulaire du pouvoir personnel dans la poésie archaïque." *Ktèma* 16: 203–10.

Cassio, A. C. (1985) "Two Studies on Epicharmus and His Influence." *HSCP* 89: 37–51.

(2001) "Il dialetto greco di Taranto," in *Taranto e Il Mediterraneo: Atti del quarantunesimo convegno di studi sulla Magna Grecia*. Taranto. 436–66.

(2002) "The Language of Dorian Comedy," in A. Willi (ed.) *The Language of Greek Comedy*. Oxford. 51–83.

Castaldo, D. and E. Rocconi (2012) "Music on Stage in Red-Figure Vase-Painting of Magna Graecia (400–320 BC). The Role of Music in the So-Called 'Phlyax Vases'," in R. Eichmann, J. Fang, and L.-C. Koch (eds.) *Sound from the Past: The Interpretation of Musical Artifacts in Archaeological Context*. Leidorf. 243–60.

Ceka, N. (2002) "I riflessi della politica di Dionisio il Grande nel territorio dell'attuale Albania" in Bonacasa et al.: 77–80.

Cerchiai, L., L. Jannelli, and F. Longo (2002) *Città greche della Magna Grecia e della Sicilia*. Verona.

Chaniotis, A. (1997) "Theatricality Beyond the Theater: Staging Public Life in the Hellenistic World," in Le Guen (ed.) *De la scène aux gradins. PALLAS* 47: 219–60.

Chen, X. (2002) *Acting the Right Part: Political Theater and Popular Drama in Contemporary China*. Honolulu.

Ciaceri, E. (1911) *Culti e miti nella storia dell'antica Sicilia*. Catania.

Clinton, K. (2004) "Epiphany in the Eleusinian Mysteries." *Illinois Classical Studies* 29: 85–109.

Collart, J. (1954) *Varron* De Lingua Latina *V*. Paris.

Collart, P. (1928) "Le théâtre de Philippes." *BCH* 52: 74–124, tav. 2–5.

Connor, W. R. (1990) "City Dionysia and Athenian Democracy," in W. R. Connor, M. H. Hansen, K. A. Raaflaub, and B. S. Strauss (eds.) *Aspects of Athenian Democracy*. Copenhagen. 7–32.

Consolo Langher, S. N. (1969–1970) "Problemi di storia costituzionale siceliota." *Helikon* 9–10: 107–43.

(1996) *Siracusa e la Sicilia greca: tra età arcaica ed alto ellenismo*. Messina.

(1997) *Un imperialismo tra democrazia e tirannide: Siracusa nei secoli V e IV a. C*. Rome.

(1988–1989) "Tra Falaride e Ducezio: concezione territoriale, forme di contatto, processi di depoliticizzazione e fenomeni di restrutturazione civico-sociale nella politica espansionistica dei grandi tiranni e in età post-dinomenide." *Kokalos* 34–55: 229–63.

Cook, J. M. (1968) "Review of Loicq-Berger, *Syracuse: Histoire culturelle d'une cité grecque*." *Classical Review* NS 18: 240–1.

Cornford, F. M. (1961; reprinted 1993; originally published 1914, London) *The Origin of Attic Comedy*. New York.

Coulton, J. J. (1977) *Greek Architects at Work*. Ithaca, NY.

Courtois, C. (1989) *Le bâtiment de scène des théâtres d'Italie et de Sicile*. Louvain.

Croon, J. H. (1952) "The Palici: an Autochthonous Cult in Ancient Sicily." *Mnemosyne* 5: 116–29.

Crusius, O. (1892) "Epicharm bei den Paroemiographen." *Philologus suppl. VI*: 283–4.

Csapo, E. (1986) "A Note on the Würzburg Bell-Crater H5697 ('Telephus Travestitus')." *Phoenix* 40: 379–92.

(1997) "Riding the Phallus for Dionysus." *Phoenix* 51.3–4: 253–95.

(2010) *Actors and Icons of the Ancient Theater*. Oxford.

Csapo, E., H. R. Goette, J. R. Green, and P. Wilson (eds.) (2014) *Greek Theatre in the Fourth Century BC*. Berlin.

Csapo, E. and M. Miller (eds.) (2007) *The Origins of Theatre in Ancient Greece and Beyond: From Ritual to Drama*. Cambridge.

Csapo, E. and W. Slater (1995) *The Context of Ancient Drama*. Ann Arbor, MI.

Curbera, J. B. (1997) "Chthonians in Sicily." *GRBS* 38: 397–408.

Daumas, M. (1998) *Cabiriaca: Recherches sur l'iconographie du culte des Cabires*. Paris.

Davidson, J. F. (1986) "The Circle and the Chorus." *Greece and Rome* 33: 38–46.

De Angelis, F. (2016) *Archaic and Classical Greek Sicily: A Social and Economic History*. Oxford.

De Bernardi Ferrero, D. (1966–1974) *Teatri classici in Asia Minore*. Vols. 1–4. Rome.

De Cesare, M. (2003) "La ceramica figurata italiota e siceliota ad Entella," in *Quarte giornate internazionali di studi sull'area elima, Erice 1–4 dicembre 2000. Atti*: 253–69.

(2013). "Greek Myth and Religion in the Sicilian Context," in C. L. Lyons, M. Bennett, and C. Marconi (eds.) *Sicily: Art and Invention between Greece and Rome*. Malibu. 67–80.

De Miro, E. (1963) "I recenti scavi sul poggetto di San Nicola in Agrigento." *CronA* 2: 57–63.

(1967) "L'ekklesiasterion in contrada S. Nicola ad Agrigento." *Palladio* 17: 164–8.

(1989) "Eraclea Minoa," in *Bibliografia topografica della colonizzazione greca in Italia e nelle isole tirreniche*. Pisa. 234–77.

(2014) *Heraclea Minoa: mezzo secolo di ricerche*. Pisa and Rome.

Dearden, C. W. (1988) "Phlyax Comedy in Magna Graecia: A Reassessment," in J. H. Betts, J. T. Hoder, and J. R. Green (eds.) *Studies in Honour of T. B. L. Webster*. Bristol. 2: 33–41.

(1990a) "Fourth-Century Tragedy in Sicily: Athenian or Sicilian?" in J. P. Descoeudres (ed.) *Greek Colonists and Native Populations*. Oxford. 231–42.

(1990b) "Epicharmus, Phlyax and Sicilian Comedy," in J. P. Descoeudres (ed.) *Eumousia: Ceramic and Iconographic Studies in Honour of A. Cambitoglou*. Sydney. 155–61.

(1999) "Plays for Export." *Phoenix*, 53: 3–4.

(2012) "Whose Line Is It Anyway? West Greek Comedy in Its Context," in Bosher (ed.) (2012a). 272–88.

Demand, N. (1971) "Epicharmus and Gorgias." *AJPh* 92: 3: 453–63.

Dilke, O. A. W. (1948) "The Greek Theatre Cavea." *BSA* 43: 125–91.

(1950) "Details and Chronology of Greek Theatre Caveas." *BSA* 45: 21–62.

Dimartino, A. (2005) "Siracusa. B. Fonti epigrafiche." *BTCGI* XIX: 59–128.

Dindorf, W. (ed.) (1824) *Julii Pollucis Onomasticon*. Leipzig.

Dinsmoor, W. B. (1951) "The Athenian Theater of the 5th Century," in G. Mylonas (ed.) *Studies Presented to David Moore Robinson*. Washington, DC. 311–30.

Dörpfeld, W. (1896) *Das griechische Theater*. Athens.

Dougherty, C. (1991) "Linguistic Colonialism in Aeschylus' Aetnaeae." *GRBS* 32: 119–32.

(1993) *The Poetics of Colonization*. Oxford.

Dubois, L. (1989) *Inscriptions grecques dialectales de Sicile*. Paris.

Ducrey, P. and O. Picard (1971) "Recherches à Latô: Le théâtre." *BCH* 95: 516–31.

Duncan, A. (2011) "Nothing to do with Athens? Tragedians at the Courts of Tyrants," in D. M. Carter (ed.) *Why Athens? A Reappraisal of Tragic Politics*. Oxford. 69–84.

(2012) "A Theseus Outside Athens: Dionysius I of Syracuse and Tragic Self-Presentation," in Bosher (2012a): 137–55.

(forthcoming) *Command Performance: Tyranny and Theater in Classical Antiquity*.

Easterling, P. E. (1993) "The End of an Era? Tragedy in the Early Fourth Century," in A. Sommerstein, S. Halliwell, J. Henderson, and B. Zimmerman (eds.) *Tragedy, Comedy and the Polis*. Bari. 559–69.

(1994) "Euripides outside Athens." *ICS* 19: 73–80.

(1997a) "A Show for Dionysus," in Easterling (1997b): 36–53.

(ed.) (1997b) *The Cambridge Companion to Greek Tragedy*. Cambridge.

Easterling, P. E. and E. Hall (eds.) (2002) *Greek and Roman Actors. Aspects of an Ancient Profession*. Cambridge.

Else, G. (1967) *Aristotle's Poetics: The Argument*. Cambridge, MA.

Facella, A. (2005) "Siracusa: fonti letterarie," in *BTCGI* XIX: Pisa. 1–58.

Favaloro, G. (1922) *Agyrion, memorie storiche ed archeologiche*. Catania.

Fiechter, E. R., (1914) *Die baugeschichtliche Entwicklung des antiken Theaters*. Munich.

(1930–1937) *Antike griechische Theaterbauten*. 9 vols. Stuttgart.

Finley, M. I. (1968/1979) *Ancient Sicily*. New York, Lanham, MD.

Fischer-Hansen, T. (2009) "Artemis in Sicily and South Italy: A Picture of Diversity," in T. Fischer-Hansen and B. Paulsen (eds.) *From Artemis to Diana: The Goddess of Man and Beast (Danish Studies in Classical Archaeology: Acta Hyperborea)*. Copenhagen. 207–60.

Fischer-Lichte, E. (2005) *Theatre, Sacrifice, Ritual: Exploring Forms of Political Theatre*. London and New York.

Fitton-Brown, A. D. "The Size of the Greek Tragic Chorus," *Classical Review* 7 (01): 1–4.

Flickinger, R. (1918) *The Greek Theater and Its Drama*. Chicago.

Forsdyke, S. (2001) "Athenian Democratic Ideology and Herodotus' Histories." *AJP* 121: 3: 329–58.

Forti, L. (1966) *Letteratura e arte figurate nella Magna Grecia*. Naples.

Fountoulakis, A. (2000) "The Artists of Aphrodite." *Antiquité Classique* 69: 133–47.

Franco, C. (1986) "Euripide e gli Ateniesi," in E. Orsini (ed.) *La polis e il suo teatro*. Padua. 111–25.

François, G. (1978) "Epicharme et Cratès." *Antiquité Classique* 47: 50–69.

Frederiksen, R., E. Gebhard, and A. Sokolicek. (eds.) (2015) *The Architecture of the Ancient Greek Theatre: Proceedings of the Conference 27–30 January 2012, Danish Institute at Athens*. Aarhus.

Frisone, F. (2008) "Tra reazione e integrazione: Thurii nel contesto magnogreco," in A. Alessio (ed.) *Atene e la Magna Grecia: Atti del quarantasettesimo Convegno di Studi sulla Magna Grecia*. Taranto. 233–75.

Galvagno, E. (2002) "Dione e i ΣΥΜΜΑΧΟΙ," in Bonacasa et al.: 405–16.

Garbini, G. (1999) "The Phoenicians and Others," in G. Pisano (ed.) *Phoenicians and Carthaginians*. Rome. 7–14.

Gebhard, E. (1973) *The Theater at Isthmia*. Chicago.

(1974) "The Form of the Orchestra in Early Greek Theater." *Hesperia* 43: 402–47.

Gentili, B. (1962) "Nuovo esempio di 'theatron' con gradinata rettilinea a Siracusa." *Dioniso* 15: 122–30.

(1988) *Poetry and Its Public in Ancient Greece.* Baltimore.

Gentili, G. V. (1959) "I busti fittili di Demetra e Kore di Siracusa." *ASSirac*, V–VI, 1959–1960: 5–17.

Gerkan, A. and W. Müller-Wiener (1961) *Das Theater von Epidauros.* Stuttgart.

Ghinatti, F. (1996) *Assemblee greche d'occidente.* Turin.

Ghiron-Bistagne, P. (1976) *Recherches sur les acteurs dans la Grèce antique.* Paris.

Gigante, M. (1953) "Epicarmo, Pseudo-Epicarmo e Platone." *La parola del passato* 29: 161–75.

(1966) "Teatro greco in Magna Grecia," in L. Forti (ed.) *Letteratura e arte figurate nella Magna Grecia.* Naples. 83–146.

(1971) *Rintone e il teatro in Magna Grecia.* Naples.

Ginouvès, R. (1972) *Le théâtron à gradins droits et l'odeon d'Argos.* Paris.

Giudice, F. (2002) "La ceramica attica del IV secolo a.C. in Sicilia ed il problema della formazione delle officine locali," in Bonacasa et al.: 169–201.

Giuliani, L. (1995) *Tragik, Trauer und Trost: Bildervasen für eine apulische Totenfeier.* Berlin.

(2009) "Review of *Pots and Plays: Interactions between Tragedy and Greek Vase-Painting of the Fourth Century B.C.*" *Gnomon* 81: 439–47.

Godart, L. and S. De Caro (eds.) (2007) *Nostoi: Capolavori ritrovati.* Rome.

Goette, H. R. (1995) "Griechische Theaterbauten der Klassik – Forschungsstand und Fragestellungen," in E. Pöhlmann (ed.) *Studien zur Bühnendichtung und zum Theaterbau der Antike.* Frankfurt: 9–48.

(2005) "Überlegungen zur Topothese von Gebauden im antiken Brauron." *AA* 2005/1: 25–36.

(2007) "An Archaeological Appendix," in P. Wilson (ed.) *The Greek Theatre and Festivals: Documentary Studies.* Oxford. 116–21.

Gogos, S. (2008) *Das Dionysostheater von Athen: Architecktonische Gestalt und Funktion.* Vienna.

Goldhill, S. (1997) "The Audience of Athenian Tragedy," in Easterling (1997b): 54–68.

(1988) "Battle Narrative and Politics in Aeschylus' *Persae*." *JHS* 108: 189–93.

Gorman, P. (1979) *Pythagoras: A Life.* London.

Green, J. R. (1985) "Drunk Again: a Study in the Iconography of Comic Theater." *AJA* 89: 465–72.

(1986) "The Beaulieu Painter and Provincial Apulia at the End of the Fourth Century BC," in E. Bohr and W. Martini (eds.) *Studien zu Mythologie und Vasenmalerei: Festschrift fur Konrad Schauenburg.* Mainz. 181–6.

(1991) "Notes on Phlyax Vases." *Numismatica e antichità classiche* 20: 49–56.

(1994) *Theatre in Ancient Greek Society.* London.

(1999) "Tragedy and the Spectacle of the Mind: Messenger Speeches, Actors, Narrative and Audience Imagination in Fourth-Century BC Vase Painting," in B. Bergmann and C. Kondoleon (eds.) *The Art of Ancient Spectacle*. London and New Haven, CT. 37–63.

(2003) "Smart and Stupid: the Evolution of Some Masks and Characters in Fourth-Century Comedy: Continuity and Innovation in the Development of a Figurative Language," in J. Davidson and A. Pomeroy (eds.) *Theatres of Action: Papers for Chris Dearden*. Auckland. 118–232.

(2012) "Comic Vases in South Italy," in Bosher (2012a): 289–342.

(forthcoming) rev. 3rd ed. of Trendall (1967) *Phlyax Vases*. [With plates.] *BICS Suppl.* 19. London.

Greenblatt, S. (1980) *Renaissance Self-Fashioning*. Chicago.

Griffin, J. (1998) "The Social Function of Attic Tragedy." *CQ* 48: 39–61.

Griffith, M. (1978) "Aeschylus, Sicily and Prometheus," in R. D. Dawe, J. Diggle, and P. E. Easterling (eds.) *Dionysiaca: Nine Studies in Greek Poetry, Presented to D. L. Page*. Cambridge. 105–39.

Guardi, T. (1980) "L'attività teatrale nella Siracusa di Gerone I." *Dioniso* 51: 25–48.

Guettel Cole, S. (1994) "Archaeology of the Sacred: Demeter in the Ancient Greek City and Its Countryside," in S. E. Alcock and R. Osborne (eds.) *Placing the Gods: Sanctuaries and Sacred Space in Ancient Greece*. Oxford. (reprinted 2000 in R. G. A. Buxton (ed.) *Oxford Readings in Greek Religion*). 199–216.

Hackens, T. (1965) "Le théâtre." *Thorikos* 3: 93–5.

Hall, E. (1997) "The Sociology of Athenian Tragedy," in Easterling (1997b): 93–126.

(1989) *Inventing the Barbarian*. Oxford.

(2006) *The Theatrical Cast of Athens: Interactions between Ancient Greek Drama and Society*. Oxford.

(2013) *Adventures with Iphigenia in Tauris: A Cultural History of Euripides' Black Sea Tragedy*. New York.

(2016) "Oedipal Quiz: little boys in Greek tragedy," online article at http://edithorial.blogspot.com/2016/05/oedipal-quiz-llittle-boys-in-greek.html.

Hall, E. and R. Wyles (eds.) (2008) *New Directions in Ancient Pantomime*. Oxford.

Halliwell, S. (1997) *Aristophanes: Birds, Lysistrata, Assembly-Women, Wealth*. Oxford.

Hammond, N. G. L. (1967) *Epirus*. Oxford.

(1972) "Conditions of Dramatic Production to the Death of Aeschylus." *GRBS* 13: 387–450.

(1988) "More on Conditions of Dramatic Production to the Death of Aeschylus." *GRBS* 29: 5–33.

Hammond, N. G. L. and W. G. Moon (1978) "Illustrations of Early Tragedy at Athens." *AJA* 82: 371–83.

Handley, E. (2003) "Theocritus on Epicharmus," in J. Davidson and A. Pomeroy (eds.) *Theatres of Action: Papers for Chris Dearden*. Auckland. 142–8.

Hansen, M. H. and T. Fischer-Hansen (1994) "Monumental Political Architecture in Archaic and Classical Greek Poleis: Evidence and Historical Significance," in D. Whitehead (ed.) *From Political Architecture to Stephanus Byzantius* (*Historia Einzelschriften* 87): 22–90.

Henderson, J. (1975) *The Maculate Muse: Obscene Language in Attic Comedy*. New Haven, CT.

(2001) "Attic Old Comedy, Frank Speech and Democracy," in Boedeker and Raaflaub: 255–73.

Henrichs, A. (1984) "The Sophists and Hellenistic Religion: Prodicus as the Spiritual Father of the Isis Aretalogies." *HSCP* 88: 139–58.

Herington, C. J. (1967) "Aeschylus in Sicily." *JHS* 87: 74–85.

(1985) *Poetry into Drama*. Berkeley.

Hesberg, H. von. (2009) "Hellenistische Theater: Zur Funktionalität der Räume und ihrer Bedeutung für die Polis," in A. Matthaei and M. Zimmermann (eds.) *Stadtbilder im Hellenismus*. Berlin. 276–304.

Heydemann, H. (1886) "Die Phlyakendarstellungen auf bemalten Vasen." *Jahrbuch des Kaiserlich Deutschen Archäologischen Instituts* 1: 260–313.

Hinz, V. (1998) *Der Kult von Demeter und Kore auf Sizilien und in der Magna Graecia*. Wiesbaden.

Hofstetter, E. S. (2004) *The Berlin State Theater under the Nazi Regime*. Lewiston, Queenston, and Lampeter.

Hollinshead, M. B. (2012) "Monumental Steps and the Shaping of Ceremony," in B. D. Wescoat and R. G. Ousterhout (eds.) *Architecture of the Sacred: Space, Ritual, and Experience from Classical Greece to Byzantium*. Cambridge. 27–65.

(2015) *Shaping Ceremony: Monumental Steps and Greek Architecture*. Madison, WI.

Hordern, J. H. (2004) *Sophron's Mimes: Text, Translation, Commentary*. Oxford.

Hughes, A. (1996) "Comic Stages in Magna Graecia: The Evidence of the Vases." *Theatre Research International* 21: 97–107.

(2003) "Comedy in Paestan Vase Painting." *Oxford Journal of Archaeology* 22: 3: 281–301.

Hugoniot, C., F. Hurlet, and S. Milanezi (2004) *Le statut de l'acteur dans l'Antiquité grecque et romaine, Actes du colloque, Tours 3–4 mars 2002*, Tours.

Hunter, R. L. (1983) *Eubulus: The Fragments*. Cambridge.

(1993) "The Presentation of Herodas' Mimiamboi." *Antichthon* 27: 31–44.

Hutchinson, G. O. (2001) *Greek Lyric Poetry: A Commentary on Selected Larger Pieces*. Oxford.

Hüttl, W. (1929) *Verfassungsgeschichte von Syrakus*. Prague.

Isler, H. P. and H. Bloesch (1973) "Monte Iato: la terza campagna di scavo." *SicA* 6: 21–2: 11–21.

(1981) "Contributi per una storia del teatro antico: il teatro greco di Iaitas e il teatro di Segesta." *Numismatica e antichità classiche* 10: 131–64.

(1986) "Un'idria del pittore di London B 76 con il riscatto di Ettore." *NAC* 15, 95–123.

(1994) "L'archittetura teatrale antica," in P. C. Rossetto and G. P. Sartorio *Teatri greci e romani: alle origini del linguaggio rappresentato* I. Rome. 86–125.

(2000) "Il teatro greco di Iaitas." *Sicilia Archeologica* 33: 201–20.

(2003) "Il teatro greco di Iaitas." *Dioniso* NS 2: 276–91.

(2017) *Antike Theaterbauten. Ein Handbuch.* 3 vols. Verlag der Österreichischen Akademie der Wissenschaften (Österreichische Akademie der Wissenschaften. Philosophisch-Historische Klasse. Denkschriften, 490). Vienna.

Isler-Kerenyi, C. (1976) "Die Stützfiguren der griechischen Theaters von Iaitas," in *Studia Ietina* I (eds.) H. Bloesch and H. P.Isler. Zürich: 13–48.

(2009) "New Contributions of Dionysiac Iconography to the History of Religions in Greece and Italy," in G. Casadio and P. A. Johnston (eds.) *Mystic Cults in Magna Graecia.* Austin, TX. 61–72.

Izenour, G. C. (1992) *Roofed Theaters of Classical Antiquity.* New Haven, CT.

Jacquemin, A. (1993) "Oikiste et tyran: Fondateur-monarque et monarque-fondateur dans l'occident grec." *Ktèma* 18: 19–27.

Janko, R. (1982) *Homer, Hesiod and the Hymns.* Cambridge.

(1987) *Aristotle: Poetics I with the Tractatus Coislinianus; A Hypothetical Reconstruction of Poetics II; The Fragments of the On Poets.* Indianapolis, IN.

Jennings, E. (1986) *Collected Poems 1953–1885.* Manchester and New York.

Jory, J. (2011) "Review of Csapo, Actors and Icons of the Ancient Theater." *BMCR* 2011.4.11: https://bmcr.brynmawr.edu/2011/2011.04.11/ (Date last accessed 1 June, 2020).

Kaarsholm, P. (1990) "Mental Colonisation or Catharsis? Theatre, Democracy and Cultural Struggle from Rhodesia to Zimbabwe." *Journal of Southern African Studies* 16: 2: 246–75.

Kaibel, G. (1899; reprinted 1958) *Comicorum Graecorum Fragmenta I.* Berlin.

Karlsson, L. (1995) "The Symbols of Freedom and Democracy on the Bronze Coinage of Timoleon." *Acta Hyperborea* 6: 149–69.

Kassel, R and C. Austin (2001) *Poetae Comici Graeci I.* Berlin.

Kästner, U. and S. Schmidt (2018) *Inszenierung von Identitäten: Unteritalische Vasenmalerei zwischen Griechen und Indigenen.* Munich.

Kavoulaki, A. (1999) "Processional Performance and the Democratic Polis," in S. Goldhill and R. Osborne (eds.) *Performance Culture and Athenian Democracy.* Cambridge. 299–320.

Kerkhof, R. (2001) *Dorische Posse, Epicharm und attische Komödie.* Leipzig.

Kleiner, G., P. Hommel, and W. Müller-Wiener (1967) *Panionion und Melie: Jahrbuch des Deutschen Archäologischen Instituts: Ergänzungsheft* 23. Berlin.

Kolb, F. (1981) *Agora und Theater.* Berlin.

Körte, A. (1893) "Archäologische Studien zur alten Komödie." *Jahrbuch des Kaiserlichen Deutschen Archäologischen Instituts* 8: 61–103.

Kossatz-Deissmann, A. (1980) "Telephus travestitus," in A. Cahn and E. Simon (eds.) *Tainia. Roland Hampe zum 70. Geburtstag am 2. Dezember 1978 dargebracht von Mitarbeitern, Schülern und Freunden.* Mainz: 281–90.

Kowalzig, B. (2008) "Nothing to Do with Demeter? Theatre and Society in the Greek West," in O. Revermann, P. Wilson (eds.) *Performance, Iconography, Reception. Studies in Honour of Oliver Taplin*, Oxford. 128–57.

Krasilnikoff, J. (1995) "The Power Base of Sicilian Tyrants." *Acta Hyperborea* 6: 171–84.

Kurke, L. (2000) "The Strangeness of 'Song Culture': Archaic Greek Poetry," in O. Taplin (ed.) *Literature in the Greek and Roman Worlds*. Oxford. 58–87.

Kutzko, D. (2012) "In Pursuit of Sophron: Doric Mime and Attic Comedy in Herodas' Mimiambi," in Bosher (2012a): 367–90.

Larmour, D. (1999) *Stage and Stadium*. Hildesheim.

Lawler, L. B. (1943) "Ὄρχησις Ἰωνική." *Transactions and Proceedings of the American Philological Association* 74: 60–71.

Lecomte, L. (1912) *Napoléon et le monde dramatique*. Paris.

Le Guen, B. (1995) "Théâtre et cités à l'époque hellenistique. Mort de la cité? Mort du théâtre?" *REG* 108: 59–90.

(ed.) (1997) *De la scène aux gradins: théâtre et représentations dramatiques après Alexandre le Grand*. Toulouse.

(1997) "Le théâtre grec hellenistique à la fin du XXe siècle," in B. Le Guen (ed.) *De la scène aux gradins*. Toulouse. 7–18.

LeGuen, B. (2007) "Kraton, Son of Zoticos: Artists' Associations and Monarchic Power in the Hellenistic Period," in P. Wilson (ed.) *The Greek Theatre and Festivals, Documentary Studies*. Oxford. 246–78.

Leighton, R. (1999) *Sicily Before History: an Archaeological Survey from the Palaeolithic to the Iron Age*. London.

Lévy, E. (1993) "*Basileus* et *Tyrannos* chez Hérodote." *Ktèma* 18: 8–18.

Lightfoot, J. L. (2002) "Nothing to Do with the *Technitai* of Dionysius?," in Easterling and Hall: 209–22.

Liou, J.-P. (1993) "Isocrate et le vocabulaire du pouvoir personnel." *Ktèma* 18: 211–17.

Lippolis, E. (1982). "Le testimonianze del culto in Taranto greca." *Taras* 2.1–2: 81–135.

(1996) "La ceramica a figure rosse italiota," in E. Lippolis (ed.) *Arte e artigianato in Magna Grecia*. Naples. 357–61.

Lippolis, E., M. Livadiotti, and G. Rocco (2007) *Architettura greca: storia e monumenti del mondo della polis dalle origini al V secolo*. Milan.

Lissarrague, F. (2008) "Image and Representation in the Pottery of Magna Graecia," in M. Revermann and P. Wilson (eds.) *Performance, Iconography, Reception: Studies in Honour of Oliver Taplin*. Oxford. 439–49.

Liuzzi, D. (1973–1974) "Ennio e il pitagorismo." *Annali della facoltà di magistero dell'Università di Lecce*: 283–99.

Livingstone, N. (2001) *A Commentary on Isocrates' Busiris*. Leiden.

Loicq-Berger, M.-P. (1967) *Syracuse: histoire culturelle d'une cité grecque*. Brussels.

Long, T. (1986) *Barbarians in Greek Comedy*. Carbondale, IL.

Lonsdale, S. H. (1993) *Ritual Play in Greek Religion*. Baltimore, MD.

Lorenz, A. (1864) *Leben und Schriften des Koers Epicharmus*. Berlin.

Luraghi, N. (1994) *Tirannidi arcaiche in Sicilia e Magna Grecia*. Florence.

Lyons, C. L., M. Bennett, and C. Marconi (eds.) (2013) *Sicily: Art and Invention between Greece and Rome*. Malibu.

MacDonald, W. A. (1943) *The Political Meeting Places of the Greeks*. Baltimore.

MacLachlan, B. (2012) "The Grave's a Fine and Funny Place: Chthonic Rituals and Comic Theater in the Greek West," in Bosher (2012a). Cambridge. 343–64.

Mafodda, G. (1996) *La monarchia di Gelone tra pragmatismo, ideologia, e propaganda*. Messina.

(2002) "Da Gelone a Dionigi il Grande: Un confronto tra due governi auto-cratici," in Bonacasa et al.: 443–52.

Malkin,I. (1994). *Myth and Territory in the Spartan Mediterranean*. Cambridge.

Manchado, J. V. (2013) "Magic and Superstition in the Fragments of Sophron of Syracuse," in G. Poulos and S. Varella (eds.) *Explorations in World Literature, from Ancient to Contemporary*. Athens. 259–67.

Marconi, C. (1994) *Selinunte: le metope dell'Heraion*. Modena.

(2005) "I Theōroi di Eschilo e le antefisse sileniche siceliote." *Sicilia Antiqua* 2: 75–93.

(2010) "Choroi, Theōriai and International Ambitions: the Hall of Choral Dancers and Its Frieze," in O. Palagia and B. D. Wescoat (eds.) *Samothracian Connections: Essays in Honor of James R. McCredie*. Oxford. 106–35.

(2012) "Between Performance and Identity: the Social Context of Stone Theaters in Late Classical and Hellenistic Sicily," in Bosher (ed.) *Theater Outside Athens*. Cambridge. 175–207.

Marconi, C., and D. Scahill (2015) "The 'South Building' in the Main Urban Sanctuary of Selinunte: A Theatral Structure?" in R. Frederiksen, E. R. Gebhard, and A. Sokolicek (eds.) *The Architecture of the Ancient Greek Theatre*. Aarhus. 279–92.

Marshall, C. W. (2001) "A Gander at the Goose Play." *Theatre Journal* 53: 53–71.

Marshall, C. W. and S. van Willigenburg (2004) "Judging Athenian Dramatic Competitions." *JHS* 124: 90–107.

Martin, A. (1995) "La tragédie attique de Thespis à Eschyle," in A. Verbanck-Pierard and D. Viviers (eds.) *Culture et cité: l'avènement d'Athènes à l'époque archaïque: Actes du colloque international organisé à l'Université libre de Bruxelles*. Brussels. 15–25.

Martin, R. (1951) *Recherches sur l'agora grecque. Études d'histoire et d'architecture urbaines*. Paris.

Martorana, G. (1982–83) "Kore e il prato sempre fiorito." *Kokalos* 28/29: 113–22.

Mastronarde, D. (1990) "Actors on High: The Skene Roof, the Crane, and the Gods in Attic Drama." *Classical Antiquity* 9: 247–93.

McGlew, J. (1993) *Tyranny and Political Culture*. Ithaca, NY.

McPhee, I. and E. Pemberton (2004) "South Italian and Etruscan Red-figure Pottery from Ancient Corinth," in L. Beaumont, C. Barker, and E. Bollen (eds.) *Festschrift in Honour of J. Richard Green, Mediterranean Archaeology* 17: 55–60.

Meier, C. (1993) *The Political Art of Greek Tragedy*. Cambridge.

Meineke, A. (1839–1857) *Fragmenta Comicorum Graecorum I–VII*. Berlin.

(1853) *Alciphronis Rhetoris Epistolae*. Leipzig.

Meinel, F. (2015) *Pollution and Crisis in Greek Tragedy*. Cambridge.

Mertens, D. and A. de Siena (1982) "Metaponto: il teatro-ekklesiasterion." *Bolletino d'arte del ministero della pubblica istruzione* LXVII 16: 1–60.

Mertens, D. (2002) "Le lunghe mura di Dionigi I a Siracusa," in Bonacasa et al.: 244–52.

(2006) *Städte und Bauten der Westgriechen: von der Kolonisationszeit bis zur Krise um 400 vor Christus*. Munich.

Miller, E. (1868) *Mélanges de littérature grecque contenant un grand nombre de textes inédits*. Paris.

Miller, M. C. (1997) *Athens and Persia in the Fifth Century B.C.: A Study in Cultural Receptivity*. Cambridge.

Miller, N. P. (1961) "The Origins of Greek Drama: A Summary of the Evidence and a Comparison with Early English Drama." *Greece and Rome* 2: 8: 126–37.

Millino, G. (2000) "Epicarmo e i pigmei." *Anemos* 1: 113–50.

Mitchell, A. (2009) *Greek Vase Painting and the Origins of Visual Humour*. Cambridge.

Mitens, K. (1988) *Teatri greci e teatri ispirati all' architettura greca in Sicilia e nell' Italia meridionale c. 350-50 a.c.* Rome.

Modona, A. N. (1961) *Gli edifici teatrali greci e romani*. Florence.

Monoson, S. (2012) "Dionysius I and Sicilian Theatrical Traditions in Plato's Republic," in Bosher (2012a): 156–72.

Morgan, K. (2003) *Popular Tyranny*. Austin, TX.

(2012) "A Prolegomenon to Performance in the West," in Bosher (2012a): 35–55.

(2015) *Pindar and the Construction of Syracusan Monarchy in the Fifth Century* B.C. Oxford and New York.

Moretti, J.-C. (1992) "L'architecture des théâtres en Asie Mineure." *Topoi: Orient– Occident* 2: 9–32.

(1993) "Les débuts de l'architecture théâtrale en Sicile et en Italie méridionale (Ve-IIIe s.)." *Topoi* 3: 1: 72–100.

(1999–2000). "The Theater of the Sanctuary of Dionysos Eleuthereus in Late Fifth-Century Athens." *Illinois Classical Studies* 24: 377–98 (= Le Théâtre du Sanctuaire de Dionysos Eleuthereus à Athènes au Ve s. av. J.-C., REG 113, 2000, 275–98).

(2008) "Les lieux de culte dans les théâtres grecs," in J.-C. Moretti (ed.) *Fronts de scène et lieux de culte dans le théâtre antique*. Lyon. 23–52.

Naerebout, F. G. (1997) *Attractive Performances, Ancient Greek Dance: Three Preliminary Studies*. Amsterdam.

Nagy, G. (1990) *Pindar's Homer*. Baltimore, MD.

Nenci, G. and G. Vallet (eds.) (1977) *Bibliografia topografica della colonizzazione greca in Italia e nelle isole tirreniche (BTCGI)*. Pisa/Rome.

Neppi Modona, A. (1961) *Gli edifici teatrali greci e romani: teatri, odei, anfiteatri, circhi*. Florence.

Nielsen, I. (2000) "Cultic Theatres and Ritual Drama in Ancient Greece." *Proceedings of the Danish Institute at Athens*, III: 107–30.

   (2002) *Cultic Theatres and Ritual Drama: a Study in Regional Development and Religious Interchange between East and West in Antiquity*. Aarhus.

Nock, A. D. (1972 [rep.] 1986) *Essays on Religion and the Ancient World*. Selected and edited, with an introduction, bibliography of Nock's writings, and indexes, by Z. Stewart. Oxford.

Norwood, G. (1931) *Greek Comedy*. London.

Novokhatko, A. (2015) "Epicharmus' Comedy and Early Sicilian Scholarship." *SCI* 34: 69–84.

Olivieri, A. (1946–1947) *Frammenti della commedia greca e del mimo nella Sicilia e nella Magna Grecia*. Vols 1 & 2. Naples.

Olson, S. D. (2007) *Broken Laughter: Select Fragments of Greek Comedy*. Oxford.

Orlandini, P. (1968–1969) "Diffusione del culto di Demetra e Kore in Sicilia." *Kokalos* 14/15: 334–8.

Orsi, P. (1899) "Pantalica e Cassibile." *Monumenti Antichi dei Lincei* 9: 33–146.

   (1966) "Eloro I: campagna di scavo del 1899." Posthumous publication with notes by M. T. Currò. *Monumenti Antichi* 47: 203–87.

Osborne, R. (1993) "Competitive Festivals and the Polis," in A. Sommerstein, S. Halliwell, J. Henderson, and B. Zimmerman (eds.) *Tragedy, Comedy and the Polis*. Bari. 21–38.

   (2008) "Putting Performance into Focus," in M. Revermann and P. J. Wilson (eds.) *Performance, Reception, Iconography*. Oxford. 395–418.

Pace, B. (1935–1949) *Arte e civiltà della Sicilia antica*, I–IV. Milan.

   (1940–1941) "Epicarmo e il teatro siceliota." *Dioniso* 8: 50–87.

   (1947) "Appunti sui teatri della Magna Grecia." *Dioniso* 10: 266–91.

Panvini, R. (ed.) (2003) *Caltanissetta: Il Museo Archeologico*. Palermo.

Papastamati-Von Moock, C. (2015) "The Wooden Theatre of Dionysos Eleuthereus in Athens: Old Issues, New Research," in R. Frederiksen, E. R. Gebhard, and A. Sokolicek (eds.) *The Architecture of the Ancient Greek Theatre*, (MoDIA, 17). Aarhus. 39–79.

Pelling, C. (ed.) (1997) *Greek Tragedy and the Historian*. Oxford.

Phillips, E. D. (1959) "The Comic Odysseus." *Greece and Rome* 6: 1: 58–67.

Pickard-Cambridge, A. W. (1946) *The Theatre of Dionysus in Athens*. Oxford.

   (1968) *The Dramatic Festivals of Athens*. Revised by J. Gould and D. M. Lewis. Oxford.

Pickard-Cambridge, A. W. and T. B. L. Webster (1962) *Dithyramb, Tragedy and Comedy*. Oxford.

Podlecki, A. (1966) *The Political Background of Aeschylean Tragedy*. Ann Arbor, MI.

Poe, J. P. (1989) "The Altar in the Fifth Century Theater." *Classical Antiquity* 8: 116–39.

(1996) "The Supposed Conventional Meanings of Dramatic Masks: a Re-Examination of Pollux 4.133–54." *Philologus* 140: 306–28.

Polacco, L. and C. Anti (1981/1990) *Il teatro antico di Siracusa*, part I and part II. Rimini.

Polacco, L. (1986) "I culti di Demetra e Kore a Siracusa." *NumAntCl* 15: 21–37.

(1987) "Rites des saisons et drames sacrés chez les Grecs," in *Anthropologie et théâtre antique*. Montpellier 1986, Cahiers du GITA, 3: 9–22.

(1988) "Alcune osservazioni sui culti nel santuario presso S. Nicola ad Agrigento." *Quaderni dell'Ist. di Archeol. dell Univ. di Messina* 3: 59–62.

(1990) *Il teatro di Dioniso Eleuterio ad Atene*. Rome.

Prauscello, L. (2014) *Performing Citizenship in Plato's Laws*. Cambridge.

Pugliese Carratelli, G. (1996) *The Western Greeks. Classical Civilization in the Western Mediterranean*. London.

Rasmussen, T. and N. J. Spivey (1992) *Looking at Greek Vases*. Oxford.

Redmond, J. (ed.) (1983) *Drama and Religion*. Cambridge.

Rheinhardt, U. (1996) "Zu den Anfängen der Mythenburleske: griechische Mythen in den Komödien Epicharms und bei Stesichoros, auf Caeretaner Hydrien und anderen westgriechischen Sagenbildern." *Thetis* 3: 21–42.

Rehm, R. (1992) *Greek Tragic Theater*. London.

(1989) "Aeschylus in Syracuse: The Commerce of Tragedy and Politics," in B. D. Wescoat and M. L. Anderson (eds.) *Syracuse, the Fairest Greek City*. Rome. 31–4.

Revermann, M. (2010) "Situating the Gaze of the Recipient(s): Theatre-Related Vase Paintings and their Contexts of Reception," in I. Gildenhard and M. Revermann (eds.) *Beyond the Fifth Century: Interactions with Greek Tragedy from 400 BCE to the Middle Ages*. Berlin and New York. 69–97.

Rhodes, P. J. (2003) "Nothing to Do with Democracy: Athenian Drama and the Polis." *JHS*123: 104–19.

Ridout, N. (2008) "Performance and Democracy," in T. Davis (ed.) *The Cambridge Companion to Performance Studies*. Cambridge. 11–22.

Rizzo, F. P. (1989) *La menzione del lavoro nelle epigrafi della Sicilia antica (per una storia della mentalità)*. Palermo.

Robertson, N. (2004) "Orphic Mysteries and Dionysiac Ritual," in M. Cosmopoulos (ed.) *Greek Mysteries. The Archaeology and Ritual of Ancient Greek Secret Cults*. London. 218–40.

Robinson, E. G. D. (2004) "Reception of Comic Theatre amongst the Indigenous South Italians." *Mediterranean Archaeology* 17: 193–212.

(1990) "Between Greek and Native: The Xenon Group," in J.-P. Descoeudres (ed.) *Greek Colonists and Native Populations*. Oxford. 251–65.

Rodríguez-Noriega Guillén, L. (1996) *Epicarmo de Siracusa: testimonios y fragmentos. Edición crítica bilingüe.* Oviedo.

    (2012) "On Epicharmus' Literary and Philosophic Background," in Bosher (2012a), *Theater Outside Athens.* 76–96.

Rose, C. B. (1991) "The Theater of Ilion." *Studia Troica* 2: 69–77.

    (1992) "The 1991 Post-Bronze Age Excavations." *Studia Troica* 2: 43–60.

    (1993) "The 1992 Post-Bronze Age Excavations: Theater A." *Studia Troica* 3: 97–116.

Roselli, D. (2011) *Theater of the People: Spectators and Society in Ancient Athens.* Austin, TX.

Rosenbloom, D. (1993) "Shouting 'Fire' in a Crowded Theatre: Phrynichos' *Capture of Miletus* and the Politics of Fear in Early Attic Tragedy." *Philologus* 137: 159–96.

Rossetto, P. C. and G. P. Sartorio (eds.) (1994) *I teatri greci e romani: alle origini del linguaggio rappresentato.* Rome.

Rossi, L. (2001) *The Epigrams Attributed to Theocritus.* Groningen.

Rothwell, K. (1994) "Was Carcinus I a Tragic Poet?" *Classical Philology* 89: 241–5.

Roux, G. (1956) "Argos: le théâtre." *BCH* 80: 376–95.

Saïd, S.(2001) "Tragedy and Politics," in Boedeker and Raaflaub: 275–95.

Salomone, S. (1981) "L'altra faccia di Epicarmo." *Sandalion* 4: 59–69.

Salviat, F. (1960) "Le bâtiment de scène du théâtre de Thasos." *BCH* 84: 300–16.

Sanders, L. J. (1991) "Dionysius I of Syracuse and the Origins of the Ruler Cult in the Greek World." *Historia* 40, 275–87.

    (2002) "The Relations of Syracuse and Magna Graecia in the era of the Dionysii," in Bonacasa et al.: 473–492.

Sanderson, D. C. (1972) A Conjectural Reconstruction from the Ruins of the Ancient Greek Theatre at Morgantina. Ph.D. thesis (Michigan State University).

Schmidt, M. (1996) "Southern Italian and Sicilian Vases," in G. Pugliese Carratelli (ed.) *The Western Greeks.* London. 443–56.

Schwarzmaier, A. (2011) *Die Masken aus der Nekropole von Lipari.* Wiesbaden.

Scodel, R. (2001) "The Poet's Career, the Rise of Tragedy, and Athenian Cultural Hegemony," in D. Papenfuss and V. M. Strocka (eds.) *Gab es das Griechische Wunder? Griechenland zwischen dem Ende des 6. und der Mitte des 5. Jahrhunderts v. Chr.* 16. Mainz. 215–27.

Scullion, S. (2002) "Nothing to Do with Dionysus." *CQ* NS 52: 1: 102–37.

Seaford, R. (1984) *Euripides, Cyclops.* Oxford.

Sear, F. (2006) *Roman Theaters: an Architectural Study.* Oxford.

Sensi Sestito, G. (2002) "La Magna Grecia nell'età dei Dionisi," in Bonacasa et al.: 389–404.

Shanks, M. (1999) *Art and the Early Greek State: An Interpretive Archaeology.* Cambridge.

Shapiro, H. A. (1989) *Art and Cult under the Tyrants in Athens.* Mainz.

Sifakis, G. M. (1962) "High Stage and Chorus in the Hellenistic Theatre." *BICS* 2: 31–45.

Simon, E. (1982) *The Ancient Theatre*. London.

Sjöqvist, E. (1962) "Excavations at Morgantina 1961." *AJA* 66: 135–43.

Slater, W. J. (1995) "The Theatricality of Justice." *Classical Bulletin* 71: 144–57.

(2005) "Mimes and Mancipes." *Phoenix* 59: 316–23.

Small, J. P. (2003) *The Parallel Worlds of Classical Art and Text*. Cambridge.

Smith, H. R. W. "A Phlyax Vase in Rio de Janeiro." *AJA* 66: 3 (Jul., 1962): 323–33.

Sokolicek, A. (2015) "Form and Function of the Earliest Greek Theatres," in *The Architecture of the Ancient Greek Theatre* (eds.) R. Frederiksen, E. R. Gebhard and A. Sokolicek, 97–104, (MoDIA, 17). Aarhus.

Sommerstein, A. (1997) "The Theatre Audience, the *Demos*, and the *Suppliants* of Aeschylus," in C. Pelling (ed.) *Greek Tragedy and the Historian*. Oxford. 63–80.

Sourvinou-Inwood, C. (1994) "Something to Do with Athens: Tragedy and Ritual?" in R. Osborne and S. Hornblower (eds.) *Ritual, Finance, Politics*. Oxford. 269–90.

(2003) *Tragedy and Athenian Religion*. Lanham, MD.

Sposito, A. (2003) "Il teatro ellenestico di Morgantina." *Dioniso* NS 2: 318–49.

(2004) "Rito e teatralità nell'architettura del santuario delle divinità ctonie a Morgantina." *Dioniso* NS 3: 284–301.

(2011) *Morgantina: Il teatro ellenistico, storia e restauri*. Rome.

Stanley, A. E. (1970; 1979) "Early Theatre Structures in Ancient Greece: A Survey of Archaeological and Literary Records from the Minoan Period to 388 BC." Ph.D. thesis (University of California, Berkeley).

Steiner, D. (2009) "Pot Bellies: The Komast Vases and Contemporary Song," in D. Yatromanolakis (ed.) *An Archaeology of Representations: Ancient Greek Vase Painting and Contemporary Methodologies*. Athens. 240–81.

Stevens, P. T. (1956) "Euripides and the Athenians." *JHS* 76: 87–94.

Stillwell, R. (1952) *Corinth. Results of Excavations Conducted by the American School of Classical Studies at Athens, Vol. II: The Theatre*. Princeton, NJ.

(1964–1965) "The Theater of Morgantina." *Kokalos* 10/11: 579–88.

(1967) "Excavations at Morgantina (Serra Orlando) 1966: Preliminary Report IX." *American Journal of Archaeology*, 71.3: 245–50.

Stobl, G. (2007) *The Swastika and the Stage, 1933–1945*. Cambridge.

Stone, L. M. (1981) *Costume in Aristophanic Comedy*. New York.

Svarlien, D. A. (1990–1991) "Epicharmus and Pindar at Hieron's Court." *Kokalos* 36/37: 103–10.

Talbert, R. J. A. (1974) *Timoleon and the Revival of Sicily*. Cambridge.

Taplin, O. (1977) *The Stagecraft of Aeschylus*. Oxford.

(1986) "Fifth-Century Tragedy and Comedy: a Synkrisis." *JHS* 106: 163–74.

(1987) "Phallology, Phlyakes, Iconography and Aristophanes." *PCPhS* 33: 92–104.

(1991) "Auletai and Auletrides in Greek Comedy and Comic Vase-Paintings." *Numismatica e antichità classiche* 20: 31–48.

(1993) *Comic Angels*. Oxford.

(1998) "Narrative Variation in Vase-Painting and Tragedy: the Example of Dirce." *Antike Kunst* 41: 33–9.

(1999) "Spreading the Word through Performance," in S. Goldhill and R. Osborne (eds.) *Performance Culture and Athenian Democracy*. Cambridge. 37–57.

(2003) *Greek Tragedy in Action*. London and New York.

(2007) *Pots and Plays: Interactions Between Tragedy and Greek Vase-painting of the Fourth Century B.C.* Los Angeles.

(2012) "How was Athenian Drama Played in the Greek West?" in Bosher (2012a): 226–50.

Taplin, O. and R. Wyles (eds.) (2010) *The Pronomos Vase and Its Context*. Oxford.

Thesleff, H. (1978) "Notes on the New Epicharmean Iatrology." *Arctos: Acta Philologica Fennica* 12: 153–7.

Thompson, H. and R. E. Wycherley (1972) *The Agora of Athens: The History, Shape, and Uses of an Ancient City Center*. Princeton, NJ.

Todisco, L. (2002) *Teatro e spettacolo in Magna Grecia e in Sicilia*. Milan.

(2012) *Myth and Tragedy: Red-figure Pottery and Verbal Communication in Central and Northern Apulia in the Later Fourth Century B.C.* Cambridge. 251–71.

Townsend, R. F. (1986) "The Fourth-Century Skene of the Theater of Dionysos at Athens." *Hesperia* 55: 423–38.

Travlos, J. (1971) *Pictorial Dictionary of Ancient Athens*. New York.

Trendall, A. D. (1936) *Paestan Pottery*. London.

(1967a) *The Red-Figured Vases of Lucania, Campania and Sicily*. Oxford.

(1967b) *Phlyax Vases. BICS Suppl.* 19. London.

(1973) *The Red-Figured Vases of Lucania, Campania and Sicily. BICS Suppl.* 31. London.

(1987) *The Red-Figured Vases of Paestum*. Rome.

(1990) "On the Divergence of South Italian from Attic Red-figure Vase-painting," in J.-P. Descœudres (ed.) *Greek Colonists and Native Populations*. Canberra and Oxford. 217–30.

(1991) "Farce and Tragedy in South Italian Vase-Painting," in T. Rasmussen and N. Spivey (eds.) *Looking at Greek Vases*. Cambridge. 151–82.

Trendall, A. D. and A. Cambitoglou (1978) *The Red-Figured Vases of Apulia, vol. I. Early and Middle Apulian*. Oxford.

(1991–1992) *Second Supplement to the Red-figured Vases of Apulia*, 1–3 (University of London. Institute of Classical Studies. Bulletin supplements, 60). London.

Triveldi, H. (1993/1995) *Colonial Transactions: English Literature and India*. Manchester.

Umberto, A. (1986) "Le commedie di Epicarmo," *Studi in onore di Adelmo Barigazzi*, Rome. 13–21.

Ure, A. D. (1955) "Threshing Floor and Vineyard." *CQ* 49: 280–1.

Vallois, R. (1926) "Le théâtre de Tegée." *BCH* 50: 164–9.

Vassallo, S. (2012) "The Theater of Montagna dei Cavalli-Hippana," in Bosher (2012a): 208–25.

(2019) "Teatro di Montagna dei Cavalli: la cronologia," in Caminnecci et al.: 33–40.

Vasunia, P. (2001) *The Gift of the Nile: Hellenizing Egypt from Aeschylus to Alexander.* Berkeley.

Versnel, H. S. (1995) "Religion and Democracy," in W. Eder (ed.) *Die athenische Demokratie im 4 Jahrhundert v. Chr.* Stuttgart. 367–87.

di Vita, A.(2002) "L'urbanistica nella Sicilia del IV sec. a.C.," in Bonacasa et al. (2002): 139–46.

de Vogel, C. J. (1966) *Pythagoras and Early Pythagoreanism.* Assen.

Voza, G. (1989) "Eloro," *BTCGI* VII: 157–66.

    (2008) "Siracusa – teatro greco: l'eccezionalità." *Numero Unico del XLIV Ciclo di Spettacoli Classici,* edito a cura della Fondazione INDA.

Walker, J. (1930) *Les fragments d'Epicharme.* Nice.

Walsh, D. (2009) *Distorted Ideals in Greek Vase-Painting: the World of Mythological Burlesque.* Cambridge.

Warmington, E. H. (ed.) (1935) *Remains of Old Latin* (Loeb). London.

Webster, T. B. L. (1948) "South Italian Vases and Attic Drama." *CQ* 42: 15–27.

    (1956; [rep.]1970) *Greek Theater Production.* London.

    (1961) *Monuments Illustrating New Comedy,* London.

    (1962) "Some Notes on the New Epicharmus." *Innsbrucker Beiträge zur Kulturwissenschaft* 7–8: 85–91.

    (1967) *Monuments Illustrating Tragedy and Satyr Play. BICS Suppl.* 20. London.

    (1978) *Monuments Illustrating Old and Middle Comedy.* 3rd ed. London.

    (1995) *Monuments Illustrating New Comedy. BICS Suppl.* 50, revised and enlarged by J. R. Green and A. Seeberg. London.

Welcker, F. G. (1835) "Epicharmos." *Zeitschrift für Altertumswissenchaft* 5: 1122–33.

Wescoat, B. D. (ed.) (1989) *Syracuse: The Fairest Greek City.* Rome.

West, M. L. (1971) "Stesichorus." *CQ* NS 21: 302–14.

    (1975) "Cynaethus' Hymn to Apollo." *CQ* 25: 161–70.

    (1979) "The Prometheus Trilogy." *JHS* 99: 130–48.

    (1989) 'The Early Chronology of Attic Tragedy.' *CQ* 39: 251–4.

    (2001) "The Fragmentary Homeric 'Hymn to Dionysus'." *Zeitschrift für Papyrologie und Epigraphik* 134: 1–11.

    (2002) "Eumelos: A Corinthian Epic Cycle?" *JHS* 122: 109–33.

West, S. (1994) "Prometheus Orientalized." *Museum Helveticum* 51: 3: 129–49.

White, D. (1963) *Hagne Thea: A Study of Sicilian Demeter.* Ph.D. thesis, Princeton University.

    (1964) "Demeter's Sicilian Cults as a Political Instrument." *GRBS* 5: 261–79.

Wiles, D. (1991) *The Masks of Menander.* Cambridge.

    (1997) *Tragedy in Athens.* Cambridge.

    (2000) *Greek Theater Performance.* Cambridge.

Wilkins, J. (2000) *The Boastful Chef: the Discourse of Food in Ancient Greek Comedy.* Oxford.

Willi, A. (ed.) (2002) *The Language of Greek Comedy*. Oxford.

(2008) *Sikelismos: Sprache, Literatur und Gesellschaft im griechischen Sizilien (8.–5. jh. v. chr.)*. Basle.

(2012) "Challenging Authority: Epicharmus between Epic and Rhetoric," in Bosher (2012a): 56–75.

Wilson, P. (1997) "Leading the Tragic Khoros: Tragic Prestige in the Democratic City," in C. Pelling (ed.) *Greek Tragedy and the Historian*. Oxford. 81–108.

(2000) *The Athenian Institution of the Khoregia: the Chorus, the City and the Stage*. Cambridge.

(2002) "The Musicians Among the Actors," in Easterling and Hall: 39–68.

(2007) "Sicilian Choruses," in P. Wilson (ed.) *The Greek Theatre and Festivals: Documentary Studies*. Oxford. 351–77.

Winkler, J. J. and F. Zeitlin (eds.) (1992) *Nothing to do with Dionysos? Athenian Drama in Its Social Context*. Princeton, NJ.

Winter, F. E. (1983) "The Stage of New Comedy." *Phoenix* 37: 38–47.

Wiseman, T. P. (2000) "Liber: Myth, Drama and Ideology in Republican Rome," in C. Bruun (ed.) *The Roman Middle Republic: Politics, Religion and Historiography: c. 400–133 BC*. Rome. 265–300.

Wonder, J. W. (2002) "What Happened to the Greeks in Lucanian-Occupied Paestum? Multiculturalism in Southern Italy." *Phoenix* 56: 40–55.

Wüst, E. (1950) "Epicharmos und die alte attische Komödie." *Rheinisches Museum für Philologie*. 93: 337–64.

Wycherley, R. E. (1978) *The Stones of Athens*. Princeton, NJ.

(1967) *How the Greeks Built Cities*. London.

Xanthakis-Karamanos, G. (1980) *Studies in Fourth-Century Tragedy*. Athens.

Zielinski, T. (1885) *Die Gliederung der altattischen Komödie*. Leipzig.

Zirone, D. "Siracusa: Storia della ricerca archeologica," in *BTCGI* XIX: 145–204.

Zortman, B. (1984) *Hitler's Theatre: Ideological Drama in Nazi Germany*. El Paso, TX.

Zuntz, G. (1971) *Persephone: Three Essays on Religion and Thought in Magna Graecia*. Oxford.

Index locorum

General Index

CPSIA information can be obtained
at www.ICGtesting.com
Printed in the USA
BVHW012043010322
630337BV00005B/37